Tales from the
Chalkface

Vernon Cutler

Matador
9 Priory Business Park,
Wistow Road, Kibworth Beauchamp,
Leicestershire. LE8 0RX
Tel: (+44) 116 279 2299
Fax: (+44) 116 279 2277
Email: books@troubador.co.uk
Web: www.troubador.co.uk/matador

ISBN 978 1780880 723

British Library Cataloguing in Publication Data.
A catalogue record for this book is available from the British Library.

Typeset in 11pt Goudy Old Style by Troubador Publishing Ltd, Leicester, UK
Printed and bound in the UK by TJ International, Padstow, Cornwall

Matador is an imprint of Troubador Publishing Ltd

This book is dedicated to all those children whom I have had the privilege of teaching and have contributed to its writing in so many ways.

Acknowledgements

My thanks are due to my family without whose practical skills and forbearance this book would never have been realised.

Preface

What follows is one teacher's recollection of teaching from the late 1960's to the late 1980's and therefore spans 20 years spent in primary schools. The book records the highs and the lows over a 23 year period; from the high of initial training to my first post and later promotion and a year's sabbatical to read for that precious degree, and the lows of my first class when I felt so desperately under resourced, in every sense, and the later low of bullying in the workplace which led to my retiring from the classroom on the grounds of ill health.

In that sense what follows is essentially autobiographical. It can be argued that any autobiography is an act of supreme arrogance, for I do not suppose that my life is any more interesting or important than any other soul's. Rather it is my hope that this small slice of teaching life will afford the reader an intimate glimpse into a world which we all experience and which, for good or ill, has a major impact on our lives, but which most of us only see from one point of view. I seek to afford the reader a view from the other side of the divide; the barrier which inevitably exists between staff and pupils. This is a behind the scenes glimpse, made the more real, I hope, by being a personal account.

Because it is a personal account, it will also be an entirely subjective point of view. For that reason the descriptions of children and colleagues should be understood to be just that, and not in any way a judgement of the person's true character. It is therefore not the author's desire to cause offence to any persons mentioned in the narrative. For that reason names have been changed or omitted to protect individual identity. Should anyone feel they recognise themselves or another from this book, if that causes offence, the author apologises unreservedly.

Rather what follows is a personal truth but I hope that renders the account the more intimate and more real for all its lack of objectivity. I have come to understand that there is very little objective truth in this world, for who of us can know the ultimate reality? Pontius Pilate asked, "What is truth?" Perhaps therefore God alone is truth. Within those limitations, however, in all that follows every effort has been made to offer an honest account as far as my own memory and constraints of the narrative permit where chronology is subject to those same constraints.

To commit such a personal account to paper is partly in an effort to answer that question often levelled at me in my own early days of teaching, "What do they get up to in schools these days?" Beyond the more obvious highs and lows of a teaching career, however, there were just the day to day challenges of trying to respond to the children's different presenting needs; those moments of exhileration when one saw the light of understanding go on in someone's eyes and just the simple trust and naive sense of fun which the young possess and can so renew our hope and faith. In teaching there was never a dull moment. I hope the reader is able to gain at least a glimpse of that joy.

Above all, what follows is about relationships. Relationships help us to develop and as we do so we are changed for good or ill. In that sense life is a process of changing; of becoming what we have the capacity to be. The very nature of that process is learning, where learning is a process of movement from discomfort to comfort; from disturbance to homeostasis. When I get something wrong I am outside my comfort zone. When I get it right I can gain a sense of satisfaction and my comfort is restored. If I must always remain in my comfort zone I can never learn. The very nature of learning takes me outside my comfort zone; it is to be challenged to learn more. In that sense to learn is to grow, where growth is the very essence of life. To cease to learn is to cease to grow. To cease to grow is to cease to live. Perhaps like a plant, it is to grow towards the light; a light we can never reach. The nature of growth, too, is that it is not reversible. We cannot go back to what we were. What we were we will never be again. Yet perhaps in essence we never change; an apple tree remains an apple tree. We may be pruned and shaped but hopefully remain true to ourselves.

Those moments of privilege and simple fun with the children, many of which have been recorded in this book, have contributed to my nourishment. Those that have not been recorded have been forced out by constraints of space. Similarly, there have been those times of pruning which, along with my growth, have shaped the person that I have become. As our journeys are unique, so are we. To all those who have contributed to my nourishment, I owe my thanks. I hope that some of the children I have taught have felt similarly nourished. This book is an acknowledgement and thank you to them.

Chapter One

Beginnings

"To travel hopefully is a better thing than to arrive"
Robert Louis Stevenson, El Dorado

As I stood and surveyed the empty classroom just two days before term was due to start, I recalled the words of a retiring headmaster of a primary school who said, "I knew on the first day it had been a mistake!"

This was where three years of teacher training had led me. Fresh from college, with high hopes of the profession I had just entered and with, I am sure, some personal aspirations too, I surveyed the classroom that was to be my domain for the next academic year as I led 1C of the junior school in the adventure of learning and hopefully fitting them for the life they were starting out on. We were to be sharing the beginning of this adventure together.

Education meant much to me and had always been precious. From the day at the age of 16, and just embarking on my A level course, when my father had said one evening in anger when his jealousy got the better of him, "Get a job or get out", and the following morning I had packed a toothbrush and whatever personal effects I could squeeze into my briefcase ready for school, I knew what was important to me.

I attended one of the ancient London foundation schools set up, in this case, by the Coopers' Company and whose badge bore three barrel rings and an adze to remind us boys of how our school had begun. Another beginning. As I was starting out as a teacher myself, so I could remember that other beginning, my first day at what had seemed such a grand school as the huge door leading into the panelled entrance hall with marbled floor was opened by the porter in impressive uniform. The school building itself was rendered the more impressive by its twin turrets and cloisters. Founded in 1536, another era in our history when education had been precious, which saw too the founding of such illustrious seats of learning as King's College, Cambridge, the present building which now housed the Coopers' Company's school was built in the 19th century and offered no end of hiding places for a boy who believed himself homeless. Fortunately, in my case, it proved unnecessary as my mother understood, that morning, my own determination and its implications. To me, at that age, the threat had felt real enough and I had, there and then, made a decision. I had understood my priorities and I knew that education was precious to me. What else could I do but teach, in spite of my father's clear disapproval and his constant assertions that, "Those who can do, those who can't teach"?

Thus it was with high hopes and even higher ideals that I had started my teacher training in 1964 at one of the then 24 Anglican church founded colleges in the country. Bishop Otter College, set amongst the rolling South Downs, was home to 471 similarly principled young men and women who, at different stages, were preparing to embark upon what was, to us, the sacred calling of teaching.

Being slightly smaller in number than the school I had so recently come from, college afforded a rather more family feel, something I so valued throughout the three very rewarding years that I spent there. That feeling of a family started as soon as we arrived at college. It was the custom for all first year students to be met as they arrived at the college entrance by one of the second year students who were then assigned to them as their college friend or 'parent'. This person would show them to their room and collect them for dinner that first evening. For many that would extend into being shown around college and there being a continued support during the first few days or weeks. Some friendships continued throughout their time in college.

I recall my parents driving me to college, complete with my trunk, on that first day and our being confronted with the sight of a large number of students all waiting near the entrance. One stepped forward and asked my name. Thereupon he said he would get someone to show me where my hall of residence and room were to be found. As an only child I had grown up feeling alone and had learned independence at an early age. I was also quite unaccustomed to people offering help. Overwhelmed by the sight of so many people, to the offer of help I replied, "I am sure we can find it". I did not know how to receive such an offer and believed that I would be inconveniencing somebody to accept help. I could not see that my independence could have been interpreted as a snub. I made my own way to dinner that evening and was asked where my college parent was. I answered, in all honesty, that I did not see anybody and did not know I had one. My insularity was to accompany me wherever I went during that first term. I sense that, socially at least, I was, as W.S. Gilbert put it in "Trial by Jury", "an impecunious party".

Having said that, it was difficult to be alone for very long in what increasingly felt like the close knit family atmosphere of college. That feeling was reinforced on the first Sunday of term when, led by the Principal, the entire college climbed one of the local high spots on the South Downs which afforded a glorious view, including that of the Goodwood racecourse. There, on what I recollect was a warm Sunday afternoon, we all had a picnic tea which had been transported up beforehand while the Principal came round to each of the new students in order to get to know us personally. In later years that was a task I got used to myself as I got to know the names of each of the children in my class, but they were just over thirty in number, not 160! She also made a point of going into the college coffee bar early that same term, again to meet that year's "freshers". "Coffee bar" is perhaps a rather grand name for what was a converted cellar, but for many of us that merely added to the atmosphere and to me it felt like the height of decadence. I recall that an espresso coffee bar had opened nearby when I was living at home; a new trend in the early sixties and the first of its kind in the neighbourhood. I remember how sophisticated I felt when I first went there with a group of friends.

Apart from the joys of tea on the top of the South Downs all the first year students were invited, in small groups, during the course of the year, to take tea with the Principal. This was another opportunity for her to get to know us and again underlined the sense of family. It started with the formal invitation, "Miss Murray requests the pleasure of the company of ...", to which the honoured recipient was expected to reply in similar vein. I was thus certainly grateful for one lecture, quite early on in our programme, which was devoted to correct forms of address and how to write or respond to formal invitations for different occasions. During the same lecture I also learned that 'formal' meant evening wear which we should all need for our first Christmas Ball, while informal, for gentlemen at least, meant lounge suits. This was certainly a very different world for me; a young man fresh from the greater London/Essex suburbs where the height of the social calendar was a visit to relatives and "eating out" was more likely to be fish and chips, while entertainment, I recollect, was limited to whatever western "movie" was showing on television. I felt a little like mole from "The Wind in the Willows", by Kenneth Grahame, who, on emerging from his little subterranean home on a fine spring morning, could only utter, "Oh my, oh my, oh my!" Indeed life in college with its lectures, societies, other activities and friends was, for me, a breath of spring, a treasure store, as I began to see new life and fresh opportunities springing up all around me. Thus we were being prepared socially as well as mentally for the world of teaching that we were hopefully to be entering three years hence.

It is a sad truth that how we see ourselves so often dictates how we are and how we behave towards others. So often I found myself not quite knowing how to respond to the many opportunities and offers of friendship. That sadly inclined me to become insular which, I am aware, some misunderstood and which attracted some negative attentions from a couple of second year students. That was quickly stopped by other members of my hall of residence. Again, I had not experienced such support before, but it helped me to look at myself and I realised that I had a choice; I could be a part of this community, or I could be alone if I wished. That first term was a difficult time for me. I was helped to confront something in myself and I realised that I did not wish to be alone. This was another part of my social development. I remain forever grateful that college was able to offer that cohesive community atmosphere that my personal development so obviously needed. Had I found myself on a campus serving 20,000 students, as is so often the situation today, I could have been writing a very different story.

It was a rather happier me that approached the end of that first term and Christmas when I was to be afforded another example of that sense of family that I had so come to value.

Situated in the cathedral city of Chichester, we were blessed with the services of the cathedral's director of music as our organist and choirmaster. At the beginning of our first term we were invited to audition for a place in the college chapel choir. Rehearsals took place every Thursday afternoon after lunch so that while the choir were rehearsing for the week's services, the rest of the college had a time without lectures. I turned up with a number of others for the first rehearsal of the new term hoping to be admitted to the choir. The choir was largely self selecting as only those with some previous experience tended to turn up and therefore it was largely assumed that we should be able to sing in tune, hold a part, and have at least the basics of sight reading, but beyond that the only limiting factor was the number that the choir gallery would hold. I had spent a couple of years singing in our local church choir as well as acting as a Sunday school teacher. Going to teachers' training college and singing in its choir seemed a natural transition.

The highlight of that autumn term was the college carol service, held in the cathedral. We were blessed with a wonderful new chapel which was large and airy but had the entire college wanted to attend a particular service we should have been a little compromised for space. The cathedral was the obvious venue and again underlined the college's roots in Anglican spirituality. In the mid nineteenth century the country was becoming increasingly aware of the need for education. It was felt that it should no longer be the preserve of the few. The church was at the forefront of that movement, but realised that if schools were to be established then there would be a need for trained teachers. Our college was an answer to that need. The Christmas carol service reminded us of that history.

I remember our first rehearsal in the cathedral standing in front of the rood screen and being told to pitch our voices to immediately above the west door for the sake of the accoustics and to be prepared for the four second delay in the echo. I do remember too that our choirmaster was not best pleased when one of his bases absented himself before the end of the rehearsal to escort his then fiancee to the train. Now my wife, we had only become engaged a week or so previously and she had spent the weekend in college, staying in one of the ladies' halls of residence, and was to become increasingly a part of that family. As our rehearsals in college gained an ever greater sense of purpose, so our choirmaster became ever more earnest and expected us to do the same. So one particular afternoon he had been haranguing us to pull our proverbial socks up with comments such as "Sopranos watch those top notes, don't strangle them", to the tenors, "For goodness sake take your music away with you. I don't expect to have to do note bashing", while to us bases he simply said "Bases, you sound like sad hoovers!" As a choir we can't have been too bad, however, as we were invited to sing evensong in the cathedral occasionally if the regular choir were not available.

After our hard work on that and subsequent Christmases we rather felt we had earned our relaxation, our Christmas dinner and our Christmas ball. My wife and I still have a photograph of her in her full length ball gown which she had made herself on the sewing machine my parents had bought her as an early Christmas present, with me in my newly acquired dinner suit which my father had bought for me, courtesy of "Burton tailoring".

Looking back to that time I can see how our social education was as much an essential part of our development as our more formal lectures. In the post Plowden years our lectures, and the teaching methods we were being encouraged to adopt, seemed like a breath of fresh air after my own experiences of grammar school.

That was particularly evident during one of our lectures which was devoted to "modern dance", more commonly known, in schools at least, as music and movement. Like all such lectures it was essentially experiential and was undertaken by all those who were preparing for primary teaching, even if, as in my case, that was junior/secondary. Thus one afternoon a week would see us moving expressively, or as one fellow student put it, "pretending to be a number 49 bus". Coming straight from an all boys' grammar school, mixed groups of male and female were new, not only to me, but also to many of the other students who came from similar single sex schools. When we were asked to, "Find a partner, go into a corner and work up into a climax" it caused not a little amusement to our young fertile minds. Clearly my social life was opening ever new and previously unimaginable horizons!

In this respect, perhaps the highlight was dinner at high table, followed by coffee and some lively conversation in the senior common room. Similarly lively conversations could be had with one's tutor both in and out of their study. It was thus the practice of many of us students to invite tutors or lecturers to coffee in our rooms after dinner. Dinner was a semi formal affair and we gentlemen were expected to wear a collar and tie. Serving was performed by whichever unfortunate soul found themselves sitting at the head of the table. The reader may understand therefore that there was usually a rush to fill all the other seats, leaving that 'exalted' position for any unfortunate late comers. There was one other motivation to avoid arriving late for dinner, namely the practice of 'bowing in' and 'out'. Those arriving after grace had been said, usually led by the Chaplain or Principal, had to make their way down the length of the central aisle, bow to the top table and wait for an acknowledgement from the Principal before trying to find a seat. With luck, at that point, somebody else may have assumed the position of server and there were usually several offers of places from those whose heart went out to any unfortunate who had just had to run that particular gauntlet. Not that it was too arduous or frightening, for the number of students 'bowing out' on a Thursday evening was often quite noticeable. The Principal, of course, was quite aware that the end of dinner overlapped with "Top of the Pops", a must for any aspiring young mind!

To the younger reader, not only may all this seem anachronistic in the present age, but also perhaps repressive and excessively regulated. My experience, however, was one of freedom within a social framework which simply afforded security, but never spilled over into repression. To rob ourselves of all social constraints does not afford us freedom. In that sense perhaps we are not so different from children, for I came to understand that children need a framework within which to function and grow safely. I was grateful to that framework. I was grateful too for the informal relationship which we were able to enjoy with our tutors and lecturing staff. There was not an 'us' and 'them' situation, but one in which we enjoyed a true egalitarianism and a freedom which was associated with that. There was a sense of students and lecturers involved in the joint venture which is education.

One example of a true egalitarianism which was so enabled in what was truly a joint venture was a production of "Noye's Fludde" by Benjamin Britten performed in the college chapel. It started life as a group of us getting together one evening with one of our music lecturers in the main music room in college and singing some of the highlights of Benjamin Britten's opera.

From a singing point of view we did not experience Britten's music as immediately accessible and so we felt it might be fun to try to work it up into something a little more musically satisfying than our first efforts could manage. Thus our evenings started to become a little more structured and we were becoming quite serious. At this point a member of the group, who was an enthusiast in the field of recording and a real electronics buff, although we never told him so, brought some of his equipment up to the music studio and busied himself recording our sessions so that we could further improve our technique. This clearly meant he was busy most of the time and thus he became the voice of God. At least we had God, we just had to find Noah, his three sons, their wives and a wife for Noah as well. This was fast developing into a production with its own conductor and pianist. But a production needs a venue and so, its being in essence a mystery play, I approached the chapel committee and sought permission to stage the production in the college chapel, as I was the then third year "chapel rep", or student repesentative on the chapel committee. That hurdle successfully surmounted, it fell to us, myself included, to get an orchestra together.

In spite of its difficult entries and contrapuntal nature, the essence of Britten's music has always been accessibility to all ages and abilities. Thus putting an orchestra together included assembling a "mugaphone" (eight mugs which when struck would cover the range of one octave) giving me a busy few weeks inviting myself to coffee in various people's rooms so that I could sample their different mugs, strictly in the interests of music, of course. Anybody who could play an instrument, but who perhaps had never thought of themselves as proficient enough, found themselves in the orchestra which was slowly being assembled. Such a description is perhaps not entirely fair as we did have some quite accomplished instrumentalists. That perhaps was one of the joys as it brought together all abilities including some hitherto undiscovered talents. Even my then fiancée, who was not a member of the college, was roped in to be two of the hands for the four handed piano part. At this stage we managed to involve a second music lecturer to conduct and rehearse the newly formed orchestra. So with chorus and orchestra rehearsing separately with me fulfilling a new found role as conductor of the choir and coordinator, the time came to bring the two halves together. At this point I could take a back seat so to speak as our newly appointed music lecturer could now conduct the whole thing. She was young, keen and needed to muster all the authority she could for this first rehearsal together. Our sound recordist, or God, to give him his other role, was, of course, kept busy and when he wasn't tweaking his sound levels or positioning a microphone he could be found engaging in conversation with anybody who wasn't actually singing or playing at the time. Perhaps as God, or at least the voice of God, he felt he should be showing an active interest in one of his children. Thus it was that on one such occasion he was so busy chatting that he missed his cue entirely and there was a pause as we all waited for God to speak. Finally our music lecturer, clearly maintaining her authority over the proceedings, broke the silence by calling out "God!". To which he immediately responded, "Yes, my daughter". Amid the uproarious laughter that ensued it was difficult to maintain any show of authority. It was perhaps a reminder that none of us can hold authority unless it has been given to us by others and that we only continue to exercise that authority with their continued consent. That applies to prime ministers and teachers alike. A teacher rules only by consent and if he or she thinks to abuse that position a class can quickly become resentful and refuse to accept their authority. The anarchy which follows can be distressing for the children and completely undermine or destroy the teacher.

Somehow order was restored and the production began to take shape, except that, at this stage, we had no animals. So it was that I and another student made overtures to a neighbouring school and enlisted the then top junior class (year 6 in modern parlance) which involved the children in art work as they each designed their own shield bearing the image of the particular animal that they were playing. We thought to avoid costumes out of consideration for their teacher and parents and, too, turning it into a pantomime (complete with horse) would not, we felt, have been in keeping with Benjamin Britten's opera. All we needed now was an ark to put them all in. So others became involved in scenery, lighting and stage management generally. All these important parts of the production needed coordinating which role seemed, largely, to fall to me, rather by accident than design on anybody's part. Thus it was that at the end of our first full dress rehearsal complete with scenery, animals etc., I sat on the end of a chapel pew exhausted. All the children had been duly collected by parents and, apart from a few people still tidying up and making sure that the chapel was in a fit state to be used for a service the following morning, all was quiet. I was spent and a perceptive member of the cast, one of Noah's daughters-in-law, came up to me and said, "You look as if you could do with a cup of coffee". That cup of coffee was a hand held out in friendship which I gladly took, aware of the true offer of sensitive support that was being made. Overwhelmed by exhaustion, I sat in her room and dissolved into tears. In that close knit community we were all glad of such support at some stage or another. We were able to respect each other's humanity and frailties and it is true that I never felt really isolated. The truth of that was borne upon me later the following term.

I was having a meeting with another student in my room. He was occupying my one armchair and I was sitting on my bed when the door to my room burst open and someone flung themselves behind me on my bed in floods of tears. The person whom I had been entertaining suggested we might perhaps adjourn our meeting and arrange another, to which I simply said, "Yes, fine, I'll be in touch. I'll drop a note in your pigeon hole", otherwise known as PIPs or people's incoming post. Before E-mail it was the hub of college communications as well as a natural meeting place.

My visitor left and I turned to the sobbing figure on my bed who was none other than the one with whom I had shared my tears the previous term. I was simply being afforded the opportunity of returning the favour and the support she had shown me.

That feeling of support was never more evident to me than as the first performance drew closer, for by this time I was both filling the role of coordinator as well as Noah. At that point everybody just seemed to pull together and said, "Vernon you've done enough!" Thus I was firmly relieved of my role!

It was not only the production which had grown. Each of us, I feel, had grown with it. That was certainly true for me, for by the time I left college I felt I had grown until I was ready to take on that first teaching post. College had been an environment not only for learning but also for growing. We are free to grow when we experience ourselves as accepted just as we are, for then we can dare to begin to develop our particular gifts or talents and perhaps see them, like the production, come to fruition. I was reminded again of that feeling of acceptance that I so valued later the following term. I had arranged with one of those who had contributed to the production as an instrumentalist to go into Chichester with her for something that was going to need our joint input. Men and women occupied different halls of residence in the sixties where gentlemen were most certainly not to be found in ladies' rooms or vice versa after 11 p.m. She had said that she would come over to my room the following morning. She indeed arrived bright and early, so early in fact that I had only just got up. I made my slightly flustered apologies and said rather in mitigation that I had only to have a wash, shave and get dressed and that I would be with her, to which she replied, "That's all right, I'll wait", and sat down on the end of my bed to do just that.

That production however, coming as it did at the end of the Christmas term in what was for many of us our final year, it left only our final teaching practice and exams to be surmounted. The time had come for us to think about our main reason for being there and to be assessed on how we might similarly enhance the lives of the children shortly to be placed in our care.

In spite of that social aspect of college life which I so valued, finals still felt very real and all the academic work which had led up to that. Part of that was our dissertation or "special study" which we had to offer in our main subject. I remember my hiring a rather old, slightly decrepit typewriter and my fiancée spending much of the Easter vacation typing it up for me. That was just one of the many reasons I had been glad we had become engaged. I recollect after I had submitted it early the following term being commended on the quality of its presentation. I owed much to my fiancée.

I recall too how a friend of mine had felt the need for support as we approached the final exams. With our education and psychology papers looming he decided that teacher training had all been one ghastly mistake and that there was no point in his sitting them. Perhaps it was the budding schoolmaster in me, but apart from reasoning with him, I pointed out that he was going to sit and pass those papers even if it killed me. I remember sitting up late with him helping him revise immediately before each paper so that he would not have the opportunity of leaving college or even the time to think about it. Each morning I would then collect him for breakfast and marched him into the examination room afterwards. He passed, which is all he had to do to gain his Teachers' Certificate. His mother was herself a head teacher and I often felt he had been pushed into a career choice. Wisely, he did not stay in teaching for long. I often wondered if I had done him much of a favour in the long term, but at least I might have spared him his mother's wrath.

Those final papers, of course, and our dissertations were but part of our assessment for that all important certificate. Arguably the more important part was our final teaching practice in which we were to be assessed on whether we could actually do the job for which we were training.

Chapter Two

Teaching Practice

"They perfect nature and are perfected by experience"
Francis Bacon, Of studies

As I approached that final teaching practice, so my previous practices in my first and second years came to mind, or should I say came back to haunt me. So my first teaching practice where it had all started "flashed upon that inward eye". I should not perhaps have been as green as some of my fellows as I had spent a term teaching uncertificated before starting college, but as the responsibilities of teaching hit me full measure during that first practice, I looked back ruefully and saw how little I had known during that term. On reflection I'm not sure how much more I knew as I embarked upon that three weeks that seemed more like three months.

The school was a single teacher school with the children's ages ranging from 5 to 11 with less than 20 children in all. The head teacher, indeed therefore the only teacher, used to pick me up each morning in his car at the end of College Lane and drive the twenty miles to his little school nestled at the foot of the South Downs. From such a description I can well imagine some of my colleagues in inner London schools feeling that it should have been idyllic and that I should have thought myself lucky in the belief that heaven had arrived early. As it was, just one week in school, saw me sitting in my tutor's study convinced that I was an absolute failure and that teacher training had all been one ghastly mistake. I sat with my tutor a dejected and trembling wreck and tried to explain to him how I was feeling. Fortunately he was able to cut through my verbiage and simply said "you're exhausted". But how could I be exhausted after just one week's teaching and less than twenty children? I can imagine many teachers asking that question, for that was the very question I was asking myself.

If there is ever a simple answer, in this case it was boundaries. As my tutor tactfully asked me to describe the situation it became clear there were none. For a start, break times were simply a time when the children could go out into the playground if they wanted to, while some would remain inside. This was their school and they could go where they liked. The net result was that there was effectively no place that the teacher could call his own and there was no place to be away from the children.

In those days too ancillary staff were few even in the largest of schools where lunch time supervision was still the responsibility of teaching staff. In the larger schools, of course, that was covered with a rota so that most teachers did actually get an hour's no contact time. The teacher bore sole responsibility not only for the curriculum and its delivery, but also every aspect of the child's educational, emotional and physical welfare during school hours. In short, the teacher was "in loco parentis" in every sense and for that reason a child could only be removed from school by a parent with the teacher's, normally the head teacher's, express permission. My experience throughout my teaching career was that staff took their responsibility very seriously. The child came first, second and third and one's responsibility and the job did not finish for the day until all aspects of that were discharged.

I was learning that in a hurry. Beyond the responsibility, however, there were a whole load of other considerations which made this situation particularly exhausting for a student teacher. As a student teacher I was starting at a disadvantage. I recall how at every teaching practice we would all be working well into the night preparing our teaching materials for the following day. I well remember one lecturer referring to the teacher's "hump". No, it wasn't a hump in the back developed from years of bending over a pile of books, marking. It was that precious stock of resources; teaching materials accumulated over the years which every teacher guarded jealously and which followed them from class to class. At this stage none of us had built up that precious resource and for every lesson we were starting from scratch. Beyond that, of course, every teacher acknowledged that some lessons would be 'mediocre' while occasionally one could admit frankly that a lesson just hadn't worked and that it was quite simply a failure. We, of course, as students could not allow ourselves such luxury, not least because our notes for each lesson, which our tutor could ask to see at any time, included a personal appraisal of the quality of the lesson and its outcome. In other words we had to perform a post mortem on each lesson to establish whether indeed it did die and whether it was due to natural causes! Such an activity could tend to lead to bouts of navel gazing which tended to increase the levels of anxiety. This was my first teaching practice and I so wanted to "get it right", while the accompanying anxiety inevitably increased my feelings of exhaustion.

As said, however, the situation was not helping. In the absence of teaching assistants or ancillary staff every little job fell to the teacher. I began to understand why the head had volunteered to take a student. Lunches, I recall, were cooked at a local secondary school and were delivered. Serving was the head teacher's preserve, while the subsequent washing up fell to the student teacher, a natural division of labour! It was my tutor's suggestion, and to his credit, that the children soon learned how to wash up. I can see that with such a small number of children the headteacher felt no need for formal structures and, indeed, probably rightly, felt that they would have been entirely inappropriate. I recall in my later years of teaching being in similar situations and so enjoying the absence of the formal constraints of the normal classroom setting. Indeed I even recall having the assistance of a student teacher on one such occasion. I hope, however, that my early experience helped me to be a little more sensitive to her needs as I tried to afford her time to herself, and to resist the temptation to use her as a 'dog's body'. She was, as I recall, remarkably accomplished and I hope she went on to a very successful teaching career. But much more of that later for at that moment I was feeling far from accomplished. Indeed I was feeling decidedly de-skilled and inadequate, and the notion of any sort of teaching career was seeming increasingly unlikely.

I said at the beginning of this particular trip down memory lane that the head drove me to his school, and therein lay the main problem - not his driving but that it was his school. It sometimes felt like his private fiefdom. It was his own little domain, and there seemed to be little room for another within it. In the absence of rules he was the rule of law. The children all looked to him. He was truly 'in loco parentis'. Such schools, I believe, had great value, for the children had one person to whom they could relate and in such a small setting could learn to relate to each other. Not for them the bewildering and impersonal environment of the large 'area' school in the nearest town where at break time they would find themselves cast out into the playground, frightened and alone, sitting in a corner trying to avoid as much attention as possible.

We hear so much about bullying these days and politicians vociferously making bullish statements about "zero tolerance on bullying". From the safety of the Palace of Westminster such statements come easily, but perhaps have a slightly hollow ring. The truth is, of course, that such large school settings, which seem currently so favoured, not only lend themselves to bullying but are a natural breeding ground for it. The large playground and the many rooms and corridors provide perfect cover for such activity where teachers cannot hope to be everywhere at once, especially at break times when just one or two will be on duty at a time. The situation at lunch time has, in some cases, become even worse with low paid ancillary staff being asked to take responsibilities for which they were never trained and perhaps, on occasions, are ill equipped. In some cases, too, in a secondary school setting, they may very well feel themselves physically ill equipped to be any sort of match for a well built 16 year old. Beyond the opportunities for bullying, however, in such a large, impersonal setting, for the less confident child, who may perhaps have size on his side, bullying can be a way of survival. The child who, on his first day, gets beaten up and finds himself having to retrieve items of clothing from various parts of the school playgound or in toilets and is then told off by the teacher for being late for a lesson and for his dishevelled appearance may quickly learn that his bullying in turn is his only way of survival.

I, of course, was not having to face up to well built or agressive 16 year olds and nor were there lots of places where bullies were wont to hide. The problem was there was nowhere for the teacher to hide. More to the point perhaps, in this particular one man band, it was difficult for me to have any role. The thing about roles is that they afford us security, they give us meaning and they can lend us a sense of authority, however limited. I, on the other hand, did not know where I belonged, but, more to the point, I had no sense of authority. This particular band only had one conductor and that was not me. It must be said that the chidren were not rude or unruly. On the contrary they were clearly happy, well adjusted children with a teacher whom they trusted, but, again, that teacher was not me.

In hindsight I see that it could not be and that the children and their teacher would be around for a long time after I left, but as a young student teacher desperately trying to 'fit in' the situation felt difficult and became anxiety laden. Beyond that my situation required me to have clear lesson plans with clear aims and expected outcomes. The notion of 'delivering' a lesson to such a wide range of ability and age was clearly inappropriate, but those were the expectations which I perceived had been placed upon me. Thus the lack of a role and any sense of my own authority, the weight of those perceived expectations and my anxiety in not meeting them, plus just no place to hide in that little Victorian village school, left me feeling totally exhausted.

It was thus that when I learned that I was to spend my second year teaching practice in a somewhat larger secondary school my initial reaction was one of quiet optimism and expectation. Somewhat larger it indeed was! Set in the middle of a sprawling estate built as part of a Portsmouth slum clearance and overspill scheme, it was huge. It dwarfed the school which I had attended in London just two years' earlier and like all attempts at resettling sections of the population it seemed that social problems had been built in with the brickwork. Some of those social problems I only discovered slowly during the course of what was to be my six week school practice. Not for me just three weeks in a tiny primary school nestled at the foot of the South Downs. This was as different to my eyes and imagination as it was possible to be. Words from the 'Sound of Music' sprang to mind as immortalised by Julie Andrews:

> "I've always longed for adventure
> To do the things I've never dared
> Yet here I'm facing adventure
> Then why am I so scared?"

Perhaps my finding out that, of one of the classes I was to be taking, 25% of the pupils, who were just the tender age of 13, were on probation orders had something to do with my apprehension. Visions of my experience of working in one of the summer play schemes held in some of the inner London schools came to mind.

Then 18 and having just completed my 'A' levels, I worked for a few weeks in a secondary school in London which was opened during the school holidays to provide activities for school aged children up to the age of about 14, aimed particularly at those whose parents were out at work and would therefore be unsupervised on the streets. For a young man given just ten shillings (50p) a week pocket money, it paid well. That was certainly part of the attraction of the work. A friend from school had introduced me to the scheme which also operated one evening a week during term time and I was duly appointed play leader grade 3. By that time I had decided that I wanted to go into teaching and this seemed a good opportunity to gain some experience, apart from which I reasoned that it might look good on a college application form! We were responsible for planning and maintaining a programme of activities to keep the children occupied during what was, in duration at least, a normal school day. Thus each day would see me leading a variety of activities from games of various sorts, through table tennis, to chasing around the playground trying to teach the children rugby. You might question how relevant rugby was, given both the circumstances, plus the fact that I had never exactly excelled in that particular area, or indeed sport in general, but the children seemed to enjoy it and enter into the spirit of the whole thing. On reflection it was probably the sight of this young man chasing round the playground with a lot more enthusiasm than skill that somehow contributed to the fun of the whole activity.

One of the activities was lunch, as a cooked meal was also provided. Perhaps under normal circumstances lunch would hardly be described as an activity, but perhaps my teaching rugby on the playground had borne more fruit than I had thought for it was rather reminiscent of a rugby scrum. I do recollect being appraised of one occasion, however, when clearly tempers between two boys became somewhat frayed. Unfortunately there was a considerable size differential between the two, resulting in the smaller of the two having his head inverted in the custard. I don't know how I managed to avoid being on duty at the time, but even so it managed to have a salutary effect upon me and I wondered if perhaps I would be safer sticking to table tennis in future. My baptism of fire, or rather the child's baptism with custard, had not managed to put me off entirely, but it was with some trepidation that I approached my second school practice.

My early days in the school did nothing to reassure me. The school itself was a maze of corridors into which the entire school population would spill every break time or between lessons, with staff and children alike trying to find the next room. I was advised by one member of staff to acquaint myself with the layout of the school as quickly as possible as it was not advisable to appear at a disadvantage in front of the children. This was clearly an authority issue, and I was beginning to gain the impression that 'might was right' or, to put it another way, that this was the survival of the fittest. How fit I was was put to the test some two weeks' later when I was asked to lead a cross country run with a group of approximately 30 fourteen year old boys.

I was given the route and was told that it simply went across a couple of fields and then headed back to school. All I had to do was to make sure I didn't lose any children or my way. At least the lesson plan was simple enough, the aim being to return all boys intact. Duly kitted out in my green tracksuit perhaps at least I might blend in with the background! The notion of disappearing did appeal. I was to supervise the boys changing and then lead them out of the school gates, turn left and left again. Fortunately some of the children seemed to know, and eagerly led, the way. This would be easy, I told myself, they were clearly eager enough. All I had to do was to keep them all together and return them in one piece. Even I could manage that, I was sure. The keener ones led the way across the first field and then came to a halt. "How thoughtful of them", I felt, "they were waiting for the rest of us to catch up and were clearly obeying my instructions not to go streaking on ahead". I duly arrived a few minutes later doing a very good impression of a sheep dog nipping at the heels of any stragglers. As I did so I began to understand the cause of the children's coming to a halt. Clearly the member of staff who had asked me to lead this particular fun run had neglected to mention that the two fields were separated by a 15' wide river! The boys seemed as surprised as I was and showed signs of turning back. Clearly this was a situation in which I was going to have to exercise whatever authority I could muster. "What do we do now?" was the question asked by a number of the boys. With the advice of the teacher not to allow myself to appear at a disadvantage, I replied, "We cross it, of course, come along". Some of the boys looked doubtful and muttered phrases to the effect of, "You're kidding". This really was turning a little difficult, with which I plunged into the river, which fortunately was no deeper than up to my knees, and waded across exhorting the boys to follow. To their credit a number jumped in after me and were soon across to the other side. Approximately half the group, however, continued to look decidedly doubtful and were clearly considering that the more attractive way back, and the quickest, was the way they had come. I knew I had to bring the group back in one piece, apart from which this was beginning to look like mutiny, in which case any authority I might have had would have been in shreds. Whereupon I stood in the middle of the river and bellowed "Come on, I'm not standing here for the benefit of my health". Fortunately a few more decided to cross and the refusers were becoming increasingly isolated. With one further bit of verbal "encouragement" from me and the rest of the class they jumped in and I immediately strode ahead and out across the field in case any of them should change their mind. It was a decidedly bedraggled, but surprisingly bouyant group on the whole, which re entered school and were even changed in time for the next lesson much to my surprise and relief. I really was not sure if the river was a normal part of the cross country course or whether I had been set up. It was clear the class had not expected it. Perhaps it had started as a stream and had been swollen with rain. At all events it was a couple of days' later that I learned from a member of staff that the run and me in particular were fast becoming a talking point around the school. My first reaction was to think to myself, "Oh dear, I might as well give up now!" I must have communicated some of my self doubt for the teacher assured me that I was being talked of in glowing terms by the children. Somehow my lunacy and determination had earned their admiration. It had also earned me a nickname of "greenback", clearly referring to the colour of my tracksuit. Little did they know that the name was even more apt than they first thought, for my tracksuit, being a particularly deep green, turned out not to be colourfast and my skin took on the same colour, courtesy of the river! Thereafter as I walked about, the word 'greenback' could be heard muttered in respectful tones in the corridors. Perhaps rather they just thought that such a lunatic at least deserved some pity. Either way that class were remarkably well behaved thereafter. Perhaps they were just frightened that I would take them on another run!

I recall one lecturer who, in speaking of the need for self awareness in our approach to teaching, quoting from another source, reminded us, "How can I hear what you are saying when what you are is screaming in my ears". I have forgotten the source of the quote, but the humbling truth of that has stayed with me. For it seems to me that it is supreme arrogance to assume that others, which includes children, should listen to or respect me just because I may believe myself to be in some position of authority. Authority is afforded to us by others or by the larger society, it is limited in its scope and only exists, in fact, where it is perceived. I do not argue against respect for particular roles. In a structured society, if it is to function, roles need to be respected, but respect is a two way street and it is too easy to abuse our perceived power.

That truth was very present for me in that teaching practice. These were not young children. In many cases they were just three years' younger than I. Thus, as I walked about the corridors into which, it seemed, the entire school spilled at regular intervals, I found myself holding the door for children following or thanking those who may have held the door for me until I was told by a teacher that is was not for me to hold doors for children, while similarly I should expect them to be held for me. That, I was told, was about exercising authority and commanding respect. Somehow I could never bring myself to comply with that particular injunction. Fear and respect can be easily confused. I am aware that in the past forty years social attitudes have changed. Perhaps we do well to consider the role and nature of respect in our present age.

Adequate lesson preparation, of course, was one way of showing respect for the children. Similarly if I wanted them to respect me sufficiently to listen or attend to my lesson, I had to make it relevant and interesting. Hence I was back to the long evenings and late nights as I prepared all those lesson plans for the following day. That, at least, was made easier than it had been during my first teaching practice. With all of the children in that tiny primary school being of different ages and stages of development and attainment it was difficult to prepare a 'model' lesson that was going to reach all of them. It was not like having a class of children who were ready grouped according to age and attainment as in my present setting. Oh the luxury of having clear lesson plans to show my tutor!

So it was that I found myself preparing a lesson on measuring. I reasoned that something as basic as using a ruler could not be too difficult even for a student teacher. Aware that I needed to make my lesson relevant, I tried to show that without measurements we had no real sense of big or small, long or short. I then tried to show how early measurements had been related to parts of the body such as an inch being based upon the first joint of the thumb and so upward through hands, spans, feet, cubits, and yards (from the tip of ones nose to the tip of the fingers of an outstretched arm). Not using a metric standard, I tried to encourage the children to see how the then imperial measures were real and easy to relate to. Thus the lesson saw the children measuring their thumbs, hands, feet etc. They were quickly beginning to get into the spirit of this and started to measure each others' vital statistics, etcetera. Unfortunately in a mixed class of 13 year olds it was the etc. which promised to quickly get out of hand as the class started to dissolve into good natured chaos. At this point I began to feel a little like Joyce Grenfell in one of her monologues, "No, Charlie, we don't want to know how big Deborah's what'sit is". Somehow, in the midst of this I managed to hear a little inner voice which said, "Well, you did ask for it, didn't you?" This was alongside the voice that said, "It's OK to start panicking now". Somehow I found myself laughing. Perhaps it was the recollection of those Joyce Grenfell monologues which managed to so amuse me in spite of the pending disaster of 30 children getting totally out of hand. Fortunately it was laughter which won the day and I managed to call the class to order. It was one of the class wits who said,

"Ah, sir, we were just beginning to enjoy ourselves". To which I was able to reply with a chuckle, "Yes, I'd noticed! Nevertheless..."

Thus, with an adequate sprinkling of humour and a dash of lunacy I had made it work for me and I had survived my second teaching practice, but I am not sure that I would have recommended my recipe to anybody else. I don't think it would have won any teacher awards.

Perhaps there is a wider lesson in that, as we seem to be into a personality cult at present so that we now have teacher awards along with the notion of 'super heads' who apparently can turn failing schools around. Teachers rule and teach by consent; the consent of the pupils, parents and other staff members. If we can enjoy the support and respect of all three it is not difficult to succeed. I am gravely concerned that the whole notion of teacher awards is ill conceived, merely serving to reinforce the sense of inadequacy of those who do not enjoy the support spoken of while contributing to the myth that there exists a special breed of particularly able or "great" people; a "master race". It was Bertolt Brecht who wrote, "Unglücklich das Land, das Helden nötig hat" (Unhappy the land that needs heroes). Perhaps such a personality or hero cult is a measure of how unhappy we are as a society.

At that point, however, I was not unhappy. If I could survive that Portsmouth overspill estate in which the planners somehow managed to squeeze all of that town's social problems into one area of high density housing, then I reasoned I could survive anything. How gratefully I returned to college with its welcoming tea, bread and jam which was just to tide us over until supper. I well remember the generally elated mood of all those students returning from the end of their second school practice in that third term of the second year. No more lesson preparation, just the swapping of horror stories and commiserating with those who at that moment felt they had not survived quite so well or those whose tutor had asked to see them or had suggested a meeting. We now had two teaching practices under our belts. We had survived two years of our course. The all important third year with its teaching practice and finals was yet to come.

I can look back on that final teaching practice with some very fond memories although the class teacher and I did not seem to get off to a very good start. He clearly felt that I was just another student without proper hold of the class; back to that question of authority again! He was probably right for formal discipline was never my strong point. My standing in his eyes, however, and my authority in the class took an unexpected upturn.

I was back in a primary school, but one that was rather larger than my earlier experience of two years previously. It was an age group that I had always felt more comfortable with and I was working with a class of 10-11 years. Part of a project I was seeking to involve the chidren in included a number of them painting. Always a risky business with a large number of young children unless there is clear organisation and discipline. How well I had managed those considerations I am not sure, but one particular boy lingers in my memory. He was clearly disinterested and could not be bothered and he became casual and sloppy in his behaviour. Sloppy is a good word for he managed to slop paint not only over the floor but upon his neighbour's work. Such carelessness of another and their work offended my sense of fair play. He had hurt another needlessly. Maintaining my composure, I suggested he might clear up the mess and started to help. His response, however, was equally careless and resulted in more spilt paint. Accidents happen, but he clearly had not learnt from his, but he was about to, as I barked at him, "Go and get a mop". He looked at me but did not move. "Now", I barked even louder eliciting a rather sullen "Yes, alright". To which I again barked, "Yes, what?" This time his manner was somewhat changed as he responded, "Yes, sir" and scuttled out of the classroom to get a mop. Once the incident was duly resolved and the classroom tidied, the classroom teacher, who had been present at this point, took advantage of a quiet moment and said, equally quietly, "Well done. You won't have any more trouble". And I didn't. I feel that discipline was a lot easier then. Teachers were still respected, even student ones.

A week or so later I understood that my tutor or supervisor was to come out to see me at work and so that Saturday afternoon he invited me to his house to discuss my work with the children. Upon my arrival I was greeted with, "Oh, I'm glad you've arrived, my wife and I just need to pop out for a moment. Could you stay with the children?" So I spent the next hour sitting on the floor playing with his three children. We were having such a whale of a time that I don't know how long he had been standing at the door before he said, "Shall we go into another room?" In hindsight I have a feeling that this very perceptive Froebel trained tutor had very deliberately set up that situation. We seemed to get on very well from then as he gave me a few pointers as to how I might further organise the rest of the project with the children in school. I took it all on board and spent the rest of that weekend and all the ensuing evenings preparing my school work.

He spent the whole day with me and his manner with the children was such that he could just blend into the background and would often be seen on the floor himself with the children. Such was his sensitivity that I hardly noticed his presence till I called the children to order at the end of a very busy and productive day and looking around saw him in a spare place at one of the children's tables, sitting up just as smartly as all the other children! Again I had learnt a lot and grown a little. Apparently I had grown sufficiently to be awarded a credit for my teaching practice which I only learned much later. Perhaps rather the credit belonged with my tutor, but I was happy enough to receive it.

Such was the ethos of the college, reflecting perhaps its roots in Anglican spirituality, but too very much in keeping with the then current educational thinking. I recall being reminded by one lecturer in our first year of the origins of the word educate, coming from the Latin "educare", to draw out, to lead away, to nurture; hence we were reminded, educo, I draw out, not I bang in.

Education was not to be drumming in a discrete set of facts, but encouraging the child's natural desire to explore, learn and understand. where each followed from the other. I drew, too, from those lectures the understanding that "What I hear, I remember. What I do, I know" We were being prepared as educators to come alongside the children and to join with them in that joint adventure of learning.

For the moment, however, I am aware of how much I was being drawn out, how much I was being lead away from what had felt an increasingly narrow home background, as I experienced interest and encouragement from tutors, support and friendship from fellow students. Thus, to go back to that other sense of "educare", I felt nurtured.

How much of those values, I question, remain in our schools today which have effectively become fortresses where children are locked in and visitors are locked out. Is there any room left for the child to discover and grow in understanding in a curriculum externally governed, politically motivated, filled with targets and punctuated with attainment tests? Attainment assessed against a set of criteria supposes an explicit set of standards instead of valuing the intrinsic desire to learn and need to grow within the individual. The implication of that explicit set of standards is that it must be externally set. Are we engendering a society in which the individual has no value beyond their ability to conform to that set of standards and their worth assessed by the extent to which they can attain those standards? My son, when he was still quite young, but old enough to have some experience of this trend in education, remarked very perceptively one day, "School teaches you how to fail". Is that the main thing we are teaching our children? I question.

Chapter Three

The Early Years

"Let us therefore brace ourselves to our duties"
Winston Churchill, 18th June, 1940

Thus full of ardour and enthusiasm I had accepted my first post and as I stood surveying that empty classroom I reflected on the frenetic activity that had brought me there.

This was where three years of teacher training had led me. Back in the 60's, in the heady days following the Plowden Report, teaching was a profession full of hope. The whole thrust of the then current thinking was "child centred". The curriculum was centred around the child's intellectual and developmental needs. The ground breaking work of Piaget many years before was now to the fore, as he had identified distinct developmental stages in understanding and we understood that, regardless of what adults might want for the child, there was no point in teaching certain aspects of the curriculum until the child had reached that stage in understanding. Thus the early school years were dominated by activities which encouraged the development of those vital concepts. Activities which to many outside the education system seemed like nothing but play. Indeed, I can recall in those early years of teaching the constant criticism levelled at teachers that, "All they seem to do at school these days is play". In spite of such objections, however, which were usually said in fun, parents were happy to allow teachers to get on with the job of educating the children in their charge. To be placed "in loco parentis" at the tender age of nearly 23 felt such a huge responsibility which I took very seriously.

With finals looming, I had, with all my fellows, started applying to Education Authorities around the country as it was usual then for newly qualified teachers to apply direct to the Local Education Authority (L.E.A.) who knew how many posts they were going to need to fill and could ensure that schools should only get their quota of newly qualified staff so that there was adequate support for the teacher concerned and that schools were not swamped with inexperienced staff. That was the theory and a very laudable principle. Unfortunately what so often happened was quite the opposite. For those schools which found themselves in less affluent or in socially deprived areas inevitably experienced the higher turnover of staff and therefore at the end of every academic year could expect to have a number of teaching posts that needed filling. It was an obvious temptation for authorities to fill those posts with newly qualified staff as they were aware that such schools would attract less applications, in the general run of things, from more experienced staff who, if they lived reasonably locally, would be aware of their reputation before they applied. Such schools quickly became known as 'sink' schools. Perhaps it reflected the understanding that the newly qualified staff would either "sink or swim". Perhaps too it reflected the feeling that, like a sink without a plug, you could keep tipping in staff and resources and that they would disappear just as quickly. Rather, I believe, it probably reflected the notion that like a sink they could be used as a recepticle for all those staff newly qualified and otherwise who could not find posts elsewhere. I am aware that the factors which breed "success" or "failure" in schools are similar to those in people. Success, like failure, however we understand such judgements, are socially and environmentally induced. Put a school in the middle of an affluent area where the parents have high expectations and, all other factors being equal, the school will flourish, for the children coming from such a background will be confident and expect to succeed. Similarly staff aspirations will be higher and will be drawn not only to teach at such schools, but also to move into the area. We are aware that success breeds success.

It perhaps would be unfair to describe the school to which I was appointed as a 'sink school', but it was certainly true that I was not the only newly qualified teacher appointed at the beginning of that academic year and that it did have a high turnover of staff. I recall the words of one member of staff who on his last day before taking up a new post elsewhere said, "I would like to say that I will come back and visit you all, but I know that if I did there wouldn't be any familiar faces, but then I'm aware too that we all have to serve our sentence here". Very clearly he felt he had been granted a reprieve and indeed there was a general understanding that if you 'knuckled down, got on with the job and kept your nose clean', your chances of an early release were greatly enhanced. It is not surprising perhaps, therefore, that the governor, sorry headteacher, had a permanent scowl and look of grim determination on his face and walked in a somewhat dogged flat footed way where, if there had ever been any spring in his step, it had long since disappeared. At least that is how he appeared to me, as a young, fresh faced, enthusiastic and perhaps slightly over optimistic teacher. Mr. Gradgrind from Charles Dickens sprang to mind. I had always believed Dickens' characters to be caricature. As I felt in awe and nervous of this determined looking figure, I started to question my earlier literary judgement. Had Dickens known our head teacher, I pondered?

Teaching and my first post were just part of a new life for me, of which, therefore, education was an essential part. Certainly that had been true as a child, when school based in London, required a 50 minute journey. Similarly I had deliberately avoided the London or more local colleges when it came to my teacher training. Now here I was, recently married, and the owner of a small house in a neighbouring village. Parents and home felt a long way away both geographically and emotionally. I had travelled a long way in the past three years. At least, that is how it felt to me as I contemplated my present situation. It was a little unnerving therefore that the head teacher in demeanour and stature reminded me very much of my father. Perhaps I was not so far from home after all!

I quickly learned that I was going to need transport to get to and from my new post and felt most grateful for my 'Lambretta' scooter as there was really only a meaningful bus service on one day a week, which was market day. On all other days, except Sundays of course, there was an occasional bus, but certainly not at a time that would get me to or from school.

I well remember those first winters, negotiating the fairly steep hill down to school on icy mornings. I still shudder slightly as I think about some of the unnerving slides and close calls that I had. How I remained upright on some occasions I still marvel at, where falling off into the path of a car seemed an ever present 'danger'. At least I had the comfort that I was most unlikely to be run over by a bus!

Buses, however, could occasionally be seen as they passed outside my classroom. A fairly small, dark room, it had a high Victorian gothic window on one side which allowed one to see the upper deck only of the buses that did pass. Next to the high window, on the adjacent wall, there was one wooden cupboard which was to hold all the resources I was supposed to need to teach the class which were to be entrusted to me.

Those two days before term started found me looking into the cupboard hopefully, for all those resources and teaching aids I had come to expect and which I believed formed the basis of every teacher's armoury. Instead I found two small piles of graded reading books which comprised those parts of two separate reading schemes which were supposed to represent the age and ability of the pupils in the class. These two piles were made up of dog-eared, very limp, cloth covered "Happy Venture" and some equally well used paper backed "Gay Way" readers. Beyond that were three piles of exercise books, one lined for 'english', one squared for 'mathematics' and another plain as a 'rough book' for all the children's jottings and calculations as this was at least 20 years before calculators started to appear. There one pile of sugar paper and paints, brushes and a box of pencils. I have a vague recollection that my "stock" ran to geography, history and nature text books. Thus resourced I was to take full responsibility for my first class. As I surveyed those meagre resources I experienced a range of emotions. At first my heart sank; I proceeded to feel very alone. This was where all my training and expectations had led me. I found any sense of hope fading. I went back outside the classroom and looked on the door just in case I had got the wrong room. No, there was no mistake, the label read clearly '1C'. There was no escaping either that simple fact or my responsibility which increasingly flooded in upon me until I felt completely swamped by it. I had signed my contract and had taken on a mortgage on the strength of it. I was on my own. I had no school practice tutor to run to, for this was no practice. It was for real. Just a fortnight earlier, my wife, who had been my wife for just the same period, and I, arrived on my scooter at our new home, with our cases, which we had not been able to carry, dumped on our doorstep where my parents had left them. I felt truly alone and my next feeling was of pure panic.

I could not, however, indulge my panic for ever. I reminded myself that I was a trained professional and must get on with the job. I procured some card from school stock which the deputy head administered and invested in a couple of fairly thick felt tip pens from the local newsagent and spent the next twenty four hours making work cards for the children, to supplement my meagre resources. It also involved my digging fairly deep and finding some resources within myself.

Resources, of course, emotional or otherwise, are what we build up slowly, normally out of surplus. The child who experiences all the love that he or she needs grows up to be a confident outward going adult with emotional resources enough to cope with the trials that life will inevitably throw at them. If we experience love as lacking, we learn to live on a "hand to mouth" basis taking whatever love we can get from wherever we can get it, but never really building up those emotional resources we need to be able to live life to its full or function at our best. That, of course, is a gross generalisation and many of my readers will point out that they had a less than perfect upbringing and have gone on to achieve great things. However, in the two years that they had already been at school, the pupils of 1C in the junior department of this very large primary school had not, so far, achieved great things in the educational field and had already been labelled as 'C' stream. As I reflected on my educational psychology lectures, I pondered those things which may have contributed to such an early label. Were they as lacking in confidence as I felt at that very moment?

As they all filed into my classroom the following morning I wondered who was most apprehensive; they or I? I guess we all brought our fears into the classroom that morning. I did not really have time for my fears however. This was it and they were firmly set aside. That first day, rather like my first year almost, seemed 'to disappear in a blur', but I do remember how gratefully I returned home on my scooter later that afternoon with my first pile of marking. I was not quite so grateful for that!

As I said, that year is now something of a blur, but there were a few highlights and low moments which went to fashion the teacher that I was to be for the years to come. My first task was to give every pupil a reading book which involved assigning each a book on the basis of their reading ability. This was to be determined by a reading test which I was informed by the head had to be completed at the beginning and end of every school year in order to determine the progress of each child. Perhaps, therefore, the observation needs to be made at this point that teachers were testing pupils using properly standardised tests long before politicians, or government in particular, felt the need to interfere and impose the dreaded SAT's. The words of W.S. Gilbert, from the operetta "Iolanthe" by Gilbert and Sullivan spring to mind:

"And while the house of peers witholds its legislative hand
and noble statesmen do not itch
to interfere with matters which
they do not understand
then bright will shine Great Britain's rays
as in King George's glorious days."

I would not single out the house of peers, however constituted, but perhaps the legislative hand is worth reflecting upon!

All that, of course, was in the days when teachers, like all other professionals, were allowed to get on with the job for which they were trained and politicians sought to maintain an atmosphere in which they could properly function. Perhaps there is a greater social comment in that which goes beyond teaching and all the other areas of our corporate living. It is, I feel, that, like the beehive, society works best as a harmonious whole when each member of it is allowed and encouraged to fulfil their own particular function within it and does not seek to stray upon somebody else's. Such straying into social philosophy, however, does not complete a reading test!

That particular reading test was based on simple word recognition, the number of words correctly read giving a score which, following a simple calculation, rendered a reading age. This was to be yet another reminder of how far I had travelled recently, in this case geographically. East Anglia felt a very long way from Essex or Greater London as my parents' home was when I had finished college. Beyond the lack of a bus service, I learned how different was this part of the world to which I had moved, including the accent. Each of the pupils had to read a list of words to me which were arranged in rows of five. The one row of words which is engraved upon my mind read in best home counties English "that, girl, day, pot, one". The majority of children in my class, however, rendered it as "the', gel, dahee, pa' wern". I was reminded of how narrow a background I had come from where regional accents were either laughed at or frowned upon. I hope that, in this regard at least, not only I, but we as a society, have become more tolerant in recent years and BBC English is no longer "de rigeur".

Again another reminder of how far I had travelled. Indeed I was in another world very different from that of home where hardly anybody knew anybody else beyond, perhaps, immediate neighbours, or college where everybody was drawn from different backgrounds from all over the country. This had been a small country town, admittedly now suffering from London overspill, but local names and local accents still survived. Thus

I was again struck by how many children seemed to be related, however distantly, or bore the same surname. The value, of course, in that small community feel is that it affords a sense of belonging and I had a vague sense that a number of children, even at that age, had an idea of what adulthood held in store for them and that whatever I did in that classroom wasn't going to make too much difference.

Perhaps such an assessment of my teaching is to take an unduly jaded view as one of the children in that class is now my local publican in the village. I recollect that his great strength was always mathematics and not only does he now serve a very good draught guinness and remarkably filling lunches, but he has never given me the wrong change yet. I like to comfort myself with the notion that perhaps not all my teaching was in vain as I see the position he enjoys and the very real contribution he makes to the community.

Increasingly, too, I was beginning to feel a part of that same community. It was for me a new and warming experience to be able to walk into shops and be greeted with "Hello, Mr. Cutler, what can we do for you today?" or to be able to walk into the pharmacist to address him by name with "Hello, Mr. Graham, what can you offer me for hay fever?" All that, of course, was in those happy days when I could open an account at the local bank without having to show photo I.D. and merely have a word with the chief clerk. So I experienced myself being accepted into a community which was certainly evidenced by two incidents in those early months. Firstly, someone arrived in the village simply asking where the new teacher lived and was immediately directed to our house. It

head teacher got that I had not? Perhaps it was that grim look of determination I have already described. In my innocence it did not occur to me that his role as head teacher alone might naturally afford some status and an air of authority. In a large school which had topped a thousand pupils just before I arrived, the head was, by force of circumstance, a rather distant figure which a child only saw if they were in trouble. That tended to apply to members of staff too. Fortunately that does not seem to have applied to me on that occasion, in spite of my unpromising start, for as he left the classroom after sitting in on much of my lesson he said something quietly to the effect of, "You'll do". I was very aware that I was, after all, a probationary teacher still serving my qualifying year. If I wanted to retain that precious ministry of education number which allowed me to teach, it would require my head teacher's assurance to the education authority that I would indeed "do".

So that first term wore gently on with the normal anxieties of a newly qualified teacher, a newly married couple and the responsibilities of a new householder. On the latter front it was good to have our own space. We always felt it had that lived in look; lived in before! For our furniture and carpets had been donated by various members of family and friends and we spent those early years still with many of our clothes stored in the trunk which had accompanied me to college and back. Such frugality became a natural part of our lives, certainly in that first year, and we tried to heed the advice of Charles Dickens' character, Mr. Micawber, "Income £1, expenditure nineteen shillings and sixpence, result happiness. Income £1, expenditure twenty shillings and sixpence, result misery". My income as a newly qualified teacher was not quite that low but I do recollect that in that first year it was not enough to cross the tax threshold. Teaching then was certainly still seen as a vocation and we all understood that one certainly did not enter the profession for its financial rewards. As Christmas, at the end of that first term, approached, I began to wonder just what rewards I had joined the profession for.

I became aware of increasing expectations upon me, not least to have my classroom looking suitably festive, showing signs of all the seasonally related art and craft work undertaken by the children. Looking back I have a sense that I had little idea on this particular front and my craft lessons were certainly on the safe side, preferring to restrict the children to those activities which did not involve them in too much exuberant activity which would still enable me to maintain class control. I was indeed "cutting my coat according to the cloth", but then not only were my professional resources at that stage limited. So, I recall, were craft materials as we were allowed two rolls of crepe paper, a small amount of gummed paper squares and not too much else. Thus the run up to Christmas arrived with a standard allotment of stock to each classroom and woe betide the teacher who said, "Please sir, may I have some more?" That is my excuse at least, but on the day of the regulation Christmas party I have a recollection that the head was somewhat underwhelmed at my attempts at decorating my classroom. Indeed on that day I gained the impression he was somewhat underwhelmed with me all the way round.

Christmas parties were held for each year in the school on a separate day. Thus all the first year juniors had their party on one day, the second years on the next day and so on. Of course it would never do to have teaching time interrupted and so children and teachers as a treat were allowed to stay after school! The "party" started with orange squash being delivered to each classroom and a regulation amount of "party fare" was to be placed on a paper napkin on each child's desk. All this took place while the children had 15 minutes' toilet break and recreation outside, and was prepared by the classroom teacher. The children were then ushered back and sat at their desks while the head came round to each class in turn to ask the children if they were enjoying themselves, to which all the children were required to respond "Yes sir". I gained the impression that enjoyment was not optional. The children then came together for some suitable entertainment before being sent home. They were, however, spared the head dressing up as Father Christmas.

I remember with what thankfulness I saw the children depart, for the day had started for me with part of a tooth breaking away whilst eating breakfast. Breakfast for me then was always a cooked one. It was comforting, beyond which it made up for the sandwich which I would normally have for lunch. In those days, in the late sixties, teachers were still expected to be on duty during the children's lunch break, but if we wanted a cooked school lunch we had to pay the full economic cost, not the one shilling that the children then paid. Taking a packed lunch meant at least a brief period to relax over a sandwich and a cup of tea while some of one's colleagues supervised the children. Lunchtime supervision was, at that time, considered a natural part of being "in loco parentis" and we all took turns. I remember the time a few years' later when teachers were no longer required to provide lunch time cover as a contractual duty and, if we did, we were allowed a free school lunch, always provided we ate it with the children. But those heady days, so hard fought for by the teachers' union, were still a few years away, which brings me back to breakfast and my broken tooth.

The tooth itself already had a crown inlay and the loss of a further part of it left me in considerable pain. Thus when I got to school I had to ask permission to telephone the dentist who conveniently was immediately opposite the school. I was offered an appointment for 11 a.m. and the head duly said he would cover my class but I was reminded that it should not take more than half an hour. It was admittedly a "no frills" or, perhaps, "no niceties" dental service; a quick injection of local anaesthetic and work started, so that if one was lucky the area started to go numb by the time the whole operation was finished. Operation seems to have been the appropriate word in this case, as the dentist took one look at the tooth and said, "I can't do much with that. It'll have to come out". That apparently was easier said than done, as on the first pull another bit of tooth came away and he proceeded to cut away at my gum to retrieve various bits of my tooth. The result could not be said to be a "neat job" and the various flaps of my gum were sown back together with black thread which I was told would need to be removed a week or so later, once it had healed. Thus I returned to school, my mouth still full of blood and looking a subtle shade of grey. Fortunately for me I had not exceeded my half hour. At that moment I was already feeling a little jaded and further disapproval from Mr. Gradgrind was the last thing I needed. I smiled faintly and muttered thank you to the head for taking my class, as much as my mouthful of blood would allow, and was left very firmly to get on with what I was paid to do. As the afternoon wore on so my local anaesthetic wore off and my mouth started to remind me, as if I needed reminding, of what had been done to it that morning, and from all it was telling me I rather gained the impression that it did not approve. Thus it was that neither my mouth nor the head teacher approved of me by now. I began to wonder what I had done to warrant such unanimous disapproval beyond eating my breakfast. I swore it was porridge for me from then on, if only through force of circumstance!

My colleagues were rather more sympathetic to my plight and did lend a hand when it came to preparing my classroom for the festivities which were to follow. Indeed by the time the "tea party", squash, sandwiches, crisps etc. had finished and the children came together, they said fairly pointedly in the head teacher's hearing that I should go home as they could manage, to which the head immediately responded that Mr. Cutler would go home "like the rest of us", when he had finished. By the time I got home that evening, I felt as if I was!

As I look back on that first term it is therefore perhaps not surprising that my birthday at the end of November found me in bed with a virus. Absence from teaching was always difficult as it meant another teacher had to be found, which often put a strain on one's colleagues until they were. Then, of course, having arrived they had to try to pick up where you had left off, so woe betide any teacher whose lesson plans were not up to date before they decided to go off sick. Thus I had had to incur the head's displeasure twice and that was just my first term's teaching. Whoever has on occasions given voice to the often held idea that teachers have nice long holidays, may reconsider their hasty judgement. If school holidays do seem long, believe me its the teachers that need them, not the children. The six weeks in the summer is normally reserved for a nervous breakdown!

This, however, was Christmas and I had survived my first term. My wife by that time also had a job in an agricultural estate office. For her too all this was a long way from the London office she had known before we were married. Indeed, our new life felt very different from the one we had come from, and I remember that some of the skills we learned quite early on included skinning and cleaning a rabbit. Plucking and cleaning pheasants was to come a little later! Money was tight on a teacher's salary then, but with my wife's job as well we were able to afford Christmas presents. Thus it was that a few days after the end of term saw us travelling back towards London and my parental home on our Lambretta scooter, with my wife sitting on the pillion seat clutching an 8 foot long-armed pruner for my father, looking something like Britannia holding her trident. Fortunately there were no low bridges on our journey.

The next term saw me starting with a little less apprehension than I had started just four months previously. I was becoming an "old hand" by now, but apprehension of a different sort was to be my companion for the next month as we enjoyed a harder winter than I had recalled in London in recent years and I had to negotiate that hill down to school. I had passed my driving test for a motorcycle just before I started college, but I had never really had to drive in icy conditions. Buses in London were frequent and routes were many, but that was not the case now. Thus I was aware I had little choice but to brave the elements. It was therefore one icy morning that I set out and negotiated the three miles as far as the top of the said hill, at which point the traffic down into the town was naturally building up, the more so because everybody was travelling that much slower. So it was that I applied my brake very gently just to check my speed, at which point with little or no adhesion to the road my rear wheel quickly locked and I sailed gracefully down the hill for the next hundred yards, still upright, but with apparently no control over how long I should continue my wavering course or where it was likely to take me. Fortunately my wheels found some gravel on the road and I came to a halt just before I reached the car in front. That salutory experience remained with me but fortunately another member of staff also lived in the village and, taking pity on this young man with as little experience of driving as I did teaching, offered me a lift in his car the following morning. He was a lot more experienced in both capacities than I and over the next few years while I remained at the school I was grateful for both his driving and his teaching experience. For if the road conditions looked in the slightest bit hazardous for two wheels I had only to telephone him to avail myself of a lift with his four. It was that, if nothing else, which motivated my wife and I to get a telephone connected fairly early on in our life in our new home. Telephones, which we so take for granted now, were even then not so commonplace and many we knew in the village still did not have one. Fortunately public kiosks were available in the village however.

My first term and the bad weather over it was down hill to Easter and the summer term. The end of the summer term promised a six week break and the end of my first year's teaching. Before such delights could even be contemplated, however, beyond the normal end of term activities, like the school sports day, there was the question of trying to assess what, if anything, the children had learned and therefore how much they had progressed. That meant repeating the reading test I mentioned earlier and the writing of reports. The latter meant going through all the records that I was supposed to keep during the course of the year for each subject area taught and trying to meaningfully convey the child's efforts and progress.

I always found the process both humbling and testing. Who was I to write a report on another or how could I begin to really convey the child's own inner struggles and efforts to engage with what I had been teaching, which lay at the heart of the educational process on which I was being asked to comment, and if I experienced him or her as failing, how could I convey that without damning or permanently damaging their future school career? How much could I know about the home background? How would my negative comments be received? If it was a difficult home background, would it result in the child receiving a "good hiding" just on the strength of my comments? What too of such terms as "lazy"? Even if I did experience a child as 'lazy' what does that term mean? Does it mean poorly motivated, in which case, does it simply mean I wasn't doing my job?

Again as much as such thoughts may have assailed me, I had to put them aside. There was a job to do and I was expected to do it. For how much would the children benefit from my indulging in what may seem philosophical questions? At least that is what I told myself. On reflection, I am aware of how much I seemed to be setting those bigger questions aside. I question how often all of us do the same because we do not feel we have the time or the place in which to look at them. Perhaps too we are afraid that if we ask them, the answer may challenge all that we do, while the practicalities of life demand to be attended to. I had been trained to do a job and thirty something children's futures needed me, and those of my colleagues they would meet along the way, to do it.

However, before I could have the temerity to write a report I needed to know how the children had progressed, so I had to repeat that reading test. I must have done something right in the ten months since the previous September for I found to my relief that the children, on the whole, had advanced between 0.9 and 1.2 years. Looking back, I am tempted to say it had nothing to do with me, but clearly the Head at least must have credited me with the results, for the following September I was given charge of 2B, second year juniors 'B' stream. In the scheme of things it seemed I had been promoted. More to the point, perhaps, I had completed my probationary year. I was a fully fledged teacher and I was being given a chance to try my wings.

Chapter Four

Growth & Setbacks

"We have as short a spring,
As quick a growth to meet decay"
Robert Herrick, To daffodils

At that stage I think I felt myself rather as a young plant being 'potted on' into a bigger pot, perhaps prior to planting out. Who could know? From my small classroom tucked away in a corner of the school with its high window I had now moved into an altogether larger room in the front of the school, near to the office and nearer too to the head's office. I was beginning to feel myself very much more at the hub of things. Indeed, with its larger windows looking out onto a rather more major road with all its busyness outside, I was beginning to feel much more a part of life in general. Coupled with that, I now found myself with a rather grand title of "Head of French". That, however, is not quite so grand when one considers that I was the only teacher taking French. At that time it was considered that language teaching in schools should start early, for it was understood that we learn language more readily when we are young. Thus it was expedient that the school should at least be seen to be going along with this trend in education. My appointment to my new post was simply effected by the head remarking, "You did French at 'A' level didn't you? I think teaching French would be good for you. Consider yourself Head of French. I'll adjust the timetable" It must be added, however, that my salary was not adjusted as well. That was to come much later in my career.

The school already had a little in the way of materials when it came to French, but they were old and few. This was beginning to remind me of my situation just one year previously as I had surveyed my meagre resources. The only difference was that now I was going to have to 'ad lib' in a foreign language. I found my stock response was fast becoming "*Je ne sais pas*" or, to put it another way, "Don't ask me I'm only the French teacher".

However, the resources problem was about to be resolved in an altogether unexpected way. We were not very far into the autumn term, being mid to late September, in the year 1968. I was in touch with a close friend from college. College of just over a year ago was almost a life time away by now, but this friend had also been present at our wedding and had recorded the service. That had included the anthems sung by representatives of the college choir who had travelled to Essex or Greater London from various parts of the country just to be at the wedding. As I look back to that time and how immediately after our wedding life caught us up and whisked us on, I regret never really having been able to more fully thank those who were there, including one of our organ scholars whom I can still remember making a very valiant attempt at Widor's 'Toccata & Fugue' on a one manual organ. Thus it was that we found ourselves with an invitation to lunch just the other side of Suffolk at the home of our dear friend, his mother and brother. In this age of fast roads and even faster cars 'just the other side of Suffolk' would represent a comparatively short journey, by today's standards, of approximately one hour, but then, with only our Lambretta scooter for transport, it took us almost twice that time. Lunch was an altogether pleasant and civilised affair such that we really paid little attention to the rain which started shortly after we had arrived. As it persisted into the afternoon we told ourselves that it would clear up before we left. However, lunch extended into afternoon tea and the rain still had not stopped. Thus it was that as the afternoon wore on we realised we were going to have to make our return journey in the rain which, far from abating, was getting heavier. Donning just our raincoats, for we were hardly seasoned bikers and certainly did not boast leathers or even proper waterproofs, we said our good-byes and thankyous for a thoroughly pleasant day and set out. With the roads by now thoroughly wet and beginning to collect puddles here and there our progress homeward was even slower than our outward journey had been as we tried to avoid skidding or aqua planing, and we arrived home shortly before a very early dusk.

On our arrival home we were completely soaked and we tried to drape our various items of clothing about the house wherever we could find a spare surface. Not yet boasting an airer, but just a clothes line and no post, doors tended to serve for that role. With only a small two bar electric fire for comfort, I set to and prepared lesson notes etc. for the coming week while the rain continued outside.

We looked in the trunk which I had had at college and still served as our chest of drawers for some dry clothes for the following morning. A teacher's starting salary most certainly did not run to items of furniture in those days especially when there were other items which seemed more pressing, like a fridge. Thus it was that, still feeling slightly damp and certainly cold and tired, we retired as soon as all jobs necessary to survival, like my lesson notes, were completed.

When we woke the following morning, the first thing that we became aware of was how quiet it was. "Oh thank goodness", I thought, "The rain has stopped and I won't have to drive to school in the rain". I didn't want any more damp clothes. Then as I listened, I realised that the absence of the rain did not wholly account for this strange absence of noise. What else was missing? It was the noise of traffic. Normally at about seven o'clock in the morning there would be the noise of people driving through our small estate of houses on their way to work in the neighbouring town and local factories, but we heard no cars. Was it a bank holiday and we had not realised? I parted the curtains and looked out of the bedroom window of our small bungalow which faced onto the road. How strange, there were people simply walking about which one never normally saw on a work morning. It reminded me again that perhaps it was a bank holiday, but these people were walking about apparently aimlessly with nothing to do. People who had clearly been up in time to go to work and had suddenly been robbed of purpose. Had there been a mass redundancy at the local abattoir and meat processing plant, a major employer in the area? I went to the door and looked out. As if seeing the nature of the question written over my face, somebody replied to my greeting of "good morning" with "You'll not get out of the village or to school this morning". Certainly within the year that I had been living within the village, everybody knew where the new teacher lived! However, my informant continued: "We're cut off, the river is over by the bridge and by the mill". As we investigated after breakfast along with a large number of other residents, we were able to confirm the truth of that statement. The main road out of the village and the houses either side were flooded to a depth of about 2 foot 6 inches in old money, or 75cms. We were greeted by our next door neighbour who was just climbing into the bucket of a digger which proceeded up the driveway of one of the flooded houses and raised the bucket until it was level with one of the upstairs windows enabling our next door neighbour to hand over some vital supplies to the marooned occupants, including, most importantly, some baby milk for the young baby. It was certain we were not going to get out of the village that day.

The following day, however, saw me back in school minus the children. I was greeted by the head who asked me why I hadn't been in school the previous day! I was tempted to say "You are joking, aren't you?" but he clearly wasn't. Clearly the head's devotion to duty and the expectation that his staff would share that loyalty was commendable, so in the face of such determination and concern for the children all I felt able to do was to explain apologetically that I had been stranded in the village due to the flood. Such concern, however, became the more puzzling when I surveyed my classroom.

The school itself was built over a brook which was, in fact, a tributary of the river which ran through our village, and rejoined it several miles further on. That same brook had itself flooded all the classrooms to a depth of about 18 inches (45cms). Apart from leaving the children's chairs in disarray as they had obviously floated about the room, it had soaked any teaching materials which had been stored on lower shelves, to whit, those precious French teaching resources. I started to make a valiant attempt at drying them by putting up lines of string across my classroom and pegging up the worksheets etc., until the head came in and reminded me that I should not be able to use them as they were likely to be infected with who knew what bacteria from the brook, which ran all the way through the town and which also took surface water. Teaching even then was not over resourced moneywise and teachers quickly became experts in make do and mend as well as simply "scrounging". However, on this occasion I was told I should have to order some more. Such luxury! I had never been able to order new materials before and in my training and hitherto short career what I could not find, re-use or adapt, I had had to make. Order some new materials! Apparently every cloud, even persistent rain clouds, had a silver lining!

My new found responsibility of teaching French was a breath of spring to me. It seemed to breathe life into what had felt like a rather dispiriting introduction to what then was still regarded not only as a profession, but a calling, although the practicalities of day to day survival can quickly dispel any notions of nobility. Hence I rather enjoyed my new found role which went a little way towards restoring some of those hopes I had had while training and when I had first started teaching. The children seemed to enjoy it too. For 40 minutes they did not have to write much, if anything, for the approach to French teaching at primary level was essentially oral. It was reasoned that we naturally learn language through hearing it spoken and learning to mime what we hear. I had always enjoyed the sound and natural cadences of the French language and tried to engender a similar joy in the children. What a contrast to my own introduction to French in the first year of my grammar school which was to learn how to decline the verb 'être', to be, while our homework had been to write out and learn how to do the same for the verb 'avoir', to have. Hence I quite quickly learned, "*J'ai un mal à la tête*". I taught the children songs and the head seemed particularly impressed when I managed to get the children to sing a French carol as we approached the end of the Christmas term. The other bonus for me of such teaching was that it enabled me to get about the school a little more and to see other classes beyond my own, while it also meant that it was one lesson which did not produce a pile of marking at the end of it. One thing about teaching my small first year 'C' stream class was that it did not inundate me with large quantities of marking. How I noticed the difference with a second year 'B' stream. Not only was the class large, 36 in number as I recollect, but they were older and more able, hence their output was greater. I quickly found myself getting snowed under. Every teacher knows how important it is to keep on top of the marking. I found myself beginning to get a little behind. Unfortunately so did the head. His way of dealing with that was not exactly sensitive, but this was Mr. Gradgrind as I explained earlier. Rather than draw it to my attention privately, he walked into my class, took over my lesson and proceeded to tell the children that I was not to be disturbed as I had a lot of marking to catch up with.

The head had his own way of stamping his authority over the whole school, staff and children alike. The net effect of his intervention was to reduce any authority I might have had in the eyes of the children. It also had the ability to wipe out any confidence I might have started to build at a stroke! I felt disempowered, which feeling was to accompany me through much of my teaching career. Confidence, for many, can be a fragile thing and is not only personal but also situational. We can all be confident given the necessary nurturing and supportive situation, but that can be quickly undermined. It was in this case!

That was evident when shortly after this one boy clearly felt that the story I was reading to the class in that last lesson of the afternoon was not sufficiently entertaining and took it upon himself to entertain the class himself. That last lesson of the afternoon with young children was a precious time, a time in which the children could be still, a time when they could be quiet and relax a little after the demands of a busy day. It was a time when the noise of the day was hushed, having a calming effect before dismissing the children and restoring them to their parents. This lesson was not to be such. Firstly the child concerned tried disporting himself in increasingly provocative positions. I say increasingly because he seemed to become more provocative with each fresh correction from me. This then escalated to noises such as belching and then saying, in a voice loud enough to address the whole class, "pardon". I felt disempowered and at a loss as to what to do. It was a fresh reminder that teachers rule only by consent and need the support of staff, parents and children alike. Any perceived authority is afforded to them. Anything which undermines that teacher's authority can make classroom control difficult and his position untenable. In an increasingly litigious age where parents are taking teachers to court for alleged physical contact of any sort children are quick to learn how to exploit that. Where staff experience themselves under increasing political pressure to meet government targets while being denied professional freedom or disciplinary powers, authority can quickly be undermined. Authority must exist for the benefit of the children. Children denied boundaries can quickly become confused and fretful. Desperate for boundaries and unable to handle the apparent freedom and to control themselves, they quickly start to indulge in anti-social behaviour.

This was the situation I found myself faced with. A young, newly qualified teacher, I felt I was just about hanging on by my fingertips by the end of that lesson. In desperation I went to see the deputy head immediately after the lesson and explained my concerns. His response was to say that I clearly must cane the offender and he informed me that he would bring the cane and the book in which the details of the punishment administered were to be entered, signed and counter-signed. I don't know whether he heard my gulp or not!

The following morning he brought in the aforesaid instrument of punishment and the child was summoned from his place. I was to administer just one stroke of the cane to his left hand, his being naturally right handed. The phrase, "This is going to hurt me more than it hurts you" is hackneyed, but was certainly true on this occasion. The thought of deliberately inflicting pain on a child filled me with horror but the child and I, between us, had manoeuvred me into this position from which I felt unable to extricate myself. I don't think I managed sufficient force even to remove the smile from the child's face. The deputy head quickly tried to come to my rescue with a salutary warning to him that it would be harder were there to be a next time. I remember quietly thinking to myself that if I had any choice there wouldn't be a next time. For the rest of my teaching career, there wasn't! I'm not sure about its effect upon the class, but it certainly had a salutary influence upon me.

I remember that the said child, who shared my first name, continued to be that thorn in my side which would give me a jab if ever I started to get over confident and to believe that life was not too bad after all. By this time it was becoming clear that I could not go to the head for that was merely to invite further censure and to be even further disempowered, while to go to the deputy head would be to repeat the previous scenario which for me was clearly not going to provide the salutary effect that might otherwise have been hoped. For some teachers at that time it perhaps provided the ultimate sanction and, if for that reason alone, was used very sparingly. In my case it was a sanction which was not available to me. I had already learned it could not work for me. I could not wittingly inflict pain on a child even if it could have been argued to be for the greater good. I was reminded of a speech by Lady Macbeth in

Shakespeare's play, "Macbeth" in which she clearly felt her husband to be similarly ineffectual and says to herself, "Thou wouldst be great. Art not without ambition, but without the illness should attend it". Macbeth lacked the hard streak that his wife clearly had, but then I was not about to invite a similar fate upon this child as met those who were an obstacle to Macbeth's career. It was clear I must needs find other means of class or child control.

I was not surprised, therefore, when a few weeks' later I found the said child chatting to the person behind him, oblivious apparently of any notion of work and oblivious of me at that point as I walked up to him. As he continued his conversation, I administered the proverbial "clip round the ear" which consisted of a tap on the side of his head with my middle two fingers, whereupon he proceeded to hold his head in a dramatic fashion and declared, "You'll give me brain damage". To which I responded immediately, "In your case it's an impossibility!" Arguably such comments were unbecoming, but this was a fight that the child must not win for his own benefit and Queensberry rules no longer applied.

One of the delights of working at that school was that the games field was situated up the hill, which I had gracefully skidded down the previous winter. Thus the weekly games lesson involved marching the children, crocodile fashion, up the hill then crossing the main road to reach the field. I could not help but muse on how much I felt like, "The grand old Duke of York, who had ten thousand men. He marched them up to the top of the hill and he marched them down again". By the time I had marched them up the hill, and got them changed, it left little time for the regulation game of football with the boys, bearing in mind the whole process had to be repeated at the end and the children returned in time for the next lesson. The short time actually available for football came as a considerable relief as I had never exactly excelled at football myself in my primary school and rugby was very much de-rigueur at my grammar school. I recollect actually making it into some sort of team in my primary school and being told to play "right back". As I proudly told my father that same evening of my obvious promotion he commented rather unfunnily, I felt at the time, "What, right back off the field?" I remember trying to laugh at his joke, but felt somewhat hurt. He clearly knew of my prowess at that particular game. It must be said that a similar level of ability in sport dogged me for the rest of my school career. Aware of my lack of skill and lack of knowledge, when I was offered the chance of doing a football referee's course at college I immediately signed up in an effort to redress my earlier failings. Unfortunately the course and course leader seemed to assume a greater level of knowledge than I possessed as I found that the sessions quickly became discussions of some of the finer points of the rules of the sport and the other members of the course would be asking the lecturer about a particular decision in a particular match. The entire proceedings were way above my head and reluctantly, but with some relief, I left the course. Thus I remained as ill prepared to supervise or organise a match as I had been at my primary school, still trying to find where right back was and rather wishing perhaps that I could be right back off the field!

On one of the occasions that I was doing my impression of

the grand old Duke of York some workmen had dug a hole in the pavement the approximate dimensions of a grave, but fortunately not as deep, and had very carefully placed cones and barriers either side. They had neglected, however, to place barriers at either end! One of the boys who at the best of times never seemed fully engaged in the process of learning and indeed gave the impression of remaining largely unassailed by the exigencies of life was happily sauntering up the hill with the rest of the class in his usual state of reverie. Happening upon the hole, and ignoring my verbal warning to the rest of the class, he stepped straight into it. Apparently completely unperturbed or perhaps even unaware of his situation he continued walking to the other end of the hole, whereupon I reached down and seizing a handful of clothing, I lifted him out, with which he simply continued walking as if nothing had happened. I remain sure, to this day, that his legs were still moving when his feet touched the pavement the other end. It is perhaps not surprising that a subject as prosaic as mathematics, dealing as it did, at least at primary level, with practicalities of quantifying our environment in one way or another, be it measuring or counting, was never one of his strong points. In history after all he could perhaps dream of castles and knights or in English be wafted away on the wings of poesy, but subtracting seventeen shillings and sixpence from one pound two shillings and ninepence, for example, or measuring the top of his desk or other such practicalities clearly did not afford such opportunities. To say, therefore, that mathematics was not his strongest subject is a gross understatement which I am sure would have been reflected in my end of year report. It was humbling, therefore, if not surprising, to be served by him many years' later in the parts department of the local garage where, as I struggled to articulate the particular part I needed for my car, he looked it up in a large book with lists of numbers, locating that number in turn in another book with equally long strings of figures with considerable aplomb, only to take that final number to the shelf returning with the precise part I needed. I was impressed. Where were my hasty judgements now?

Apart from the weekly outing for the games lesson there was also the delight of P.E. or physical education lessons. I remembered how, when I was at school, they had been P.T. lessons. This, however, had given way to P.E. by the time I had started training. The stress was very much on education, that is helping the children understand not only how to do something, but also what they were doing and why. Also, again, the stress was away from teaching particular activities and then getting the children to copy them.

Although I say "teaching" various activities, again my experience when at school or rather at my grammar school was being lined up with the rest of the class and being presented with a four legged piece of equipment with a very firm leather padded top which I was informed was a "horse" and told to jump over it, legs astride. I had never done this before in my life, for that matter I had never even seen such equipment before. The teacher, an ex sergeant-major did not demonstrate, he merely lined us up and commanded us to jump over it. So I stood awaiting my turn watching how the other boys did it. Most of them seemed to manage it. Those that did not were told to go round again where those who had cleared it stood out or rather stood "at ease", which meant standing legs slightly apart, hands behind one's back in military fashion, and watched the attempts of the less able. The rest of the failures seemed to manage it on the second occasion with suitable verbal encouragement from our teacher until it left only me. I was made to go round again and again with the ex sergeant-major shouting at me the while, "You bloody yellow belly!" By the time he had managed to utterly destroy any little confidence I may have had and had completely humiliated me in front of my classmates and his clearly being in danger of bursting a blood vessel, he told me, much to my relief, to join the end of the line. That was my introduction to P.T. equipment, which we had not possessed at my primary school. P.T. then had simply consisted of standing in rows out in the playground doing exercises with the teacher standing at the front of the class demonstrating. P.T. for us was simply callisthenics (jumping on the spot - begin!) It must be said that latterly the school had invested in some large coconut mats and I had learned to do a forward roll, the total sum of my gymnastic prowess. In fairness to me, that is all we had been taught, and I was not, at that time, really any worse than any of my fellows. It took the grammar school to completely destroy all my self confidence and make me the failure at sport and P.T. that I began to feel I was clearly intended to be. As I reflect on that experience I see how true and how perceptive was my son's remark that school teaches us how to fail.

Thus it was that it came as considerable relief to learn when I got to teacher training that the stress was now on education and encouraging the children to explore the equipment. Presented with the dreaded "horse", the children, which meant us students for most practical purposes, for this was essentially experiential learning, were encouraged to get over it or round it in as many ways as possible. For me, in the first instance, I remember that meant simply walking round it. How creative could I get? The wonder of this totally different learning environment, however, was that I could do so entirely legitimately. Above all I could encounter the equipment at my own level of ability without being judged as inadequate and therefore feeling free, with suitable encouragement, to try ever more adventurous activities and to develop different skills. Two of those skills, I remember were a head stand and a hand stand. Again, I had never done this in my primary school. I remember watching the girls not only doing hand stands in the playground, but then going all the way over and walk about crab fashion. The boys never did this and so I grew up to believe that boys simply did not do such things. By the time I got to grammar school our teaching consisted of being told to stand facing the wall bars, to place both hands on the floor and kick our legs in the air, the wall bars being there to prevent our going right over. In my case there was never any risk of that for my feet never got more than a few feet off the ground no matter how hard I kicked and I certainly never even approached the point of balance, let alone going over it!

It was only at college that, by having the mechanics of a hand stand explained, stage by stage, so that I could be aware of the function of each of the groups of muscles involved in turn, I finally learned how to do a hand stand. Similarly for me any attempt at a head stand had always finished up as a forward roll until I again understood the mechanics. For me it reinforced the truth of the adage, "To know all is to understand all". Thus I began to understand the role of the teacher in P.E. was truly to educate and the Latin word 'educare', to draw out, had ever more meaning for me. My role was not to be that of an instructor, of demonstrating or setting a precise skill and getting the children to replicate it, but to teach through enabling their understanding and encouraging the growth in confidence and ability where the one leads to the other. In an increasingly skills based society and education system that would seek to reduce the role of teachers to that of instructors where children are merely required to learn whatever skills politicians and industry may deem that society requires, perhaps we do well to reflect upon that.

In my case, however, faced with the reality of teaching P.E. there was little room for social philosophy or educational philosophy for that matter. Indeed room was all I had; the room being the old corn exchange immediately opposite the school. Thus instead of marching the children up the hill, I now marched them across the main road already spoken of, doing my best impression of a "lollipop lady", but without the "lollipop" Would I perhaps be given one if ever I got promotion I reflected? Again I was presented with a large empty room with rough boards. I did not need to encourage the children to explore the equipment. There was none! Thus team games and music and movement without the music became the order of the day. I don't know how much I was "drawing out" of the children, but my teaching environment was certainly drawing resources out of me that I never knew I had. These days we are becoming ever more aware of our use of dwindling natural resources. That seemed to summarise my situation fairly well as during that year my wife seemed to comment frequently on how tired I looked. I recall too that it was about this time that my wife started doing some secretarial work for an industrial journalist and, apart from learning a great deal about the scanning electron microscope, now perhaps a part of our every day vocabulary, but truly ground breaking work then, I also spent some time cataloguing his library. When he, too, commented on how tired I looked, perhaps it was time for me to reflect upon my personal ecological sustainability! Clearly the head had, for at the end of that year, I was told I should be taking 2C the following year, which area of responsibility continued for the rest of my time at that school. So much for my short lived promotion. I was fast gaining the impression that when it came to teaching, I was a 'C' streamer!

Chapter Five

The C Stream

"To be, or not to be? That is the question."
William Shakespeare, Hamlet

In spite of the question which exercised Hamlet's mind in Shakespeare's play, in my case 2B was not to be, for here I was in charge of 2C and, significantly it felt, at least to me, I was tucked away in a small classroom in another far flung part of the school, rather as I had been in my first year only at the opposite end of this vast Victorian building with its labyrinth of tiny rooms. Built shortly after the 1870 Education Act, it had been the town's first and only "National School" as they were then known. This room again had one window, only rather wider and not so high as the gothic shaped window of the classroom I had first inherited when starting at the school and embarking upon my career. That first room had been at the east end of the school and its high window had caught the morning light. This room, my new domain, was at the west end and the only time a ray of sunshine entered it was when it was time to go home. That, in itself, felt significant. There were too, the words of Horace Greely, founding editor of the New York Tribune, echoing in my head, "Go west young man, and grow up with the country". I had certainly been told to go west but somehow this did not feel like growing up. On the contrary it began to feel to me that I was not going to get the opportunity to grow while I was already feeling so disempowered and inadequate to the task of teaching. After what felt like my demotion, I was not even sure that I had the capacity to grow. How true any of those assumptions were it is difficult to say, for indeed I have to acknowledge that in such a large staff there were many teachers far more experienced than I and who naturally seemed to get the greater opportunities. I guess that can feel like the problem for many working in a large organisation and at the beginning of their career. Its effect upon me was to leave me feeling demoralised, which further undermined my personal sense of authority. My childhood background had ensured that I had never had much sense of it and what I had was very fragile.

Teaching can be a very exposing job and can thus make heavy demands upon our emotional resources. Children need the confidence of the significant adults in their lives to afford them a sense of confidence in turn. Parents and teachers alike can so easily convey their own fears to children, leaving them to grow up feeling timid, afraid and quite ill equipped to deal with what, sadly, can be a predatory society which inevitably exploits those whom it sees, or who see themselves, as its weaker members. Similarly, when we feel ourselves to be disempowered or ignored, such conditions can quickly find out our own emotional Achilles' heel and leave us feeling even more vulnerable and inadequate to the task. How inadequate I felt I am not sure and I have a sense that I would not, and could not, afford to allow myself the luxury of such feelings, but I do have an enduring sense during that year of feeling isolated. If I felt professionally isolated, the children, however, seemed to respond to me. Perhaps my lack of confidence showed itself in a gentleness which allowed the children to flourish a little, for, as has already been observed, lion tamer I was not. Tucked away with my 9 year old charges, I found myself feeling some affinity with those whom the system had already pronounced as failures. Perhaps there was an understanding on both our parts that we would not benefit by exploiting each other's vulnerabilities.

Becoming accustomed, by now, to the lack of resources, with my basic set of graded readers, some mathematics text books with little or no maths equipment and some rather uninspiring history and geography text books, with just one pile of each of lined, squared and plain exercise books, I was to embark upon the task of educating the thirty or so children in my class for the next year. There was, for me, a strong sense of "You're the teacher, get on with it!", and so somehow or another the children and I did just that, their writing in their exercise books, me writing on a blackboard. Each week saw me submitting my lesson plans to the head for the coming week, trying to make "muddle along as usual" look philosophically sound and educationally inspiring. I must at least have succeeded in that as I never received any adverse comments, or indeed any comments at all for that matter. In short, having 'gone west' I have an enduring sense that "all (was) quiet on the western front". Indeed in our quiet little backwater, all was quiet enough for the fungus to grow and the mice to roam unhindered. Perhaps both allusions deserve a little explanation.

Running all round the classroom to a height of approximately one metre was wood plank panelling, painted in grey, with a small ledge surmounting it. When the room was sufficiently quiet, one could hear the mice happily scampering around behind it and it became clear, by the droppings left behind each morning, that when the classroom was deserted at night they were in the habit of coming out and scampering along the ledge at the top of the panelling. Not being a 'country boy' by upbringing I was not able to immediately recognise the little black deposits that I found each morning. This, however, was not so true of the children. Even though the majority of them lived in the town, it was still sufficiently a country market town for them to be acquainted with field mice. Thus it was that the children took to leaving crumbs and little bits of their break time snacks along the panelling for these smaller members of the class, who were clearly grateful as a substantial amount of their offerings had disappeared by morning. The appearance of the titbits clearly alerted the caretaker who had not bothered before, for he started to leave traps on top of the panelling. I can only assume that the mice were sufficiently well fed not to bother with the traps as, to the best of my knowledge, they were never sprung except by the children if they were still there the following morning! In our quiet little backwater perhaps the children found room to grow.

They, however, were not the only things to be growing in the classroom, for apart from the mice who were arguably growing fatter, a large fan shaped fungus also started to grow out of the wall. As we were provided with little in the way of maths equipment, clearly the good Lord had provided for us, for I immediately put a frame around it and a chart to record our measurements of its daily growth. No, it did not appear in my weekly lesson plan! From these measurements we then proceeded to draw a graph. I rather felt this was all perfectly educationally sound and was relating mathematics, in a real way, to the children's environment. I was, I felt, trying to make the study of mathematics relevent to the children's understanding. Surely philosophically and educationally commendable. If only my teaching practice tutor were here now. I felt he would be sure to approve! Clearly, however, the caretaker did not, for, in spite of my notice next to it, and our chart, I found it had been removed on coming into the classroom a few days' later. Clearly educational philosophy was not his strong point, neither was respect for teaching staff apparently. So much for our mathematics project!

One of the head's own projects, started during that year, was a new approach to craft teaching in the third and fourth year juniors, (years 5 & 6 in current parlance). I was recruited to teach basket work and was told to order whatever materials I needed. Such luxury, of actually being able to order teaching materials. Thus I found myself learning about such things as grades of cane, warp, whaling and the like! One afternoon a week saw me sitting with a group of children with huge lengths of soggy cane, weaving baskets destined to become flower pot holders etc. Indeed I recollect that basket weaving was not the only thing going on. Around me was woodwork, metal work with mild steel, as we did not run to a forge, and even enamalling which involved the children making tiny brooches or pendants and finishing them in a tiny electric kiln. It was not only the children's education which was being broadened. This, of course, was before the health and safety culture had crept into our society and teachers were still more concerned about protecting children from harm than themselves from litigation.

One afternoon each week saw me returning to my classroom after the lesson with an assortment of unfinished baskets awaiting completion in the coming weeks. On one such occasion I encountered the head who complained that he only ever saw me with uncompleted work and said he should like to see some completed for a change. As soon as the children had finished their basket they took them home and it had never occurred to me that the head would be interested in seeing a canework basket, but I had yet to learn that he tended to judge by results and visible success was important to him. Thus, thereafter, a queue of children would be seen one afternoon a week outside the head's office holding canework baskets.

All the way round I began to gain the impression that the school must have had a large increase in its L.E.A budget or was the recipient of a bequest from some wealthy benefactor, for, beyond the craft materials, one of the rooms in this sprawling Victorian building found itself set aside for P.E., and equipment like a horse and gym mats started to appear. This was an unexpected and unaccustomed luxury, although, with a school population still approaching 1,000, it remained an occasional luxury with twenty something classes to be timetabled into it.

French teaching continued for the upper classes and in my

continuing post as head of French, indeed the only teacher of French, I found myself emerging from my little room tucked away in a corner of the school rather more often. I could also be found leaving my classroom carrying a recorder on occasions. I have a feeling I must have put music as an interest on my original application form, either that or I must have let slip that while at college we were all required to purchase a descant recorder and to learn at least the rudiments of the instrument. Either way, I now found myself teaching music to some of the 'A' stream classes, although it must be said that my grasp of the subject was considerably less than that of French. Thus, armed with my recorder and the "New National Song Book", I found myself contributing to the music curriculum, although I found the children sometimes rather preferred some of the latest 'pop' songs to "Barbara Allen" or "Bobby Shaftoe". It may, of course, simply be that the head was so impressed by the French carol that I had taught the children that he felt I was a natural to music as well. Clearly I would have to learn a few more French carols!

Perhaps my felt sense that I was not going to get the opportunity of growing was a little unjust as I began to contribute to ever more aspects of the curriculum; a curriculum which was itself growing, as during that same year we were to see the arrival of a pottery wheel and a hitherto unused tiny room was pressed into service. The room concerned was at the end of two classrooms built out of concrete blocks and roofed in corrugated asbestos. The roofing would not be allowed now, but I would guess these rooms had been built in the 1950s to accommodate the growing school population. It was clear that the school dining hall had been built at about the same time, as all three rooms formed the fourth side of the now enclosed playground. These rooms were considerably larger than the classrooms in the main building, so it was clear that Victorian class sizes were not as great as those experienced in the post war years and well into the 60's & 70's. Either that or they were packed in a lot tighter.

The growth in school population had been largely the result of the huge growth of the town in the 50's and 60's as part of an overspill scheme which displaced a proportion of the London population some 70 miles away to a hitherto small market town which clearly had neither the services nor infrastructure to cope with such a huge influx. Thus the town saw two huge council housing estates being built each accommodating a population in excess of a thousand. As so often happens with such schemes it would seem that our then political masters thought "Wouldn't it be a wizard idea if we moved some of the unemployed or those without adequate housing out into the country!" and proceeded to sell the scheme as a "fresh opportunity", leaving the local council planners to find somewhere to put the sudden increase in population. Inevitably services, including schools, would take time to catch up, as would employment opportunities. Thus the school found its population being fed by the newly built council housing estates and inheriting the social problems which inevitably seem to accompany such development. High density housing and little in the way of services, entertainment or space for recreation all provide the ingredients for social problems. The creation of unlit areas of no-man's land within the estates, which often are not even overlooked by windows, create ideal areas where those social problems can find expression. All these elements were feeding into the greatly enlarged school population. I began to understand why I had so readily been offered a post in the town. It is to the school's and the head's credit that it responded to these challenges, firstly with its hastily built classrooms and now, later, with its widening curriculum.

Indeed, this felt like a period of widening horizons in so many ways, for as that school year drew gracefully to a close, the reading tests and reports completed, I learned that I was again to take a second year 'C' stream class the following year. That, at least, would ease the amount of preparation that I had to undertake for the following year, for it was to be a busy summer vacation that year. But before we reached that time of blessed rest, time hopefully to unwind from the stresses which I seemed to experience at the end of term, there were still the leavers' parties, as our 11 year olds prepared to go on to the one secondary school in the town. Although at that stage we still had a two tier education system, there was no 11 plus examination and there were no opportunities for going on to grammar schools and the like. That, at least, had the advantage that it avoided divisiveness and all the children knew where they would be going. For until that time there had basically been one large primary school and one secondary school in the town. Even the secondary school had been built in the post war years, for until that time our Victorian built school had been the only school providing "elementary" education to the entire population of the town. Indeed some of the parents and grandparents rememebered those days and would relate their memories to me of their school days and "how things had changed!" I remember being grateful for their memories, for again it gave me a sense of history; a sense I was lacking, feeling in many ways something of an outsider.

Village life was quite new to me. Indeed the notion of a village was something I had only come across in my reading of fiction until then and therefore had a strangely romantic feel to it. Those early winter journeys into school soon dispelled the romance, as one thing I learned was how isolated a village can be without adequate public transport. Perhaps rather I should just say adequate transport. Yes, we were still reliant on my trusty scooter as, apart from anything else, the cost of a road tax and insurance suited our limited budget far better than that of a car. Even that was to change, however, during what was to prove a time of widening horizons, but I could not yet look to the horizon until the end of term was completed.

It was the school tradition, maintained, if not started, by the head, for the entire school to form two lines across the playground through which the leavers would walk, rather like a guard of honour; a rather nice touch, I felt. Once that ceremony was completed it only left us to take our own children back to class, there to complete the end of term formalities and dismiss them. Another school year had ended and the vacation and a blessed "letting go" beckoned. I had always had the same sense when a child and this strangely did not feel substantially different.

That vacation started for me with a French summer school

run for teachers of French. It meant that for a week we immersed ourselves in the language, theoretically speaking French almost exclusively. The leader of the course was bilingual and was equally at home in both English and French, as were her children, who put the rest of us to shame or at least myself as I found I was struggling to remember all my 'A' level French of some 7 years' previously. That experience, after the initial shock, was so much fun that I determined that French lessons in future would, as far as possible, be conducted in French. From a teaching point of view it was a wonderful discipline as it made me ensure that I had sufficient teaching materials at my disposal, while it encouraged the children to think in French and, I found, afforded them a new confidence. I remembered my own 'A' level French teacher exhorting us to think in French and to avoid trying to translate, which inevitably caused halting, clumsily constructed phrases.

Back then, as a schoolboy myself, I had taken it to heart and my studies were put to the test when my great school friend had suggested a trip to Paris one Easter. He had booked the tickets as he was much more experienced in such things than I and so, just a couple of days before Easter saw us sitting on a bus bound for the airport, during which journey he showed me the booking which read "*Chambre a grand lit*". When I drew this to his attention his comment was "Oh good, I like a big bed". To which I responded, "No, you fool, it means a double bed!" However, upon arrival at a small hotel in Montmartre, the "*chambre a grand lit*" did not materialise. The agent had clearly failed to book it properly as the concierge showed us a form, and said in his broken English, "See, cancell-ed!" Apparently we were not the only ones to be so affected for a Dutch person was also standing there desperately trying to make himself understood. The notion of the universality of language or indeed that English is spoken all over the world did not seem to apply then or there. My cousin had had a Dutch boyfriend for a period and I had learned that Dutch was similar to German which I had studied to, and failed at, 'O' level. However, I managed to rise to the occasion and translate for this similarly unfortunate guest to the concierge. Thus, that evening saw us crossing Paris, complete with suitcases, just before the French office of the travel agents closed, trying to find somewhere to stay and again explaining our position to the assistant there who had equally little understanding of English, if any. With my French teacher's advice to think in French ringing in my ears, I wondered if I could panic in French. It should be added that my friend was doing Geography at 'A' level, not French, and while he had some ideas of all the places we could visit, the problem of making ourselves understood he left firmly to me. Having spent some five nights with him in a double bed and acted as translator, at the end of our stay I wanted to say with feeling that our holiday would not have been the same without him.

I had, however, been immensely grateful for that experience. A lad from the suburbs, I always regarded my school friend, who himself lived quite near our school and therefore within the confines of that great metropolis, as so much more sophisticated than I. I have always been glad of our friendship and what I felt it had afforded me. It was only later that I learned that he had actually envied my living in the suburbs where I so admired what I felt was his living near the hub of things with access to London theatres, art galleries and the like. I had become a real "culture vulture". Perhaps part of that was my love for the French language which so received a boost during that brief holiday that when it came to my French oral examination as part of my 'A' level, I received a particular commendation from the examiner, via my French teacher, on the quality of my accent and my confidence in the language. I did not say that it had been born of necessity and that while in Paris I had felt far from confident. I just received the comment and chuckled quietly to myself. That Easter had also seen me travelling across Paris trying to find a church in which to take my first communion. The service was conducted in a mixture of Latin and French; another experience. Truly I felt I had been enriched then, as I was by my summer school now. Could I convey something of my love of French and the richness of my experience to the children? I wanted to.

Later that vacation saw me expanding my horizons a little further as I journeyed to London to sit an examination as part of my becoming an Associate of the College of Preceptors. It must be said that it later changed its name to 'College of Teachers' which perhaps made it a little more accessible than 'Preceptors' which reflected the Victorian age in which it had been founded. Having been offered an opportunity while at college to go on and do another year to gain a degree in Education, I had always felt hungry for further qualifications. I had felt unable to take up that offer of a place at the time as my then fiancée, who was also partly supporting me financially while at college as my parents were failing to meet their contribution, was experiencing increasing unpleasantness at home. I was deeply concerned about this and felt that to take another year would have been the utmost selfishness at that time. My examination and the previous year's study at home was part of my addressing that. So it was that the November of that year saw me graduating as an Associate of the College of Preceptors and I could now sport the letters A.C.P. after my name which apparently afforded me Chartered Teacher status. In a society in which status appears to be everything it was certainly a time of hope and broadening horizons for me.

Chapter Six

Broadening Horizons

"The real way to travel! The only way to travel!
Here today, in next week tomorrow ...
always somebody else's horizon!"
Kenneth Graheme, Wind in the Willows

That was true for the school as well, as the new academic year saw me in another classroom even if it was another 2C! Not only that, but all the second year classes were together in the same part of the school and I found myself working alongside two colleagues. That again felt an enriching experience for me. Hitherto I had felt myself rather isolated, either because of the geographical position of my classes, or, as in my second year of teaching, because of my perceived inadequacy. Now, my two colleagues and I were able to cooperate in some areas of the curriculum and we started to take each other's classes for some lessons, enabling us to capitalise on our particular strengths. Essentially we were beginning to work together and teach as a team.

That was particularly evident as the first term drew to a close and we started to prepare for Christmas. Each year every class would contribute to the Christmas concert, this year being no exception, and so the band of three second year teachers cooperated in its different aspects, which involved our meeting in each other's houses from time to time to plan our magnum opus. Clearly wandering about the school with a recorder was sufficient to establish me as the music expert in the minds of some of my colleagues and so the rehearsing of the massed choir fell to me. Thus we squeezed one hundred or so children into my class, which at least afforded my colleagues opportunity to get a bit of their marking done, which was reciprocated when it came to other aspects of the production. However, come the full dress rehearsal where all the school came together to have their efforts viewed, or rather judged, by the head, the fact that ours was a joint effort seemed to have eluded him, such that he rather assumed that my class were just singing a couple of songs. The fact that my class had also grown in size to somewhat in excess of a hundred also escaped his notice. Thus after the first musical offering he turned to me and asked, "Is that it? Is that all you're doing, becuase if so they had better stand out the front?" I tried in vain to point out that this was just part of the whole production and that we needed the music to complement rather than dominate it. To which he simply retorted, "If that's all your children are doing get them to stand out the front". I felt judged, unheard and disempowered. This, I felt, was not the time to argue, beyond which I had the distinct impression that there would be little point. The power structure in the school was very much from the head down and nothing happened without the head's explicit approval. That was to become more evident as the year progressed, but more of that later!

The Christmas concert duly happened and apart from the apparently meagre offering from that chap in charge of 2C the head seemed satisfied. We could all breathe a sigh of relief. The term came gracefully to a close and the last day saw us taking the decorations down which had been made by the children during the preceding weeks. It was always my practice to share them out between the children as I could not bring myself to destroy all their efforts and the cupboard certainly did not offer space enough to store them. That year, however, I had got some children to make a life size picture of a "Father Christmas" using a variety of materials, as the regulation couple of rolls of crepe paper and gummed paper squares would not really have run to that. Thus it was that I felt deeply honoured when the children refused my offer of a draw to see which child should take it home and said, "Sir, why don't you take it home and decorate your house?" Which I duly did, and I recollect it adorned one of the doors making onto our entrance hall so that it could be seen as soon as anybody entered the front door. Teaching had its own rewards in those days, which most certainly weren't financial.

After our collaborative efforts with the Christmas concert, the next term saw us second year teachers teaming up on a more regular basis. In particular we got together once a week for a classroom assembly which we took it in turns to lead. I often found it difficult to think of something original which might hold and perhaps even fire the children's thinking. None more so than one Wednesday when I still found myself without any ideas in particular that I might use the following morning. Afternoon came and school ended. I arrived home later on my scooter and after a welcome cup of tea I recall our walking to the outskirts of the village to one of the telephone kiosks, as our finances still did not run to a telephone. The village lay in a valley and was served by one main road or 'B' road which ran across the top of the village. Thus it has always tended to be simply referred to as "the top road". Having made our telephone call a car stopped and the driver asked us directions to our house. It was only then that I recognised the driver as a friend from college who had driven up to the wilds of Suffolk from the other side of London. It felt as if a shaft of light had suddenly entered my lonely exile and reminded me of those heady college days when I had been fired with enthusiasm and teaching to me had seemed such a noble profession. The practicalities of day to day survival had dimmed those feelings a little but now suddenly school, just three miles away, could have been on a remote island. So far as I was concerned, at that moment, it simply didn't exist. Our friend and welcome guest explained she was looking for a bed for the night and I recall how the evening just sped by as we "caught up" over dinner and beyond. The following morning school came back into my consciousness and I remembered my morning assembly. I recall asking our guest if she had any ideas and she suggested a box of matches. I have never forgotten that assembly, for having said our goodbyes, and duly armed with the said "prop", I headed off to school. Many teachers will be aware of this old 'old favourite', but for those who are not, I likened our tongue to a match which can do so much good and bring warmth to a home or it can be used destructively, such that what it destroys can never be rebuilt. The light of understanding in the children's eyes that morning reminded me of the fellowship my wife and I had enjoyed just the previous evening and the value of relationships. Perhaps I had shared just a little bit of that light with them.

Our Lord said in Matthew 5:16, "Let your light so shine before men..." and I guess that meant children too, for after that, similarly fired with enthusiasm, my colleagues and I started cooperating ever more widely such that we started taking each other's classes for different lessons, bringing our particular strengths into the curriculum. At least that was our rationale. The head did not quite see it that way when he walked into my colleague's class, only to find me standing there instead, and demanded to know where Miss.. was. I explained that she was taking my class at that moment. His only comment was that it wasn't timetabled as he turned and walked out. Clearly to him this was not so much about enhancing the curriculum as straightforward anarchy. I recall that the head had a "master timetable" on the wall in his office which detailed the class, the teacher, the subject and the room in which it was to take place. Thus he could know the who, when, where and what at any time of the day and was in the habit of swooping down on any unsuspecting member of staff who might have the temerity to stray from the timetable. That particular unsuspecting soul which had "erred and strayed like [a] lost sheep" that morning was me. As explained previously, the school was a large one and I guess took considerable organisation. The head's method was to govern the entire operation from above with a rod of iron. His was a clear style of leadership which he imposed with his own unique dogged determination. Questions of curriculum were not up for discussion.

Thus it was with considerable surprise that my colleagues and I were asked to see him in order to discuss our teaching of mathematics. It seemed that he had an idea for collaborative teaching which he wanted us to develop. I was tempted to question whether his seeing our moves towards collaboration had made him reflect, but, given the head's natural leadership style, that seemed unlikely. It would have been comforting to think that he was inclined to encourage his staff's efforts and welcome any positive contributions to our delivery of the curriculum, but, as said earlier, the head did not feel happy with devolving power. However, here we were discussing how we might develop our mathematics' teaching into a topic based approach. I recalled my own training and I remember with what enthusiasm I responded to this challenge. This felt a lot more like what I had trained for and I started to fantasise about eager eyed children absorbed in their learning with the hum of happy work focussed chatter pervading the classroom. This began to resemble what I felt teaching was all about. But it got better.

We were to take one topic each which we would teach to each of the three classes in turn so that at the end of the given period of a few weeks each of the classes would have covered the three topics, by which time we would have prepared the next set of three topics between us. Furthermore, we were to prepare work cards, and materials were going to be made available. Indeed, not only materials, but resources generally. Thus I found myself designing a series of work cards on area starting from the basic concepts of bigger and smaller through mapping the shapes and on to the more familiar length x breadth. The thrust of such teaching was to afford the children a sense of the underlying concept and a real understanding of what they were doing rather than their being told, "You multiply length times breadth" and in answer to the question, "Why?" being told, "Don't worry about that, you just have to do it".

To go back to that precious word 'resources', I now learned that all I had to do was to prepare 'masters', and to give them to the secretary so that they could be duplicated onto card. I didn't even know, until that point, that we had such facilities! Had I been backward in coming forward over the past three years? Rather I began to see that if the head wanted it to happen, it was amazing what could be made available. I remember how my finished work printed on cream card really looked quite professional. As I luxuriated in all these resources and rejoiced in the support which team teaching can afford, I began to feel like 'Toad' from Kenneth Grahame's "The Wind in the Willows" as he declared, "This is the life".

Teaching, at its best, can offer some unique rewards where the staff room can be a place of mutual support and a much needed haven even to the most dedicated teacher. Similarly, it can be the sort of job which is never boring and the classroom a place where children and teacher alike feel nurtured by each other; where both can find the place to grow. The reverse of that can be equally true and become a very destructive reality for all involved, but for the moment this certainly felt like a time to grow.

There was admittedly for me a lingering question in the back of my mind which I didn't really want to hear. "Enough", I told myself "to be getting this level of interest and resources". Nevertheless the question remained, "Why?" After three years was there another reason for all these resources; the pottery wheel, the enamelling kiln, woodwork tools, and basketwork? Suddenly this feeling of plenty was extending into other areas of the curriculum too, as I contemplated the luxury of the very professional looking workcards which I and my colleagues had just created.

There had been a few teachers' meetings within the county where all the philosophical strengths and educational advantages of a three tier system had been advocated. First schools 5-9 years, Middle schools 9-13 years and Upper schools 13-16 or 18 years was felt to be the way forward. Much research was cited to support this move which showed that children learned more effectively, that these ages coincided with natural stages of development and that the resulting smaller schools provided a friendly and manageable environment to which the children could relate and therefore develop both socially and educationally, where maintaining the village school for those vital early years was seen as a key feature. I cannot help but reflect a little wryly that 40 years on, research is again being cited along with other grand sounding philosophy to support the county's policy of re-establishing a two tier system which again, apparently, enables educational development and those ever precious higher grades.

Perhaps the cynic in me then was not quite so well developed. However, it was early the following term that we learned that a new middle school was being built not too far away which would take the top two years from the present school, which would itself become a first school. It was sometime after that we learned that the head of our existing primary school had been appointed to the headship of the new middle school. Could all those facts go some way to answering my question?

It was certainly a time of growth, and one thing about growth is that we cannot really stop it. It may be stunted or slowed but it can never entirely be stopped. That, I believe, is true of children and adults, of physical and mental growth. The thing about growth too is that we can never be the same afterwards, although we may try to halt change. We find it comforting and reassuring when something remains the same. It affords us a sense of stability such that we know where we belong and how to behave. Children and adults alike need stability. We find a constant bombardment of fresh projects, ideas or legislation unsettling. This was true, I recollect, for teachers and children at this time, as I felt "the writing was on the wall". This, it seemed to me, was perhaps the time to be looking to pastures new.

Although I had been trained to teach the 9-13 age range and this proposed restructuring should have felt like the chance I had always wanted, my entire, if limited, teaching experience had been with 7-8 year olds and I had grown to love the openness and unaffectedness of that age group. Nevertheless I was somewhat reassured to be offered the post of "Head of French" at the new middle school. Perhaps I had not been found quite so wanting as my own fears and self concept would have had me believe.

Perhaps it was the apparent vote of confidence which afforded me the motivation to look at my own situation a little more critically. Confidence bred confidence until I came to believe that I did not necessarily have to accept the first offer of a post that came my way. Rather, I began to see that I needed fresh compost and a different pot if I was really to be able to grow. At least I had grown sufficiently to dare to contemplate a fresh challenge.

Thus I found myself eagerly scanning anything from the Times Educational Supplement down to the job pages of the local paper looking for another teaching post. With my horizons broadening it was becoming increasingly clear that my trusty scooter was going to have to give way to something a little more stable and comfortable in cold or frosty weather, preferably therefore with four wheels. A scooter did have its drawbacks. One of those was that we thought it might be difficult to manage a carry cot on the luggage rack at the back. We had managed a suitcase and hamster complete with cage, but we felt that carrying a baby in the same way might not be quite the thing. If we were to start a family we understood that a car had to be a part of that. I had taken driving lessons whilst still at college, paid for by my then fiancée. Even before we married, we learned increasing independence, or rather perhaps interdependence, and my learning to drive was thought to be a part of planning for our future life together, post college. Unfortunately that part of our planning didn't really come to fruition. With finals looming, trying to negotiate the purchase of our first small house (the one we still live in!) while planning and sending out invitations to our wedding and sorting out a thousand and one other details, by the time it came to my driving test, to be told that I hadn't passed was a sort of relief. In truth we couldn't have afforded a car and my fiancée couldn't keep paying for the driving lessons and so my failing my test just helped draw a line under something which was almost doomed to failure from the start.

However, by the time I started my driving lessons some four years' later, my motivation was greatly improved. So too, I felt, was the motivation of my driving instructor who clearly enjoyed his work. He was also one of the most "laid back" instructors I had ever met. As I found myself doing about 45m.p.h. within a 30m.p.h. limit, he merely gently brought it to my attention with the quiet question, "Are you aware you are travelling at 45m.p.h?" I wasn't. I was too busy concentrating on trying to steer a reasonably even course between the grass verge on my left and the white lines on my right. I rather gathered that as long as the white lines weren't on my left I didn't need to worry too much! He also certainly didn't seem too worried as I found myself trying to negotiate my way by the old watermill in our village where the road went round a bend, over a narrow bridge and up a hill, more or less all at the same time, and he happily regaled me with stories of how many of his pupils had left a part of the car on the bridge. As I was trying to change gear and avoid the side of the bridge at the same time I don't know if such stories were meant to relax me! He must have done something right, because by the time of my test I had acquired sufficient confidence for the examiner to thank me for a nice ride! Again, it is perhaps a reminder how fragile a thing our confidence can be and is very often situational. Jim Smith, for that was my instructor's name, I felt had given me much and it was both a great privilege for me, as well as a sadness, when I conducted his funeral some 30 years' later at the request of his family. A lot of water had flowed under that particular bridge by then and I was a licensed lay minister within the diocese, but all those years previously, of greater importance to me then, I was licensed to drive. We could think about a car, and I could think about a new job.

The latter materialised later that term. A new school was opening just 10 miles away in a neighbouring county and was advertising for teaching staff. It was then widely recognised that education spending per capita in that county was higher than some others at the time. The lure of educational resources and a new school were sufficient to prompt me to put in an application. I must have made my application look sufficiently convincing as I was duly called for interview which was held at the local secondary school. I recall that during the interview, having been introduced to the newly appointed head of the school, I was asked about my relationship with the head of my present school. I pondered what manner of question this might be. Could it be that the interviewing panel knew Mr. Gradgrind as well? If they had contacted him, what had he said about me? Perhaps it was the pleading "Get me out of here!" look on my face. How could I answer the question? I finally said that I was aware that some found him a little difficult but that I experienced him as 'fair'. The answer seemed to satisfy the panel sufficiently for I was called back into the room after my initial interview and was duly offered the post as assistant teacher at what was known as an 'area' school. Essentially it was a primary school large enough to accommodate children from about three very small village schools which were then housed in old Victorian buildings of the same vintage as the one at which I was teaching. Having said this was larger than the schools it was replacing, its total population was still going to be under 200 and therefore about a fifth of the size of the school at which I was presently teaching. With the promise of a new building housing a school whose numbers made it sound positively 'cosy', where even the head was to be a woman, I felt it must be a change from my present situation. Indeed, I felt nothing short of euphoric as I telephoned my wife to tell her my glad tidings.

Interviews completed and a deputy head and at least one teacher appointed we were invited to view the new school, then more or less approaching completion. As I drove back from the school I became aware that I was going to need that car sooner rather than later. Fortunately the person who lived more or less opposite us at that time was a salesman with the local garage. We had seen him carry his new wife over the threshold shortly after we had moved into our own home. I had very little idea of what car I wanted, but he arrived late one afternoon with a white Ford Anglia with the distinctive rear window which sloped back on itself and had the advantage that it did not need a wiper when it was raining, or even snowing.

With a car and a new job I felt as if the world was my oyster. I was so full of hope and "great expectations". This seemed to be reflected in my attitude and general bearing at school. My manner was different with the children. I was more confident and could afford to be more patient; confident not only because I had managed to get another post, but because I did not worry so much whether I pleased the head or not. It was not exactly a devil may care attitude, but it was the closest that my newly appointed escape route could afford me. I felt a little like a prisoner of war who has just completed his tunnel, so I knew I was not going to be there much longer and nothing short of gross misconduct, professionally speaking, was going to stop me. Again, I can reflect upon that period and see that the children must have observed a difference as well for they seemed to become more relaxed and better behaved. We may be tempted to think that those two conditions are slightly contradictory where we may naturally associate good behaviour with discipline. My experience as a teacher was that when I felt sufficiently in control of myself and the class, then formal discipline became unnecessary, on the whole. The children became more relaxed, free perhaps to attend to the task of learning where busy, well motivated children were also well behaved children. Thus as I could relax so I became more confident and growth enabled more growth. We could grow together.

How different it had been just a few months' earlier when I recall working in my classroom after the children had gone home one day and two boys, not from my class, had felt free to taunt me by making faces through the window and calling my name in a mocking fashion. I did not know their names, but they knew mine. They had an advantage. They also had the added advantage that if I were to go out to confront them they could run away. My threats to inform the head the following morning therefore did not seem to carry much weight. I had felt then as much alone and diminished and deskilled as I felt confident now, just a few months' later. Confidence, as I have observed before, is very often situational, but it is too a state that we develop with help over the years. One could very often see that confidence developing in even very young children. Some on their very first day in school as they walked into their reception class bore that quiet happiness, while others would be timid and appear so much afraid. I could find myself even as the adult identifying with those latter souls and was able to reflect on my own upbringing and early school years which had contributed to my own timidity. What backgrounds had these chidren come from? I often pondered. Increasingly, such questions were to surround my approach to teaching, but for now I could enjoy a confidence and freedom in the knowledge that my escape route was secure. I had formally accepted my new post and had submitted my written resignation, leaving only the reading tests and other standardised ability tests to be administered, my own individual child records to be summarised and those end of term reports to be written, before finally updating the children's record cards (pink for girls and blue for boys). All that to be achieved within the last month, or few weeks of term!

The final sports day was, for me, only a brief interlude to that process and did not greatly involve me, beyond marching the children up that familiar hill and marching, hopefully the same number, down again, road works permitting! Sports day was always a formal affair and was not complete without the head crowning the victor and victrix ludorum. I was always rather uncomfortable with what felt like divisive competitiveness, but such exalted awards were never likely to involve those children of 2C who, like their teacher perhaps, felt rather like onlookers or, at best, also rans. Again that had rather been my own childhood experience of school sports day. I, at least, was able to take part and always gave it my best effort, and always came last. Perhaps it afforded me a greater affinity with, and sensitivity towards, these children within my charge for whom school was serving to remind them in so many subtle ways of the failures that society was gradually and unwittingly labelling them.

All those tasks completed, there was a feeling for me that I had, in the words of a colleague, "served my sentence". I had perhaps not excelled myself or made a great mark in the history of the school, but I had performed all that was expected of me and the day of my release was approaching. There was just the final assembly and then the tea break in the staffroom that afternoon.

This was one of those rare occasions when the head would be seen in the staffroom to say goodbye to those members of staff leaving at the end of that particular term. I was one of four staff leaving on that occasion and when it was my turn for the head to say goodbye, his only remark was to say, "And this teacher is leaving us for another school, although I don't quite know why!" But for me the scent of fresh pastures was sweet in the air.

Chapter Seven

A New School

"To fresh woods and pastures new."
John Milton, Lycidas

It was not so much to pastures as a meadow, for the new school had been built on what had been a meadow and that part of it which was not taken up with the building or tarmac for play areas served as a playing field. I wouldn't have to march the children up that hill any more. That in itself had to be worth the ten mile drive to school.

Here I was in a new school and a recently purchased, but not so new, car. This really did feel like pastures new. Thus, perhaps a little like my first day in teaching, I was full of hope, but I did not feel my hopes fading quite so fast this time. As I surveyed the new classroom that was to be my domain for the next year I'm sure I must have appeared a little wide eyed like a little boy that has just walked into a sweet shop for the first time. From that sweet shop I must at least have had a 'gobstopper' for I remember standing there and gazing in silent wonder.

Firstly there were the large floor to ceiling windows and a door leading directly to the playground and that hedge boundaried meadow. There was the new type revolving plastic "green board" which could also be a white board for projecting filmstrips and the like and next to that another door. Where could that lead to? Ever more full of wonder, I investigated. On opening I found it led into a walk-in stock cupboard with floor to ceiling shelves all round. This was all mine; I could hardly believe such good fortune. The remaining walls of the classroom were covered in pin board for displaying children's work; again an unaccustomed luxury compared to the tiny display area I had been used to. The classroom opened onto an area with quarry tiles and a sink; my own sink! This area, in turn, opened onto boys' and girls' toilets serving just the one classroom. Indeed every classroom had its own toilets. Apart from the children being spared the long walk across the playground to the toilet block, it also made teaching a lot easier as I did not have to worry about where the children had gone or try to keep such an eye on time if they were longer than expected. And that was something else. I could keep any eye on time, for each classroom had its own electric clock.

In my previous school I had always been dependent upon my little travelling alarm clock which I had sat on my desk. That had worked well enough until one parents' evening when I was walking around the class talking to parents about their child's progress, when the alarm on my clock rang, signifying 7.30, to which, rather embarrassed, I remarked to those assembled, "At least you know what time I get up in the morning". I remember no one laughed. Perhaps they were as embarrassed as I was or even were wondering what I was doing getting up so late. That was one benefit being just 10-15 minutes from school. In my new situation I would have to get up a little earlier, but not too early, for I was never an early riser, even in childhood. I remember that if we were going on holiday my father would always pack the sidecar, for we had a motorcycle and sidecar in my early teens, the night before, and would then rise at about 4 a.m. in order to avoid the traffic. In my later teens the motorcycle had given way to a car, but the same routine prevailed. I remember I would always leave it till the last minute before getting up and felt tired for the rest of the day. That was before I had helped pitch the tent at the other end of the journey which was the pattern of holidays then. When my fellows at school told me of the hotels they had stayed in or the foreign climes they had visited, I just kept quiet or pretended we had stayed in a farmhouse. To my child's mind that did not seem quite so 'non you' as a tent.

It was, of course, still during the school holiday that I was making my tour of the new school and its facilities. Having said that, in spite of the wonderfully appointed new premises that was all we had at the moment. There was no stock as yet. The P.E. equipment had not been delivered or fitted and there was no furniture. I remember the teaching staff and head meeting in the staffroom. There was much to talk about and to do if, between us, we were going to be ready to open the school and welcome about 180 children into it in the September. Even that, in itself, felt so different and encouraging to me. Yes, we were going to receive the children in September. This was a venture in which we were all involved; a feeling of joint responsibility and joint involvement. That feeling was quite unaccustomed to me. In my previous post everything had happened from the top down. To put it in terms rather more familiar to today perhaps, it was a different management structure. As I reflect upon that I can see the many factors which contributed to the situation in my previous school. To start with, it was large both in terms of population and layout. It was a sprawling Victorian building with rooms everywhere, leaving staff isolated from each other, except at break times. In truth, mayhem could have broken out and no one would have been the wiser. The staffroom serving such a large staff spread over two rooms which had been made into one, but the resulting space was L-shaped with only a small opening between the two parts. Thus one tended to be the 'infants' staffroom and the other 'juniors', with little dialogue between the two. In fairness, therefore, to be the head of such a large sprawling establishment required considerable organisation and a very clear leadership style which would have been entirely inappropriate in this small school situated in a village where some of the staff were local and therefore not only knew a lot of the children but also their families and where they lived.

Here we were just seven staff and the head, with a brand new building without any furniture, stock or equipment and the arrival of children from all the surrounding villages expected in just a few weeks. At this stage too we did not even have a name. Although situated in the largest of the villages, it was intended to serve as a school to the entire area. We could not just name the school after the village in which it was situated. Having finally settled upon a name which we felt was both inclusive and reflected the nature of the position in which it was situated, at least now we felt as if we had an identity.

The head promised that we would have furniture and stock for the beginning of term. Equipment might be a little slower in coming. We were thus invited to say what we wanted in the way of equipment and stock. Never having been presented with such choices I really had little idea of what might be available. We were back to the little boy in the sweet shop for the first time who did not know the difference between a gobstopper and a sherbert dab, or between a flying saucer and a quarter of dolly mixtures. Such allusions are, of course, a part of our history. Again, like the little boy, to be presented with such choices felt rather bewildering and as I listened to my colleagues talking of paper backed foil and various other unheard of luxuries, and, too, as I heard them enthuse to each other's suggestions, I could only feel like something of an onlooker, desperately hoping that my lack of experience and knowledge, so obvious to me, was less apparent to them. There was an unheard voice in me which was saying, "I agree with whatever you say. I shall be grateful for anything I get". In retrospect that feeling of being an onlooker while busily trying to pretend to be an equal part of the school was to remain with me throughout my teaching career, but more of that later. I write it now for colleagues within the profession who feel able to identify with that feeling, which can be so personally disempowering.

I remember, when a couple of weeks' later, the stock arrived, the head bringing some of it over to my classroom. I was so taken aback by her willingness to work alongside her staff I just did not know quite how to respond. Thus, to the question, "Where would you like me to put it?" referring to a large pack of sugar paper, I could only respond rather lamely, "Oh, in the cupboard, I think". She sensibly put it on one of the lower, larger shelves and said, "It will be easier for you to get at it here". I have a feeling she was already beginning to be slightly sorry for this young, inexperienced but very willing teacher.

I duly accompanied her back to the main stock cupboards where I was again to be put into that, now familiar, 'child in a sweetshop' feeling with the invitation to help myself. I found myself going for all the safe options that I had known in my previous school; one ream of plain, lined and squared paper. Even the question of exercise books and pencils felt a little overwhelming as the books came in packs of 25 and the pencils in boxes. I had always been accustomed to being told how many there were to be in my class and being allocated the exact number of books and pencils. Should I take two whole packs of books for a class of thirty? Was that being greedy? Was that allowed? Such agonising may seem a trifle pathetic in these days of plenty, but it reflected not only my hitherto limited professional background, but also my childhood. For I remember being five years' old before I tasted chocolate and a little older before my mother bought me a threepenny (3d) bar of chocolate, the smallest then available, and told me it was all mine. I recall staring at it in wonder and disbelief before carefully breaking off just two tiny squares; one for my mother and one for me. I had thus grown up in an era when frugality was a virtue, indeed a necessity for many families. Being an only child with both parents working, I was perhaps largely spared such economic strictures, but whatever my childhood had afforded me, confidence did not number among the qualities.

Thus stocked, as I tried to organise my cupboard I found things I had never even seen before, including hollow tubes for blow painting. Dare I show my ignorance and ask? All we now lacked was the furniture. New furniture had been ordered but would not arrive until after term had started and thus another call from the head ensured the delivery of tables and chairs from county stock until that which had been ordered should arrive. This temporary stock arrived the day before term was due to start and I recollect the head's apology for this second hand furniture. Even so, to me it still looked like luxury in comparison to the old, heavily scored desks and ill assorted chairs that I had been used to in my previous post, for these were modern plywood tables and chairs matched for size all bearing a red spot for second year junior (year 4) pupils. By this time we had all been in school for about a fortnight before term had started. The caretaker had been busy getting all the floors polished before 180 pairs of feet were to walk upon them at the beginning of term. Again I reflect that, now, child contact hours and total hours are all contracted so that even parent evenings and marking time is counted into the contractual duties. I recall how, then, there was no actual holiday entitlement and we were required to work whatever hours the head or education authority may "reasonably require". In short, we put in as many hours as we needed and we finished when we were finished.

In practice, for me, that tended to mean 10 o'clock at night, but I am also aware that it afforded professional freedom.

I could do my marking when I liked and if I needed to leave school as soon as the children had left, I could. That would also apply to any courses that one might attend which tended to be held early evening and normally gave teachers just enough time to get from school to where it was being held. Those who lived closer even had the chance for a cup of tea. In an age which loves abbreviations, we now refer to such activities as C.P.D. (continuing professional development). The point of abbreviations, of course, is that they create their own particular in-group or 'cogniscenti', while those who do not understand are established as 'outsiders'. Groups thus develop their exclusivity which, of course, can then extend across society such that even shops can be exclusive. This must surely be true of the world of computing with its RAM, CD-ROM, Gigabytes and the like, where young salesmen can try to blind older customers with abbreviations in the hope that, once sufficiently confused and disempowered they can be persuaded to buy whatever equipment is the most expensive and least suitable to their needs.

When it came to expensive equipment I was already of the belief that surely this early Christmas at the new school would come to an end, but it didn't seem to, when I learned that the P.E. equipment had been delayed and would not be installed in time for the begining of term. Installed? What on earth could we be going to get now? I had been accustomed to managing without equipment, and even latterly in our new found luxury at the old school, that had still only extended to coconut matting and little else besides. As I recollect it was finally after Christmas that the equipment did arrive; but what equipment! Extendable wall bars, deployable ropes suspended from the ceiling, ladders, climbing frames/tressles, bars, benches, boxes (adjustable heights) and even the dreaded horse!

Amidst this impression of luxury, I reflected that there surely could not be any more. Thus it was that when the head showed us samples of fabric for curtaining, I seriously thought she was joking. It was clearly felt that the staffroom should feel a homely space in which we could relax in those brief but all important breaks. This was to be our personal space, our refuge, and in those early days it did indeed feel like a family. However, curtains were not restricted to the office or staffroom. We were to have full length curtains in the assembly hall/dining room/gymnasium. Such a versatile space it was felt must also have curtains if it was to offer a place where we could welcome parents to P.T.A. (parent teacher association) meetings and the like. Please accept the writer's apologies for slipping in another abbreviation! All the way round, the school was beginning to feel a thoroughly civilised place where, it was expected, children should behave in a like manner. Serving a largely rural population where the only housing estates were either small private developments or a few post war built council houses, the school did not have the same behavioural problems that I am sure many urban schools experience now. For many children it felt perhaps more like a natural extension of home, as I recollect that some were the children of members of staff, while others lived within sight of the school. Parents would come into the classroom to collect their children in the afternoon and clearly felt able to come into the classroom during the day to drop off things such as forgotten P.E. kit.

Such an atmosphere made it easy for staff and parents to keep in touch so that behavioural difficulties could be addressed if they occurred and not be left to grow into real personality problems such as ADHD (attention deficit hyperactivity disorder). Surely a condition of our present time which we now delight in treating with drugs. Thus society creates the problem and then uses drugs to control the symptoms when they become inconvenient. These children, however, did not suffer from a deficit of attention for teachers and parents could communicate on an ongoing basis so that the child should feel held in a secure and nurturing background. All this sounds perhaps rather idyllic, but is an honest recollection of how I felt about my new working environment.

That first day of term felt rather like starting school all over again. All that preparation had somehow still felt a little removed from the reality of what we were preparing for. That first morning of term as 180 children filed into the hall reminded me. At least I had had a fortnight or so to become accustomed to our new environment. I wondered what these children must have felt, many coming from one or two teacher schools in surrounding villages, and just having got off a bus to school for the first time in their lives. The children seemed remarkably quiet after my previous experience of teaching, but I felt I could relate to their feeling slightly overwhelmed and bewildered. At least, I reflected, this was a fresh start for me and any children whom I had experienced as difficult would not be following me as the school was in a different county. How wrong could I be, for I noticed among the sea of faces a few familiar ones; all members of one particularly difficult family. A "difficult" family to a teacher is one in which the children display particularly 'challenging' behaviour but where the mildest censure on the part of the teacher will almost certainly elicit a visit from a very irate parent the following day, threatening dire consequences, or at least legal action, if you dare say a word to their obviously innocent little darling who will usually be standing beside the parent with a look of satisfaction on their face that says, "You can't touch me". Fortunately in my time at the school I encountered very few such families and enjoyed the trust of the parents; a precious commodity indeed. These children, however, as I said, were from one such difficult family. My immediate reaction was a rather persecutory thought of "They're following me". It transpired that a rather more logical, if unlikely, set of circumstances furnished the explanation. The family concerned lived right on the county boundary and with the opening of a new school we became their nearest, and the original county would no longer provide transport. In other words it was simple economics and the family concerned, as so often happens, were just the bystanders. In the previous school the eldest had been in my class and as I was taking a second year junior class again and, by now, she was a third year I trusted that our paths need not cross again. The names of the younger children were called out first and thus I duly marched my second year class out before the next class was assembled. On my way out we exchanged glances and I saw a worried look on the child's face. Was it her guilty conscience, and which of us was more afraid?

I soon put such thoughts from my mind as I told the

children where to hang their coats, went through the register, trying to remember some of their names, and gave out new books. I usually took a few days to learn all their names but always managed the process within the first week. A teacher is always at a disadvantage until they can name the children and therefore, inevitably, it is the naughty or "challenging" pupils who are remembered. We were under way and the remainder of the morning until lunch time and our first real break sped by almost unnoticed.

Lunch at the previous school had always consisted of two members of teaching staff walking up and down a rather large concrete block outbuilding, feeling a little like prison warders. The new situation felt as different as it was possible to be and altogether a lot more civilised even if our new curtains had not yet been delivered! The tables were arranged such that each could seat 8 people. A number of the tables, as I recollect, had one slightly larger chair, to accommodate a teacher who took the role of serving. It solved the problem of lunch time supervision at a stroke, while in such "family" groups the children need not have anything they did not want and the whole eating experience was relaxed and friendly. It also meant that the staff had a proper meal at lunch time free of charge, for we were effectively all on duty.

Those early days felt so civilised, almost gracious, after my exerience of a large 1000+ pupil school where, at the end of my four years' service there, I still did not know the names of all the staff, let alone children. I did indeed feel like a young plant which had been replanted from a huge seed tray to a smaller pot to grow on and perhaps even to bloom. Certainly the compost felt a lot more nourishing if one's colleagues can be described as compost. I recollect the breaks in the staff room where the conversation was relaxed and friendly. Similarly if teaching resources could be likened to compost, then the compost was a lot richer. The only downside was that the head teacher insisted on keeping the key to the stock cupboards and stock was given out once a week, always provided that one had submitted a list of requirements in adequate time. Clearly the head did not want us to get indigestion on such rich fare.

As Christmas approached we began to turn our minds to decorating our classrooms. Such huge floor to ceiling display areas could be a blessing as well as a curse; a blank canvas just awaiting our creative urge to give itself full expression or a daunting area that had to be filled somehow! Being all newly appointed, I think there was a slight tendency for the staff to compete with each other for the best looking classroom. It therefore became quite difficult to find a balance between the teacher creating their own work of art and truly reflecting the children's work. Beyond angels suspended from the ceiling and snowflakes dotted around, I decided to use the two largest walls for two panels; one of father christmas and his sleigh and the other of the three wise men, somehow trying to strike the balance between the religious and the secular. But such grandiose designs need resources in order that they should be realised. Thus it was that on my stock list, just a couple of weeks before the end of the Chrismas term, I put 'tissue paper', not knowing how much, if any, I might reasonably expect or indeed ask for. Not for the first time the head asked me, 'how much?' and did I want all colours? Again my response to the second question was, 'Oh, I guess so'. I was still so unaccustomed to being given any choice that not only was I still slightly frightened to ask, but also I did not always know what to ask for. My experience had always been, in my first post, that of being given an allotment of stock at the beginning of each term and having to limit my needs to what I was given. To put it another way, I had become a master at cutting my coat according to the cloth. Perhaps such skill had come from my working for a month at a local draper's shop immediately after I left college in order to raise enough money to get married. Either that or I had missed my vocation entirely and should have become a tailor!

To my tentative request for tissue paper, therefore, the head brought over a pile of different coloured sheets, enough to require her using both arms to carry it and it was not for the first time in my short teaching career I found myself feeling a little like mole from 'The Wind in the Willows' saying to myself "Oh my, oh my, oh my!"

Having lined the walls with lining paper (another luxury) I set to and drew the outlines of my grand designs. Such opportunities were clearly uncovering my latent artistic talents. I can remember those weeks as feeling precious and relaxed as occasionally the head could be found in my classroom helping the children and involving herself, sticking crumpled tissue paper on the wall along with them. I remember her too saying how delightful the room looked. All the way round there seemed a relaxed, happy atmosphere as the children engaged in making their decorations with the head and I, all working together with a common purpose. There is something rather special about a class of children absorbed in a creative atmosphere and working and cooperating together. This was such an atmosphere. How different, I reflected, from my previous post where the children all had to stop work and stand up if ever the head walked into the room, and woe betide any child who happened to be absorbed in their work that they neglected to stand to attention immediately. Such omissions, beyond the castigating of the said child, were usually accompanied by comments from the head to the class teacher along the lines of, "Clearly your class have forgotten their manners. Perhaps you need to remind them". This usually elicited a rather lame, "Um yes", from me, leaving me feeling even more inadequate than usual without the vaguest idea of how I might "enhance" the discipline of the class and perhaps not even sure that I wanted to.

Thus the present situation and this, my fifth Christmas in teaching, felt as different as I was able to imagine. I really began to enjoy teaching for the first time since leaving college. The years in college had felt so special while, during the next four years, I had almost forgotten why I had joined teaching as my aspirations had become swallowed up in the day to day considerations of survival and earning enough money to pay the mortgage. The following term saw the delivery and fitting of the new P.E. equipment with all the teaching possibilities it offered. This began to feel rather more like what I was trained for and the notion of encouraging the children to encounter the apparatus at their own level made a lot more sense. I began to see a general truth that professional practices are often required to change in order to reflect current socio-political trends, but so often resources are slow to be put in place and fail to keep up with the changes that are expected. That had certainly been the case in my previous school. Hence professionals, be they teachers, doctors, nurses or the like find themselves under increasing pressure to do the impossible and implement policies in settings in which they are not designed to work, thus creating increased stress on staff and little, if any, gain for pupils, patients et al. I well remember my wife some years' later, while working as an estate secretary, being confronted with a new computer, as the landowner concerned had been seduced into purchasing it with the promise of all the functions it could perform and how it would save time. Hence with the promise of being able to do more things and reduce secretarial hours at the same time, he had invested in this new system. My wife was thus presented with a wish list and in response to her question of what she was supposed to do with the machine was told, "I don't know. You're the secretary, make it work!" I am concerned that often our political masters assume a similar position and, when schools fail to deliver, 'OFSTED' inspectors can then officially describe the school as "failing". I have met and talked to more than a few otherwise good caring teachers who have either been forced to take "sick leave" as a result of depression or have left the profession altogether because of the stress induced by such an inspection.

This school, however, was not failing, and was not subject to such judgement. Indeed, almost for the first time in my career, I began to feel adequately resourced and, dare I say, even adequate to the task.

Winter thus gave way to spring. By this time, too, the junior play area had been tar macadamed and, the area immediately outside my toilets, paved. Where all the children had been confined to one play area we now had infant and junior playgrounds. It therefore made sense that the toilets to my classroom should serve the junior children during break times.

With the reduction in numbers on each play area it was easier for the teacher on duty (for two play areas now required two staff) to be aware of the movements of all the children. Thus it was that I noticed the prolonged absence of one boy and girl, both of whom happened to be in my class. In spite of my earlier comments that the toilets attached to the classroom meant I did not have to worry so much, in practice, of course, it is the teacher's duty to be aware of the whereabouts of all the children in their charge at any given moment and if two children were in the toilet for longer than seemed normal, as was the case on this occasion, I needed to know why. They could have been taken ill. The possibilities that flooded into my mind seemed endless. I clearly needed to investigate. Thus I entered the boys' toilet, being reticent to enter the girls' area without very good reason. There was no sign of anybody. I came out thinking to check the playground again when I heard voices emanating from the area of the girls' toilets. I went to the door and listened and recognised the voices of the boy and girl mentioned. I entered quietly and stood outside the cubicle door. It became clear that they were indulging in some mutual exploration and were playing a game of "you show me yours and I'll show you mine". Clearly they were unaware of my presence and were engaged in more interesting matters. I wondered how I might respond to this. Clearly spring was in the air. I did not want to criminalise what was perhaps a little harmless exploration and a natural part of development, leaving them scarred by the experience and their attitude to male and female sexuality marred for life. Equally, I could not be seen to encourage their behaviour for this also felt like a matter of discipline. I could not be party to, or help foster, an 'anything goes' atmosphere. Children need to experience boundaries sensitively maintained otherwise they quickly become distressed, and unable to contain themselves, indulge in increasingly challenging behaviour until they experience the boundaries they so desperately need. We fail our children if we let their anti-social behaviour go unchalleneged only to confront them with harsh penalties in some sort of kneejerk reaction discipline. At the risk of being a spoil sport, I felt I needed to curb their activity in case it went too far. So I merely addressed the two children from outside the cubicle and said, "Would you care to come out now and join the rest of us". They emerged looking a little flushed and shamefaced. To their obvious shame I simply retorted that the quicker they went back into the playground and the less said the better. I also assured them that I would not tell the head if they didn't. They both looked obviously relieved. Their relief, however, was short lived for somehow the head had been appraised of the incident, although by whom I never knew, who duly remonstrated at length with the two miscreants. Their humiliation in front of the entire class had been the one thing I had wanted to avoid. What could I say when the head turned to me and asked if I was aware of their 'dreadful' behaviour. Perhaps in hindsight I was not lying when I said "No". For I had not been aware of any dreadful behaviour. It appeared that this was not the only thing I had not been aware of.

When the new school had opened it was intended that the old two classroom school, just a short walk away, should continue to function. Thus in the early years we continued to work on a split site. I had been glad to work in this new building, which indeed had been my understanding at my original interview. I was therefore a little unhappy when our welfare assistant told me that I would be working in the old school the following academic year. I was the more unhappy that it had taken the welfare assistant to tell me and questioned why she should have taken the trouble to come over to my classroom to impart the news. The deployment of teaching staff, I felt, was the responsibility of the head teacher. I was equally wondering why she should show so much interest in how I felt about that. Thus resenting being informed in this manner and suspecting that she was seeking to make mischief, I replied that as I had been appointed to a new school and as that had been the object of my application, then I should have to seriously consider my position but then added rather curtly that I would have to wait to see what the head teacher intended. I don't know if my reply satisfied her, but she looked a little alarmed and scuttled out of my classroom. The situation was resolved the following day when the head came to see me and asked if I would be prepared to teach at the old school, as she was hoping that I would thus relieve the deputy head who had been working there, freeing him to work closer with the head. I had now been consulted and felt respected. Honour had been satisfied, and faced with what felt like a fresh opportunity for growth, I readily agreed.

Chapter Eight

The Old School

"I love everything that's old; old friends,
old times, old manners, old books."
Oliver Goldsmith, 1773

The old school was situated the other side of a small housing development which also provided the quickest route to the new school and all its facilities, such as the games field, which by now had been marked out with a football pitch, and the hall which continued to serve all the children as a gymnasium and dining hall. Thus when it came to any of these activities I could be found doing my best impression of the Grand Old Duke of York again, except on this occasion there was no hill to climb. Also, I recollect, that, being a village, the school felt rather more a part of the community and as a number of children from the school lived in this development, parents would sometimes wave as we made our way to or from the old and new establishments.

I recollect that the old school soon became known as the "old establishment". This was courtesy of the deputy head who, when answering the telephone, had simply announced it as the "old establishment" much to the amusement of the rest of us. He had clearly felt safe in doing so in the knowledge that all calls would be from the new establishment. Thus he became ever more daring in his mode of address when answering the phone, on one occasion responding with "Chinese laundry", again the cause of much hilarity. Did I say all calls came from the new school? Well, nearly all, but on one occasion a call came from the Education Department and the deputy head answered in his same humourous vein. He related that there was a long silence the other end of the phone before the caller said rather abruptly, "This is the Education Department here. Is that...?" Clearly the person concerned had not updated their file with the new telephone number and perhaps like Queen Victoria was "not amused". While, as a result, the title of the "Chinese laundry" did not last long, the "old establishment" stuck.

So here I was teaching in the old establishment. I remember that year we had 1st, 2nd and 3rd year juniors in the old school; two classes situated in the main building and the third year housed in a separate prefabricated building. This, however, was where any resemblance to my previous school finished. The building was admittedly pre-war, but this was pre World War II not Crimean War. Furthermore we continued to enjoy all the new stock while also benefitting from the old stock of text books that remained from the previous village school that had been housed here. Thus I felt rather like the teacher who, as our Lord put it in Matthew 13:52. "can produce from his store both the new and the old".

Thus the new and old continued to peacefully coexist, the old feeling very much a part of the new as all lunch breaks were taken at the new school as well as physical education or rather most of it. One thing the old school boasted, which the new had not yet acquired, was a swimming pool. Such luxury! Again my previous experience had been marching the children in yet another direction to a public pool. This school boasted its own. Changing facilities were a little limited, being either the toilets or classroom. In practice most of the children opted to change in their classroom. The pool was eventually moved to the new school and changing rooms were built, but more of that later. For the moment with the pool on the spot and the children changing in their own classsroom, swimming felt a rather relaxed affair, which was reflected in the children's respect for each other and their obvious enjoyment.

Being an outdoor pool its use at the beginning of that winter, or Michaelmas, term was limited to the first few weeks as beyond that it became far too cold. Thus swimming gave way to indoor pursuits such as music, as slowly we began to look forward to Christmas. The classroom next to mine boasted a piano' and with the sliding doors pushed back we could bring both classes together for singing. Sadly neither I nor my colleague were able to play the piano' and so, not for the first time in my teaching career, my wife came in for one afternoon a week as our pianist. I remember the BBC had produced a pamphlet for that winter term to accompany a programme which contained predominently Christmas songs. I recollect that these were thoroughly enjoyable occasions with sixty to seventy children all together gently raising the roof with their singing, my wife playing and my acting as coordinator, choirmaster and conductor. Indeed the songs and those Friday afternoons left such a lasting impression on me that when my son was born a couple of years' later I can remember sitting in his room nursing him at bedtime singing some of those same songs, sometimes with my own words to render them a little more appropriate. They seemed to have a remarkable effect, working very well as lullabys, getting him to sleep quite quickly. That was always a relief as it allowed me to get on with my marking!

For the moment, however, the songs formed part of the Christmas concert and nativity play. Again I had been able to contribute to that and felt a member of this family and community. Indeed I remember a number of parents welcoming me to the village and the school. In a school of 1,000 pupils, one was substantially insulated from parents, arriving before school started and departing complete with a pile of marking shortly after the chidren went home in the afternoon. I had no sense of their home or family background. As mentioned before, many of the parents would come into the classroom to meet their children after school which afforded them an opportunity to talk to the teacher. Thus, although we still had the customary parents' evening, it was by no means the formal affair I had become accustomed to where the classroom teacher became a rather distant figure seen only briefly once a year. This was an altogether more relaxed affair where I already knew a number of parents. This very much smaller school had many advantages. I am aware that one of the main arguments advanced for larger schools is that they are able to offer a wider curriculum. Again that was not my experience.

The "old establishment" had within its grounds, dividing

the playground into two areas, the 'old' old school. This single roomed building again would probably have been built shortly after the 1870 Education Act and was heated by a single large tortoise stove. One look inside told me that this would make an ideal craft room. More to the point, I could just see it as a carpentry room and in my mind's eye even had the carpentry benches arranged.

I could remember watching my father working in his shed doing woodwork of various kinds, but was never allowed to touch any of his precious tools. Perhaps therefore it was in an effort to redress such childhood deprivation that I put my suggestion to the head who not only encouraged the idea, but also helped me order the tools and benches. I certainly remember something of a childlike joy when the tools arrived. I am not quite sure which of the children most enjoyed those lessons, but I have a sense that it was probably my own inner child. Perhaps indulging my own inner child was a legitimate reason for joining the teaching profession. I began to understand why, in my own training, we were encouraged to engage with the children in their own way of experiencing; relating, perhaps, as one child to another. Again, I remember how my own grandmother had that very special gift; a childlike quality that enabled her often to be my playmate. Perhaps again, being an only child who very often felt isolated, there was a part of me that could enjoy the company of the children. Although I did not, at that time, have the leisure or inclination to so analyse my inner psyche, the ability to simply enjoy the children's company continued to be a valued aspect of my work throughout my teaching career.

Thus with my woodwork/craft room established and my wife's regular contribution to the music in the curriculum, school, particularly the "old establishment", began to feel like home, although it must be admitted, as homes go, some of its facilities were a little limited. For a start, it lacked a staff toilet. The toilets, as explained earlier, were situated outside and had obviously served the "old, old school" as well as the present one. In practice one of the cubicles was set aside for staff use which was capable of being locked. This was the closest I ever got in my career to a key to the executive loo. The toilets being situated behind the old building effectively closed the gap betwen the two halves of the playground, joined only by two narrow passages. This made supervision during the children's playtimes difficult, such that often two teachers would be on duty at a time, but with just three staff in total, that effectively meant that only one third of the staff could have a break at a time, while the other two clearly needed to at least pour themselves a cup of tea. As break times also tended to be the time when the old and new establishments could keep in touch via the telephone, even the one teacher who was not on playground duty was effectively left to man the phone, thus ensuring that all three members of staff did not get a break. Though some would argue that a teacher's day is not a long one, yet 8.45a.m. to 3.45p.m. can seem very long without a break. With my own memory of working in a small rural school during my first teaching practice still fresh in my mind, I was determined that we should not replicate my earlier experience. Thus, in practice, duty was rather informally managed with at least one teacher outside, and nominally in charge, at any one time with staff able to drink their tea and spend at least some time to themselves.

On one occasion, however, I recollect that the normal harmony seemed to be disturbed as the teacher on duty came into the tiny room at the end of the corridor which served as a staff room and said, "Things are getting ugly out there. I don't quite know what to do". Even then, I was aware that children need boundaries and if those are not made clear, then their behaviour can begin to break down. At that point children can become distressed and bullying can ensue. If, as adults, we fail to provide sufficiently clear boundaries to our children then not only are we encouraging a generation which needs ever more external constraints in terms of legislation, but also we abdicate our responsibility. If, as seems increasingly to obtain, our political masters prevent parents and teachers from enforcing those boundaries in an effort to protect our children, then we do not do the children any favours, for nature abhors a vacuum and where clear authority is lacking then a different authority in the form of bullying or gangs becomes quickly established in its place.

That awareness was very much present for me as my colleague came in looking slightly pale and worried. It was to her credit that she was able to see what was happening and to come in to ask for reinforcements. Clearly some artillery was needed. Filled with a sense of warm indignation for my colleague and concern for the children, in response to her statement, "I don't quite know what to do", I jumped up and, with the words, "Well I bloomin' well do", strode out into the playground.

At that point I was sufficiently aroused that I did not need a whistle or anything else to attract their attention, I simply stood in the middle of the playground and bellowed, "Stand still". I must have sounded a little like a sergeant major in the middle of a parade ground for it seemed to have a similarly salutary effect. I stood waiting for any sound or movement. It only needed one child to provide it and I swung round and repeated in similarly stern fashion, "I said stand still". I continued in stern tones to say, "Right, break is over and in a moment you will get into your lines in silence". At this a few sullen boys made as if to go into their class line, at which point I really did begin to feel like the sergeant major saying, "Wait for it, wait for it". As it was, I simply barked at them, "When I say so". Following a period of shocked silence, I said in slightly quieter but still sufficiently stern tones, "Right, you may line up quietly" and approximately one hundred crestfallen children duly obliged, as by this time my colleagues had strategically positioned themselves alongside me to receive the children in their respective classes. Their support was timely and essential at that point and it was a reminder to me again that teachers rule by consent and with the support of their colleagues and parents. If that consent or support is absent we quickly learn that control can become illusory.

As I watched the very subdued children filing into their classrooms I felt quite sorry for them, but I knew too that I had had no alternative, for the sake of the children's welfare which had at all times to be paramount. It was only at that moment that I reflected that it had not been my intention to disempower my colleague. The presence of their support, however, was perhaps their reassurance that they understood. It was not the first time, nor was it to be the last, that the use of artillery was to feature in my teaching, although I hasten to add that I do not believe it reflected my normal teaching style!

Rather, increasingly, I found myself wanting to come alongside the children and encourage them to explore and to grow in that adventure which was education. Coming from a boys' grammar school whose values in many ways reflected its ancient foundation, I had found my teacher training something of a culture shock, where so much of our learning was experiential in nature. At school my experience of physics teaching, for example, was sitting at a desk in the tiered lecture theatre making notes, while the master performed an experiment at the front. The hands on approach at college, therefore, did not feel like "proper teaching". There was a guiding principle behind such an approach that, "What I hear I remember, what I do I know". Thus I can remember blowing glass to make my own test tube and winding my own rudimentary electro-magnet. Not that such an approach was limited to science teaching. It extended through mathematics and the teaching of reading. So at least we were covering two of the 3Rs! Even P.E. and 'modern dance' or music and movement were experiential. From sitting at a desk I found myself becoming increasingly at home sitting on the floor!

I could not have known, at that time, how increasingly such an approach to my own teaching was to become important to me. I can still remember the thrill that I experienced when a child managed to grasp a concept and I saw the light of understanding in their eyes. Could I encourage that same love of education and learning in others? I was to be given an opportunity to find out later that same year when at the beginning of the summer term I was assigned a student teacher from the local College of Education. She was to be the first of a number of students I had the privilege to work with during my career. To be in the position of mentor to an aspiring teacher where, just 7 years previously I had been a student myself, felt like another sign of my own personal growth.

The first thing I remember of this young woman was that she was an accomplished guitarist so the music curriculum received another boost. Although from early childhood I had enjoyed singing and had always found myself in the choir, both in my primary as well as my secondary schools, and later in the chapel choir at college, I had never learned to play an instrument. It is something I had often wanted to do but which had never come to fruition, such that I always admired those who possessed such a skill. This particular student was able to teach the children a number of songs including "My grandfather's clock" and what I believe had been a popular song at one stage, the refrain of which included, "Let me take you by the hand and lead you through the streets of London". I remember again seeing that sense of enjoyment in the children's eyes and I knew that she was truly engaging with the children, a quality which increasingly I found myself looking out for in students in later years.

It is, of course, a lot easier to engage with a group of children when you have them grouped around you, especially if you happen to be holding a guitar at the same time, another reason perhaps why I envied this student her skill, but it is altogether more difficult to hold a group of children together on a games field. If you are to avoid the problem of blowing a whistle till you are red in the face, gesticulating or shouting and generally making a spectacle of yourself to no avail, it is essential to be able to engage with the children. That, however, as I said earlier, is easier said than done as a colleague of mine found out to his cost. He had been a friend at college and we had qualified together. He had specialised in junior work (7-11 year olds) and I had specialised in the slightly older intermediate or junior/secondary (9-13). For all that, I was to spend my entire career teaching junior children except when I was teaching reception infants! I remember visiting my teacher friend and his wife about a year or so after we qualified, for he, like me, had married shortly after he left college. After we had caught up with events of the past couple of years and began to relax we started to swap our experiences of teaching, or perhaps I should say horror stories. I began to gain the impression that he had not fared any better than I as he related one of his more memorable games lessons in which he took the children outside, that being effectively the last he saw of them as they ran off in all directions, including through a hedge! As he related it, it seems he spent the rest of the lesson doing a fairly good impression of a sheep dog. My heart went out to him as I reflected on my experiece of the cross country run when I was training and I thought ruefully to myself, "There, but for the grace of God, go I!" It was that and a few other telling moments which decided my friend to leave teaching shortly after his qualifying year. I recalled when I was still training, in one lecture, the question being raised of how long one should remain in teaching. It had seemed such a redundant question at the time as the answer that naturally came into my mind was, "Surely for the rest of our working life?". I began to revise my initial aspirations a little as I saw what a uniquely demanding job it could be.

That rather brings me back to my student who, a couple of weeks into her practice, was clearly gaining in confidence such that I felt she could take responsibility for the games lesson with me on hand in the background to do the sheepdog bit, if necessary. It became increasingly clear that I was going to be redundant. For a start she had changed completely into track suit and plimsoles, as trainers per se had not really been invented at that stage. She clearly looked the part, which is often half the battle. To engage with a group of people, especially children, in an outdoor setting one really needs to be able to project one's personality so that, given all the other possible distractions, you are the main presence. As I went outside to bring the children in, I made it clear that this was her lesson. I duly played my part by making sure that they came into the classroom quietly and in an orderly fashion, but from that point on, I need not have worried as she supervised the children's changing and marched them down the road and onto the games field with me obediently bringing up the rear. Her lesson was well planned with equipment put out ready. She quickly had children in groups and doing warm up activities and from that point it was clear that she had control. Her organisation and confidence were everywhere apparent. I simply joined in with the children and I recall how much I enjoyed that lesson and wished that games lessons had been like that when I was a child. I might have related to that area of the curriculum a little more if they had. Suddenly I didn't feel like the teacher any more. There was only one teacher on that field and it wasn't me. Rather than feeling usurped I quietly thought back to my own final school practice and how my own tutor had just quietly disappeared into the background. Teaching can sometimes feel a great privilege. When we can learn from someone younger and less experienced than we then our humbling can be an even greater privilege.

I recall this student's willingness to learn and her eagerness to contribute to and widen the curriculum. Thus it was that I suggested she might like to organise a village study with the children. I met her at school during that half term holiday and introduced her to the more prominent features of the village and suggested that she may care to prepare some work cards or sheets around that and indicated my willingness to fit in and support her leading of the project; in short that she should regard me as a resource to be used as she thought fit. Again the following week saw her fully prepared. As, over the next couple of weeks, I saw the walls of the classroom fill with the children's work I was filled in turn with a sense of joy as I saw both children and teacher blossom. It was hard sometimes to see her as a student. How could I have the temerity to sit in judgement and write a report on this young woman's teaching? That, however, was my part of this process. I hope it reflected something of my sense of privilege.

As my career continued I recall a number of students with whom I worked, all from the same college. Indeed as time went on that became increasingly my role until I became the member of staff responsible for students unless they had specifically requested a different age group. During my years of teaching only one of the students from the college failed to make the grade. It quickly became clear that she had not made the right career choice in teaching and she withdrew from the course after 3 weeks in my classroom. Clearly the shock had been too much for her. In this present case, however, I felt I had learnt a lot and grown a little. It was clear that the children had, as they showed their sadness at her leaving. That, I felt, was the greatest testimony to her work.

As the term drew to a close, life and teaching were feeling good and I learned that I was to be restored to the new school the following year. A different year group, a different challenge and six weeks in which to prepare materials and myself in order to meet that.

Chapter Nine

Back Home Again

"A good book is the purest essence of a human soul"
Thomas Carlyle

In spite of the changes spoken of in my last chapter, one thing remained constant, my room; the classroom I had started in when joining the school. Thus it really did feel like going back home again; back to the luxuries of a walk-in cupboard, a sink and wet area and inside toilets. I find it interesting how apparently little things can feel so important to us. Regardless of the larger issues, be they educational philosophy, theology or whatever questions may exercise our minds, yet it is our bodily needs and comforts which clamour to be met first. It is as if they have first claim upon our attention and will not allow us to consider the broader issues until they are satisfied. I came to learn, but slowly, that children thus need to feel comfortable and secure before they are free to learn. It was during that year the floor to my classroom became carpeted with carpet tiles. This greatly reduced noise, and, being tiles, meant that in the event of accidents the individual tile affected could be lifted, replaced and scrubbed. Life at that time, after my experience of the previous school, just seemed to be one unexpected luxury upon another.

It was also very early on in that term that the head discussed with me the possibility of establishing a library. I was really enthusiastic about this and a room was duly set aside and converted to make a very comfortable sized reading area. In order to support this venture a new post of librarian was created. I was invited to apply for that and had to attend a formal interview. As a result I was offered a scale post which meant that I moved from the basic assistant teacher scale to a post of responsibility or PSR as it was commonly known. Again, I experienced the luxury of ordering materials, including library tickets, so that the children could borrow the books and have the experience of using a 'real' library.

I thought back to my own experience of the school library especially during my sixth form years when free periods could be spent working in it. As a new pupil at the grammar school in London I was firstly struck by the its size which was similar to that of our local public library. The notion of being able to look in a card catalogue, find a book on any subject I wanted, then to locate that number on the shelf and go straight to the book seemed absolutely amazing to me. You may imagine, then, that when, later, I had the opportunity to become a library monitor, I jumped at the chance. Such a position also carried with it a lunch pass which meant that instead of having to line up with my class I could go up to lunch early to free me for my library duties. I was truly in my element. The library, it seemed to me, had a book for just about every conceivable subject. Perhaps that reflected in part my then rather limited horizons. However, my horizons broadened when I was trained in cataloguing and later promoted to head librarian, responsible directly to the master in charge of the library, with whom I worked increasingly closely in cataloguing new entries, which often saw me consulting the British National Bibliography at the local library or visiting one of the larger London libraries to see how they had classified a particular book. Beyond the fact that the post carried with it a "priority lunch pass", which meant I could have lunch whenever I wished, the world of libraries and the notion of maintaining the "body of knowledge" and making that knowledge available to others fascinated me. I remain forever grateful to the master, also my english teacher, who took this rather shy boy of limited horizons under his wing and introduced me to a whole world of knowlege at my very fingertips, which it, in turn, became my responsibility to make available to others.

Could I convey something of my enthusiasm to the children and imbue them with the same sense of wonder at this school where I now was the teacher in charge of the library? Perhaps one way of doing that would be to give these rather younger children the opportunities that I had been given, but perhaps at a slightly humbler level. I was not about to send them off to the university library to ask how they had classified a book. Thus I appointed library monitors whose role it was to keep the library tidy and operate the lending system. During my years at the school the post and the library grew with me and I like to think that the children involved in that also grew. Perhaps I succeeded in that hope to a certain extent as it was some years' later that a child wrote in her 'goodbye', "I will never ever forget the pride I had when you appointed [me] as a librarian. [I] was so chuffed". When we are afforded responsibility we are afforded, too, a sense of worth.

Beyond the many advantages of this present home already mentioned, there were again those large display areas in the classroom. Thus I remember that as Christmas approached I applied my mind to how the children and I might decorate our room. There being three main display areas within the classroom, I adopted three different aspects of Christmas. Thus one area depicted a crib scene, another the three wise men and the third was Father Christmas, again complete with sleigh. Thus the religious and the secular were represented. Of greater importance they were designed to represent the children's understanding and images of Christmas. The children seemed really pleased with their efforts in decorating their classroom, but delight grew when the head asked them if they would be prepared to loan their depiction of the three wise men for display in the main hall. The head had previously spoken to me and I was unsure how they would feel about one of the walls in their classroom being robbed of its decoration and so partly out of simple politeness and because it was important that the children should feel that it was indeed their decision, I suggested that the head ask them herself, which she duly did. The light in their eyes as they readily gave their consent and the beam on their faces as they proudly carried them through to the hall said it all. The empty wall left behind was quickly filled with paper snow crystals, candles and the like, the making of which filled another art/craft lesson and all was restored.

I was taking older juniors, i.e. nine to ten year olds, and

one might have expected the younger children in the infants department to produce rather humbler offerings. Not a bit of it, for I remember being slightly bemused to hear one of the infant teaching staff talking in the staff room about the colour scheme she was going to be using that year! Where the decorations in my own classroom and those of some of my colleagues were rather more on a mix and match basis, with the emphasis more on mix than match, hers were colour coordinated. I remember that the scheme was predominently blue and white, including a white artificial Christmas tree to complete the effect. The result, I recollect, was truly stunning and left me feeling quite inadequate. It must be added that the teacher concerned had many years' experience within the profession; so many, in fact, that she was by then approaching the age of 70. She had transferred from the old village school into the new building and the education authority had either overlooked her age or from my experience of the teacher concerned she simply had not told them on the grounds that she would have judged it none of their business. She had sufficient presence about her that any clerk daring to ask would quickly have demurred from pursuing such an enquiry. I remember too that she informed me that one of the advantages of a walk-in stock cupboard was that if things got on top of her she could shut herself in and have a "good swear"! Somehow, I just could not imagine anything getting the better of this formidable lady!

One child, however, did get the better of me. Indeed you might say he got right up my nose, for when his thumb wasn't in his mouth, to the amusement and distraction of the rest of the class, his finger was up his nose while he busily unpacked his trunk. If that did not distract the class sufficiently he could be relied upon to talk endlessly, apparently quite unaware of or unable to heed my admonitions to the contrary. There was no guile about him and in another setting one may have described him as perhaps slightly socially inadequate, although such a term feels rather harsh and judgemental on a child who was after all merely a little immature and saw no reason to be otherwise. Thus I was reminded of the compromise that teaching very often presents; a compromise between respecting the needs of the individual child, while trying to balance those against the wider needs of the rest of the class. To put it another way, I had to maintain an atmosphere in which all the children were free to learn. This can be difficult when the behaviour of the one impinges upon the rights of the many. It becomes the more difficult when we understand that such behaviour is not actually criminal or destructive of another, but merely sufficient to cause others to tear their hair out! That was the stage I had got to. The child seemed to be as unaware of my emotional health as he did of the effect he was having upon the rest of the class. Finally I felt that a slightly sharper reminder of his social responsibility was necessary as talking the while, he managed to get up, knock his chair into somebody else with sufficient force to cause them pain, then trip over somebody else's feet on his way to see me. Perhaps again it was that sense of injustice that caused me to judge his behaviour sufficiently unacceptable that he needed a sharp reminder to help him amend it. Thus it was that with the flat of my hand I slapped his bottom. I recollect that a past government introduced what the then Home Secretary described as a "short sharp shock". My recollection is that it was just as ineffective as the one that I administered to the child concerned who ambled back to his place with the same vacant grin, apparently undisturbed. I had administered what might have been described as corporal punishment just once before to similar effect. I told myself that we are all allowed two mistakes, but I vowed to myself there would not be a third. In the years that followed there never was. Beyond not being a lion tamer, (I could never quite see myself with a chair and a whip), I wasn't much of a child tamer either and I slowly realised that I would have to find other ways of achieving an atmosphere in which children were free to learn.

Discipline is a funny word. We so often associate it with something which is externally administered, sometimes with sufficient harshness so that the will of one is imposed upon another. Perhaps that was the problem, for I never actually wanted to impose my will upon another, least of all children. I merely wanted to maintain an atmosphere which was respectful of the needs of all and conducive to learning. I am aware that such a stance can be misinterpreted by many, but for the moment that was my truth. I had not joined the profession because I wanted power. Although I felt under pressure, on a number of occasions, to exert it, I equally knew there must be another way, and I knew I had to find it.

Not that my class were an undisciplined rabble for I recollect that I always managed to bring them into the main hall quietly each morning. Perhaps I should say they always managed that quietly, for again I am not sure how much of it was my doing. Each morning after registration the entire school, all 200 of us, would assemble in the hall for what was then simply known as 'assembly', which really consisted of a few notices from the head and what was essentially a simple act of worship, which meant a hymn, a story, another hymn and simple prayer, and dismissing the children as quietly as they came in. For my part I always managed that by asking the children to line up in pairs, then standing at the front of the line and trying to engage the gaze of each of them, usually just by standing quietly and looking at them. The message seemed to go round fairly quickly, I was lost if it didn't. I would then smile, raise my finger to my lips and set off in a rather exaggerated tip toe gait. I believe that there has to be something of a showman in every teacher, while I also believe that children respect genuineness and honesty. A teacher also has to be able to project those qualities to the children. Every actor talks of the need to engage the audience. It is no different in teaching except that at the point of engagement, it ceases to be an act. I had to be prepared to be real, to allow myself to be seen for who I was, while still remaining within my role as a teacher, never forgetting that I was also in loco parentis.

So rather like little miss bo'peep, I would set off for the hall, hopefully with my flock intact at the other end; that is if they hadn't called into the toilet on the way. We always seemed to get there. Perhaps I was learning slowly that there are other ways of class control.

Once in the hall it was over to the head, except one day a week when each class would take it in turns to lead the assembly. This was something which had been instituted by the head and agreed in a staff meeting once we had got established. The children seemed to enjoy leading the assemblies, but inevitably it tended to entail a lot of work for the teacher concerned. This is part of the art of good teaching; to be organised such that the children are able to give of their best and to make it look at the end as if it is all their work even if the teacher, now a shadow of their former self, is saying "never again". That seemed to be rather the effect of class led assemblies for inevitably the teacher would tend to feel that their own ability was on show, each trying to better the previous class' efforts, such that within a comparatively short time, the assembly began to resemble a "Cecil B. De Mille" production.

I don't know whether it was my natural flair for class control or my abilities as a producer, but I became aware of the head's encouragement. Looking back I have a sense that I was not particularly strong in either role. Rather I suspect that the head just saw that this young man meant well and was generally harmless. At all events, it was fairly early on in the spring term that my wife and I received an invitation to dinner. Again, looking back, I must have been rather socially naïve as I was simply glad to accept the invitation. I could not see that she was in truth trying to encourage me and to enable my own growth.

The extent to which I was being asked to grow should have become clear later when the head confided in me that she had been appointed to a headship of another new school, closer to her own home, and she invited me to apply for the deputy headship. I duly sent for an application form and applied in the usual manner and, not surprisingly on reflection, I was invited for interview. I say on reflection because I honestly do not believe I fully comprehended what I was truly being offered.

I observed earlier that I came from a world of limited horizons which perhaps contributed to my naivity. Having said that, school was in London, and its proximity to the bright lights of the West End and the great metropolis in general meant that when I reached the sixth form, some friends and I would often go into the city, particularly the theatres, after school. On one occasion I recall we were walking through the Soho district. One might say that the district had a certain reputation. Its reputation, however, had not reached me, such that when a young woman approached me and asked for the time, not having a watch, I simply called ahead to a friend and said, "Tony, this young lady wishes to know the time". His retort was "Come away, you fool." He explained later that I was being 'propositioned'. I did not even quite know what that meant. I was very clearly an innocent abroad.

Here, I was again perhaps being 'propositioned' only in a rather different manner. Again, however, I was unable to recognise what I was truly being offered. I did not interview well, but at the end of the afternoon was called back and offered the post. The head showed me round the new school after which I drove around the area a little and obtained details from a couple of estate agents. The first thing that struck me was the proximity of a cement works, the second was the price of property; somewhat higher than where we were presently living. My wife was expecting our son at that time and I realised therefore that we were going to lose her income. One might argue that a deputy head's pay would be higher, but not a great deal to start with. My own background had not endowed me with a great deal of confidence which was also true of my wife, such that when the letter confirming the offer arrived I did, what perhaps would seem to some, the unthinkable; I refused the post. On reflection, it seems like the unthinkable to me now, and I certainly deeply regret the difficulties I obviously caused the head. I could not see any of that at the time. All I could see was the threat of penury and uncertainty. Unlike Julie Andrews in the "Sound of Music", I had not always longed for adventure.

As to whether I regret that decision from a personal standpoint many years' later it is difficult to say. It was certainly professional suicide, but I am equally aware that there are other considerations beyond ambition. Perhaps too ambition needs to be understood in different ways. It was two years later that I applied for another deputy headship, but I had by that time also applied for a place at the University of Nottingham to read for my first degree. Thus, when attending for an initial interview I felt it incumbent upon me to warn them that I was waiting to hear about a place and that, if offered, I would feel bound to accept it. Not surprisingly I was not offered the post. I have a suspicion that anyone reading this may think that I "need my head testing" or at least needed to sort out my priorities. With regard to the latter, I have a sense that at a deeper or subconscious level I already had. As said at the beginning, education had always been important to me and having given up the chance of going on to read for a degree immediately following my initial training, I had remained hungry, and that deeper hunger clamoured to be satisfied.

All that perhaps reflects the benefit of hindsight. At the

time I only knew how uncomfortable I felt about the new post and felt I could do no other than refuse it. The head and I had to continue to work together and she showed, I feel, remarkable restraint. The atmosphere became strained in the staff room and I tried to quietly get on with the job of teaching.

Thus that momentous year drew to a close and I remember that my wife and I went pony trekking that summer. We wondered if after such an early introduction to the saddle my son might go on to become a horse rider. He turned out to be no more proficient than we, which was not very! We did, however, enjoy that break and mother and child were none the worse for the experience.

The following term felt a lot more relaxed, not only from a personal point of view as I recollect, for the present deputy head became acting head and, his being of a rather more "laid back" personality, that became reflected in the general atmosphere of the school.

For a start the stock cupboard remained unlocked affording staff access. For the first time in my teaching career of seven years, I could now actually have access to stock whenever I needed it. Things had been better under the previous head than in my first appointment for at least we could ask for what we needed to support our teaching, but our asking was limited to a Tuesday morning via our stock list, which the head filled for us and brought to our classrooms or left out for our collection. Thus we had moved from a shopping list, (I often felt like adding 1/2lb. sultanas and 1/2lb. butter) to a supermarket setting. The only thing missing now was the supermarket trolley!

I find it interesting too how during that interregnum period with its very much more relaxed atmosphere, staff became slightly more supportive of each other. There is perhaps a wider social implication here as we move ever more towards a culture of surveillance and punishment. For we see an increasingly insular or "look after number one" atmosphere prevail in the workplace. Work becomes restricted to contractual duties and exceeding those to help an individual is not encouraged.

By contrast, I was to learn just how supportive my colleagues were later that term when the baby whom my wife had been carrying during our pony trekking holiday duly arrived three weeks' early. He had been expected on Christmas Day but, in fact, arrived on December 6th. That being St. Nicholas' day what else could we call our newly born son, but Nicholas. That day started early as my wife began to experience abdominal pains. She felt it could not be our baby as that wasn't due and became concerned as to what might be the cause. I duly telephoned our doctor's surgery number, but was told to telephone again during surgery hours! Clearly then, as now, one could only be ill or have a medical need during those hours. Beyond the fact that I should need to be with my class in school, as the pain seemed to be increasing in severity, I telephoned the maternity hospital and was advised to bring my wife in. So having telephoned our acting head and explained that I should be a little late that morning, we duly set off. Having seen my wife settled into a bed I headed for school, arriving, as I recollect, more or less on time!

One aspect of teaching that I have always experienced is its capacity to demand all our attention. It is not something one can do while thinking of something else, or in this case, somebody else. While this may perhaps sound uncaring, at that moment, for me, the needs of the many outweighed the needs of the few. I reasoned too that the latter were being taken care of better than I was able to do. Thus again, I was confronted with that familiar voice which reminded me that I had a job to do and that thirty odd children would suffer if I did not do it. Beyond thinking briefly about my wife at lunch time when I had a moment to think of anything beyond the more immediate demands of teaching, I found myself totally immersed in the needs of the children. In fairness to myself, such a capacity is, I understand a feature of the masculine brain. I was glad of lunch, because breakfast had been little, if any, that morning as I recall that the hospital had advised me that my wife should avoid food in case anesthaesia was required. Apart from which, I was too concerned that she should receive medical attention as soon as possible. Four o'clock that afternoon saw me tidying my classroom rather peremptorily and gathering my marking and books together before my departure for the hospital, with the good wishes of my colleagues.

The hospital did not provide parking facilities for patients or visitors and thus I had to leave my car in the nearest multi-storey car park and walk the rest of the way. By the time I did arrive at the hospital my wife was beginning to wonder where I was, but I also gathered that little had happened. My wife's pains had subsided and thus it had rather been decided to keep my wife in overnight to "monitor the situation". The "situation" did not need monitoring for too long, however, as shortly after my arrival my son obviously felt that now both his parents were present he might as well join them. That, however, proved to be easier said than done as late afternoon became evening and evening gave way to night. I stayed with my wife trying to do my inadequate bit until the midwife realised that there just was not room for even a smaller slightly premature baby to be born. Having consulted my wife's notes and realising that the vital statistics just were not there, she called the consultant who, I understand, was at a dinner party. To his credit he came immediately, I was duly ushered out and shown into a waiting room, and from where I sat, it seemed that all hell broke loose as nurses dashed to and from the room where I had left my wife. Thus I sat for about an hour trying to contain my mounting anxiety until at last I approached a nurse as she left the room and asked how my wife was, to which she simply replied "Oh, we're just trying to get some more blood!" as she hurried by. In the absence of any further information, I now had to assume that my wife and child were bleeding to death. That helped my anxiety levels considerably!

It was some time later that the consultant came out to me and said that I had a son, but explained that they had given my wife an anaesthetic and had had to perform a forceps delivery as there was insufficient room for my son to be born otherwise. He went on to explain that as my son had had difficulty breathing he was in an incubator, while the pressure of birth had caused slight facial palsy. He duly took me to a room where there were a number of incubators and showed me one in which my sleeping son lay. He went on to explain that hopefully the palsy would wear off with time, but at that moment I really could not take any more information in. My son looked wonderful to me and I just didn't care about anything else except to ask anxiously how was my wife. I was told she was still asleep from the anaesthetic and that I should see her in the morning.

Thus I left the hospital at about 3.45 that night and made my way back to my car. It was only then that I realised that I did not have any change with which to feed the automatic barrier. I wondered about going to the police station, but did not know where the nearest one was, and being without the said change could not even telephone from the local kiosk to find out. In our increasingly automated society there seems little capacity to cope with the needs of the individual, while the individual must remain ever more vigilant to survive within it. A society which cannot cope with deviance is itself impoverished where history shows that it is its eccentrics which often make the greatest contribution.

As it was, I was now seeking the contribution; the change to enable me to get home. Thus I approached a lone passer by and asked for some change. Fortunately he was able to provide for my need and I duly reached for my wallet to recompense him, to which he nervously retorted, "keep it, keep it" as he hurried on. It was only later that I learned that a rapist had already made a number of attacks in that area. Had this obliging stranger mistaken me for him? It was just a little later that night that my true criminal nature was to be discovered.

The multi-storey car park and indeed the city centre were well lit and there was little traffic such that I was able to negotiate my way through the streets and fairly quickly left the light of the town behind me so that I now found myself on the open unlit road leading homewards. There being little, if any, traffic, I remember how grateful I was to be spared the dazzling lights of oncoming cars. Did I say there was little, if any, traffic? There was one car directly behind me, whose head lights were shining straight in my mirror. Undaunted I continued on my way until the said car started to flash its headlights. I slowed in order to let it pass, but it remained behind me. As I continued to slow it became apparent that its driver was not going to overtake. By this time I had almost stopped. So had the car behind me. More questioning than afraid, I finally stopped in a layby and a figure got out of the car behind. After my experience of the previous few hours I felt too tired to be afraid. By this time the approaching figure had reached my car and had tapped on the window, and I discovered it to be a police officer in uniform. Apparently, not only had I been too tired to be afraid, I had also been too tired to switch on the lights of my car! Having politely reminded me of my oversight, I simply responded, "Oh, have I? I'm awfully sorry". Having duly switched on my lights, the officer concerned simply said, "Drive carefully". I thanked him and proceeded, suitably chastened, on my way.

I cannot help but ponder whether, if in a similar situation today, I would not have been asked to step out of my car, been breathalysed, then spreadeagled against the side of my car and been searched for drugs or offensive weapons before finally being charged with failing to drive without due care and attention, such that my son could so easily have had a father with a criminal record! At that point I should have failed a CRB check and therefore arguably been unemployed as well. How different my own son's future could have been had he and I been born a few years' later. Again I am forced to reflect that, "There, but for the grace of God, go I".

As it was, I completed my journey home, now able to see where I was going, threw some fuel on our solid fuel room heater in the hope that it was still alight and crawled into bed. I did not know any more until I was awakened about 9 o'clock that following morning by someone banging on the window. It was a friend who had also been my colleague when I had been teaching at my previous school wanting to know if I and my wife were all right. Clearly news had gone around the village the previous day although I still do not know how, and seeing the curtains still drawn, our friend, later to be my son's godmother, was sufficiently concerned to enquire. I gave her the glad tidings, "Unto us a son is born". She seemed genuinely delighted. I still felt dazed.

My wife remained in hospital for a week until I received a call at school on a Friday morning saying that, "It would be convenient to pick your wife up at 3 p.m." "Convenient for whom?" was my first question as I reminded the caller that the children did not finish until 3.15 p.m. I was tempted to try to explain that teaching wasn't like nursing and that you could not simply get one's colleagues to cover for you by sharing the extra work load between them. One could not simply "absorb" a class of children. Such an explanation I sensed would be lost. I simply said that I would not be able to be there at that time. As I had taken the call in the office, the secretary was fully aware of its nature and had obviously had a word with our acting head. For at lunch time he said that the afternoon had been sorted out; that I would go and collect my wife from hospital and that a colleague would go out to my house and ready it for my wife's return, including putting the room heater up and bringing up the radiators. He clearly had it all worked out and I thanked him just feeling held in the warmth of such a supportive atmosphere. As the children went out for a break that afternoon, I drove to the hospital. On our arrival home my colleague had not only got the house warm but had set tea ready, and, having made sure everything was tidied for our return, waited to welcome us before making a tactful withdrawal. At that moment I was somehow not sorry that I had turned down my promotion. I had, in my own way perhaps, asserted what values were important to me even without being consciously aware of them. As I had turned down the earlier opportunity of a degree, so now I had refused promotion, because in each case another person was being put first. If we fail to put people at the centre of our social structures, be they schools, services or companies, then we negate their very purpose.

Chapter Ten

A Growing Family

"Now sits expectation in the air"
William Shakespeare (Henry V Act2)

A very busy Christmas, as my wife and I tried to adjust to the new routine imposed by a new baby, gave way to a slightly more settled new year. The interregnum at school continued with our acting head such that I was conscious of being a member of two families; a family of three at home and a family of eight, including our secretary, at school and just sometimes those families would mix, as our acting head's young children and our own baby with their respective mothers could also be found in our staff room.

School had a relaxed feel about it. As I recollect that also seemed to be reflected in the behaviour of the chidren as I did not experience any discipline problems in spite of my declared lack of prowess in that area. Again my experience is that children are very sensitive to the prevailing atmosphere at home or school. If school is a quiet relaxed atmosphere, so the children likewise become quiet and relaxed and are thus free to grow and learn. Children also need motivation and structure in order to facilitate that learning, but the place at which motivation spills over into stress is a remarkably fine line and from that point onwards intellectual performance begins to drop away. As stress increases and performance decreases, the atmosphere becomes increasingly strained and competitive, so the other element to increase is the behaviour, or rather misbehaviour. It is very easy for a school to descend into a battlefield with embattled staff desperately trying to maintain order. In that atmosphere children and teachers quickly become exhausted and learning is just one of the casualties.

Perhaps it was my own role as father that made me a little more gentle with the children at school, but I had a sense, as once before in my career, that we were gentle with each other. I recollect that term, as was regular practice, we held a parents' evening at which parents were free to come to discuss their child's progress although it was my experience that increasingly parents would often call in immediately after school to discuss any concerns. The only difference was that our mark books would have been gone through such that staff had a rather more precise indication of individual performance, although again my experience was that parents were often more concerned as to whether their child was happy, for parents and teachers alike understood that happy children made happy learners.

That parents' evening was even happier than normal! Half way through the evening, which lasted from 7p.m. to 9p.m., the head had very thoughtfully brought coffee round to all the staff. What a nice gesture, I thought! I remember that the coffee tasted a little strong and added to that I was so busy talking to parents I didn't actually finish it all. My only concern during that otherwise very relaxed evening was that I noticed what I thought was the smell of alcohol on the breath of a number of the parents. I thought this was in rather poor taste as it was apparent, to me at least, that they must have come on from the local pub in the village and I remember a rather judgemental me thinking quietly to myself, "Please don't let me or concerns about your child's progress interrupt your drinking time!" Indeed when the evening had finished and the last parents had left, I quickly opened all the windows for a while as I tidied my classroom ready for the following morning. Having closed the windows again and returned my washed cup to the staff room, I returned home about 10p.m. It was another reminder that teaching was most certainly not a 9 to 5 job, as I hadn't even started my marking at that time. Perhaps I could allow myself to give it a miss just this once!

The following day during morning break the head asked how we enjoyed the coffee. Being polite I thanked him and said it was very thoughtful. Somebody else said it was a little strong while another member of staff commented that it had a slightly different flavour. The head replied that that would be the rum! A couple of my colleagues commented that they thought it "had a bit of a kick to it", while I admitted to my hasty judgements about the parents I had seen. The only person who had been drinking was I!

I remember how I continued to enjoy that relaxed atmosphere which spilled over into so many areas of the curriculum. It was about that time that the swimming pool, which had been housed at "the old establishment", was moved up to the new site where it could be plumbed into the boiler house, which meant not only could the water be constantly circulated and filtered, but that also it could be heated. O, the luxury of a heated pool!

Again I could think back to my years in the grammar school and our swimming lessons which meant lining up on the side of the pool, military fashion, and then being told to "jump in, get your head under", which instruction was barked at us in a similarly military fashion. I remember too the sickening shock of cold water. Those weekly excursions to the pool occurred evey summer term for the first four years of my time at the school. I don't know if it was intended to "make men" of us. All it achieved in my case was that, by the time I started teaching, I vowed I would never put any child through that same degrading, traumatising process. The one thing it did not achieve was to teach me how to swim!

Thus here I was charged with the task of teaching others to do what I could not do myself. Thus I recalled my father's words, "Those who can, do, those who can't teach". Many a true word is spoken in jest! In this particular instance I had no choice. It was about a year later that one of the county advisors came to instruct us in some of the basics of the teaching of swimming and to remind us of basic safety procedures and requirements, which included the presence of at least one member of staff who could swim outside of the pool at all times. Clearly that made sense as, if the teacher was in the pool, then approximately half of the children would be behind them at any one time. In an ideal world one was meant to have teaching assistants in the pool while it was clearly intended that the class teacher would also be the qualified swimmer.

This, however, was not an ideal world and whatever role needed filling, I was it. That, for me, was one of the joys of primary teaching; rather like the parent, one brought one's strengths and weaknesses and gave one's whole self to the task of teaching the children. Over the years that I continued in that role I often pondered that it was perhaps my very weaknesses that were my greatest strength for I recollect that I never had any children who did not want to go swimming, save just one occasion, when the child concerned pretended to have forgotten his swimming costume. That afternoon after school I was accosted angrily by his mother for not allowing her son to go swimming. When I pointed out to her that he had supposedly forgotten his costume, it became clear that he had given different explanations to each of us. She quickly apologised and turning to the child said "Wait till I get you home." He did not forget again.

At this point, although the pool had been moved, we did not boast a changing room. Adjoining the wet area of my classroom, however, there was another room of similar size which had been built to accommodate phase two of the new school. By standing a couple of blackboards on their edge supported by two portable clothing racks, the area was divided into two - girls' and boys' changing areas.

Now with a fully functioning pool our deputy/acting head devised a swimming award scheme geared specifically to the age group and to our pool which was approximately 5 by 10 metres and stood on the ground, such that the sides came up to about 1 metre, or my waist height. This had some distinct teaching advantages, but some practical disadvantages. From a teaching point of view you could talk to the children at a natural level instead of shouting at them several feet below or kneeling down and going head to head. It also meant one could put out a hand to the less confident. The downside was that any water coming over the side of the pool lay in puddles, most likely having drenched the teacher's front in the process. To this latter practicality there were really only two answers; one either donned a waterproof and boots or wore as little as possible, such as a tee shirt, shorts or light trousers and beach shoes. I tended to opt for the latter, while female colleagues tended to opt for a plastic mac.

Thus prepared, we could attend to teaching the children to swim, hence our award scheme which consisted of green, blue, red and gold ribbons. Green was awarded for swimming one width of the pool and was the first one awarded. Blue was for one length of the pool, red for one circuit front stroke and one circuit back stroke, while the prized gold was for two circuits front stroke, two circuits back stroke, one width glide across the pool and retrieving an object from the bottom of the pool, this being a small rubber brick, but latterly, when the brick seemed to be missing, I found a 10p piece provided sufficient incentive. I don't know if that constituted bribery and corruption! As the children became more proficient the number wanting to do the red and gold ribbons increased such that it was no longer sensible trying to fit testing for awards in with the regular lessons, which were necessarily limited if all classes were to have time in the pool. This was a particular problem for the older 10 and 11 year olds. Latterly we boasted purpose built wooden changing rooms which again our acting head had organised and, with some parents to help him, had erected one weekend on a concrete base which had been laid the previous weekend. With improved facilities and the need becoming more apparent it became my practice to keep the swimming periods for teaching and to concentrate on the awards after school. This after school period became increasingly popular as those trying for awards very often had supporters with them, while for others it was an excuse for a bit more time in the pool. This quickly expanded to two sessions a week. As a number of the children were "bussed" in from the surrounding villages, it meant that those two afternoons would often see me making a tour of the villages with a car load of children. I remember that my car was insured through a company which operated a scheme for N.U.T. members which meant that I could arrange for passenger cover while using the car in a professional capacity. So for an extra sum, the children were covered in the event of an accident. Teaching in a school of under 200 pupils in a rural area had the advantage that one was known and trusted by all the parents where very often one may have taught some of the children's siblings in previous years. I am not sure that any of my colleagues teaching today would dare to expose themselves to the risk of accusations of impropriety and the accompanying litigation.

I am reminded of one such occasion when most of the children in that after school swimming session were from the village in which the school was built, with just one girl coming from one of the surrounding villages, who was therefore going to be dependent upon me for transport. Thus I had seen the other children do their ribbons first and had left her till last. I remember how determined she was to complete her award and seeing her keeness I had overlooked the fact that she might be getting cold, having to wait in the pool for some of her classmates to finish theirs. It was clear, by the time that she got out of the pool, that she was beginning to shiver. I enquired if she was all right and having received her assurance that she was, through chattering teeth, I urged her to go and get changed, while I returned to my classroom to gather my books and marking for that evening before returning to the pool area. Knocking on the changing room door, I enquired if the child concerned was ready. On receiving no reply I opened the door to see if she had already vacated, only to be confronted with a shivering child still in her swimming costume. She clearly needed help - and fast. Reasoning that this situation was the result of my negligence and the child was my responsibility, I simply enquired if she wanted me to give her a hand, to which she nodded through chattering teeth. By the time I had delivered her home safely she seemed none the worse for her brush with hypothermia and simply could not wait to tell her mother that she had got her gold ribbon! If ever I needed one, that was a very precious reminder of the immense position of trust, responsibility and privilege in which one was placed by children and parents alike.

Swimming was restricted to the summer term as it was an outside pool and while the new changing rooms provided proper girls' and boys' changing facilities they were still little more than large wooden sheds on concrete bases, Had it not been for the enterprise of our deputy/acting head, indeed we should not have been provided with that. Thus I, in my naïvety, rather felt that the headship should have gone to him. At that stage I was unaware of the politics of such appointments, while a school of that size tended to attract applications from existing heads from smaller schools and therefore rather more experienced candidates. Thus that summer term saw interviews for the headship being held at the school. We met the successful candidate briefly, who, having been formally introduced said, "just call me Bill". My entire experience of heads up to this point had been of rather distant figures, and even though my experience of our previous head had been like a breath of spring after my first appointment, I had still been aware of a slight distance. This new approach felt a little bit of a culture shock which was reinforced for me when his parting words were T.G.I.F. On enquiring the meaning of the abbreviation, he simply said, "Thank God it's Friday", and was gone. So this was to be our new head. I remember feeling slightly shocked. Even after eight years in the profession there was still something of the young idealist in me and I suspect that I expected at least a slightly greater show of dedication.

That saw half-term arrive and as we returned the following week the appointment of a new head seemed a long way away. He wouldn't be starting until September and this was still the end of May. May of that year also saw the baptism of our son. The church had originally been built in the twelfth century and I don't think the heating had been updated much since then, with the result that during the winter it was difficult to raise the temperature sufficiently even to take the chill out of the air. Given that he had been born prematurely decided us that May was the earliest we could sensibly manage. There was very much a feeling of being a member of a family both at school and in the church and wider community. My son found a welcome in all those families as he could be found at different times in staff room and church alike. I remember the parents' evening that term felt equally like a family affair, although without the assistance of alcohol on this occasion. As one of the members of staff lived even further from school than I did, I invited her for a meal before we both returned to school to see parents. The boundaries between home and school became comfortably blurred. As that term and academic year drew to a close, I began to feel relaxed for the first time in my teaching career.

The following term saw the arrival of the new head just a few days before the children were due to start. The first change was that both our restored deputy head and I were to be down in the "old establishment" again as phase two of the new school building was due to start during that year. This was indeed the beginning of another period of change as it saw, first, the appointment of a new 'head of infants', while later saw the appointment of another member of staff to replace a colleague who had left to have a baby, which was born about the same time as my own son. Both the head of infants and our new teacher in the 'junior' school were capable pianists who began to contribute to the curriculum in an increasingly wider sense. It was clear that my own limited contribution to the music curriculum and my wife's rather more accomplished input would no longer be needed. "The partial vanishes when wholeness comes". It soon became apparent that the services of in-staff musicians were to become ever more important to the life of the school. Shortly after the arrival of the new head of infants saw members of the school involved in a production of "Joseph and his Technicolor Dream Coat". Thus the West End came to a corner of East Anglia. Indeed over the coming years there were to be Christmas concerts conducted by the head, complete with baton, and various other productions organised by the now rather more active P.T.A.

It became clear that our new head was a showman. As the years progressed I began to feel he had missed his true vocation. I began to understand too that perhaps sometimes teaching required one to be just that. For the essence of a showman is that he commands our attention and human nature is such that we are very often unable to see, and therefore appreciate, something unless it is sufficiently bold or clear. Advertisers are quick to learn that simple truth and to exploit it. That, I feel, was the essential difference, which became increasingly apparent as the years went on, between the head and I.

For the moment, however, his showman type nature made him easy to engage with and I began to understand a little of why he had been appointed. I appreciated this new informal atmosphere and this man who was so eager to engage with his staff. I recall some afternoons after the children had gone home and "the busy world was hushed" would see the head, deputy, and I discussing educational philosophy. I recall too how Bill, as I had to remember to call him, was very much taken with Edward de Bono and what he termed as 'lateral thinking' and our discussing how that might influence our teaching. Looking back, those discussions were indeed precious for I am aware that there is little room in teaching now for discussions about educational philosophy and our children are most certainly not encouraged to indulge in lateral thinking. My concern is how much we may now encourage children to think at all in a society where every aspect of life, including the home, is closely regulated and that therefore compliance, rather than thinking, seems to be the order of the day. The same culture is clearly prevalent in schools where not only what one should teach and how one should teach it is regulated, but also for how long each day! It was the character of "Inspector Morse" created by Colin Dexter, who said to his sergeant, "Thinking, Lewis, old or new, would be a welcome change". For the time being, I enjoyed that professional freedom. Such an approach was clearly the underlying philosophy of, and had been very apparent in, my own training. This felt like what I had indeed been trained for.

What I had not been trained for was acting as a theatrical prop, which, as the head's latent showman came ever more to the forefront of the life of the school, seemed increasingly my role. On these occasions teaching staff opting out was not an available option. Thus, instead, I always asked, as choosing was also not available, for a minor role. I guess roles did not come any more minor than crouching at the head's feet under a table. Did this, I pondered, somehow summarise my position on the staff? This particular occasion saw the head in a situation in which he was clearly at home, on stage before a hall full of people and the focus of everyone's attention. What he was doing in order to gain their attention was to sit at a table dressed up as a gypsy, complete with a crystal ball. Various people from the audience had been primed to ask him questions, to which I was duly required to write down the answer, and hand to him while hidden under the table, thus creating the illusion of his being clairvoyant. That perhaps should have told me something of his approach to running the school. The act finished with his leaving the table to take a bow, pulling the table cloth with him, revealing me beneath!

Such "fun" evenings were to become increasingly the norm as the head sought to involve the P.T.A. (parent teacher association) ever more closely in the life of the school and it began to organise more social events, which afforded the head more opportunities to indulge his latent showman or alter ego. Again staff presence at such events was de rigeur as apparently was the purchase of raffle tickets. In fairness the P.T.A. funds sometimes enabled the school to buy an occasional item of equipment which perhaps the normal budget would not extend to. I always try to avoid raffle tickets like the plague on the grounds that I never win anything, while, in that setting it would tend to mean my waiting until they were drawn so that I could throw them away with a clear conscience. In the unlikely event that I should win anything then my absence would be noticed. My other problem is that the raffle prize may very well be somebody else's unwanted item which has been kindly donated, which again, should I be the holder of a "lucky" ticket would then involve me in a trip to the local charity shop.

On one occasion, however, I had bought the regulation strip of 5 raffle tickets and managed to win first prize which was a duck dinner for two. As I related this to my wife later that evening I had visions of a cosy table for two, perhaps in one of the better restaurants in town, with candlelight glinting through a wine glass showing the deep ruby hue of a moderately aged chateau bottled claret as an accompaniment to the perfectly cooked tender duck breast, brought to us by an attentive waiter. I assumed that I would be given details of the restaurant or perhaps vouchers later during the week.

I did not have to wait too long as our deputy head gave it to me the following morning at break time. Our 'duck dinner' came in a vegetable box and consisted of a duck, still in feather, three carrots which looked like young tree trunks and a pound of potatoes! At least I could tell the vegetables were local produce by the soil that still clung to them. The duck was not in a position to say where it had come from as my one comfort was that it was already dead. I could already imagine the look on my wife's face when I took it home that evening. Her only comment was "Well I hope you're going to pluck and clean it". Perhaps I could do it after I had finished my marking!

When the head wasn't dressed up as a gypsy, he could be seen dressed up as a "dinner lady", complete with wig. Fortunately that was restricted to the last day of term, immediately before Christmas. Less fortunately, on one occasion, he seemed to feel that his staff should also dress up. Hence a few days before the end of term saw me going along to a local theatrical costume hirer and hiring a bear costume, complete with head. Now I could, in truth, be a bear with a sore head!

The end of that year too saw my return from exile down at the old school as the new extension was finished. I remember three chairs being set in a line in the staff room with a label declaring them to be for the "three wise monkeys", being the three staff returning from the old establishment. It did indeed feel like 'returning to the fold'. All the staff were to be united, at least geographically, and now teaching on one site.

The new extension was formally opened and would accommodate the three older classes, namely the 2nd, 3rd and 4th year juniors or years 4,5 and 6. Our new premises were built such that they were largely self contained although additionally they did boast an audio-visual room which was intended to be used by the entire school. Thus this largely self contained extension became known as the 'wing'. Intended for three classes, it contained three teaching areas, each furnished differently. One was supplied with tables, chairs and a teacher's desk; a second was supplied with collapsible desks allowing the carpeted area to be used for informal groups; while a third area contained a sink unit, benches and storage units which was intended for an art and craft area. This, in turn opened onto a new kiln room so that pottery could now be incorporated into the curriculum. Such an arrangement sounds like a teacher's dream accommodating formal teaching, informal groups and a dedicated craft area. Indeed it would have been if it had been designed for one class.

Unfortunately the dream quickly became a nightmare as three staff and three classes tried to share three separate areas. In order to accommodate such sharing the head had decided that team teaching along with vertical grouping was the way forward. This effectively meant that the children had no fixed room and no fixed teacher while vertical grouping meant we had ages ranging from eight to eleven in each class, thus making any formal or class teaching an impossibility. Hence the formal teaching area could not be used for what it was intended. Beyond that, while staff would cooperate on use of the different teaching areas it was clear that no class would want a third of its time doing art or craft. Nor, equally, would they want to spend a third of their time sitting on the floor in informal groups. Add to that the problem that only one class had a teacher's desk and it will quickly become apparent that staff and children alike began to feel like displaced persons of no fixed abode. Teachers could be found perching on a stool at any spare table or other work surface trying to mark children's individual work as the vertical grouping meant every child was at a different level of attainment and all needed individual help before they could progress.

In fairness to the head, team teaching was in vogue at the time and he clearly felt we ought to be seen to embrace such an approach. That could have worked if all the other variables had not been introduced at the same time. As it was, the 'wing' quickly degenerated into chaos. From time to time the head would provide further input which basically meant his placing even more requirements on the staff or targets to meet. By the end of that year neither staff nor children really knew what they were meant to be doing or where they belonged. It was into this situation that one of the county education authority's inspectors found himself inducted. He had clearly waited until we were well into the third term before visiting to see how we were making this "exciting new wing" work. That we weren't was immediately clear to him as this new visitor found himself totally ignored beyond a passing nod or smile from a harrassed teacher. I recollect that the best I could manage by way of greeting or indeed conversation was something to the effect of, "Hello, do feel free to have a look round. I'm just a little busy at the moment" as another child clamoured for my attention.

He didn't stay long before finding the head and making it clear to him that his staff were totally over stretched. There is perhaps a wider lesson in that as now, increasingly, politicians are doing the same to our education system. As ever more targets are placed upon schools and staff, when the stress begins to show in staff absences, as evidenced in the high proportion of supply staff whose first language may not be English, and attainment levels drop, as indicated in the "league tables", so the school is labelled as failing.

It is perhaps not surprising that the deputy head and I both started to look to broader horizons.

Chapter Eleven

You're in Charge!

"Happy he who has found wisdom
and the person who has acquired understanding"
Proverbs 3:13

Perhaps the stress of the previous year, or perhaps a recognition of a deeper voice within, but the following year found me applying for a place at university to read for that precious degree in education which I had felt unable to pursue when I was still at college. Increasingly I found it was a voice that would not be silenced.

Mrs. Thatcher had just been elected to her first term as prime minister and it seemed to mark a new era in education. Until then, education had largely been teacher/pupil led and succeeding ministers had seen it as their responsibility to provide an environment in which teachers could teach and children could learn and professionals be left alone to do the job they had been trained to do. Now we began to see a shift in stance as government sought to become ever more closely involved, firstly in the curriculum and later in its delivery. The professional freedom I had enjoyed I saw being increasingly threatened and as I saw political agendas beginning to creep into the curriculum through ever changing "guidelines" I realised just how much I cared about education. My care extended beyond just wanting to get promotion and thus further my own career and perhaps increase my salary. I found that deep down I cared about the broader issues and how those same issues may impinge upon the children in my class. This, it must be said, was long before the days of league tables and the dreaded SAT's; dreaded, that is, by teachers and pupils, but seen as an essential tool in gaining ever more political control over what and how schools taught.

That term thus saw me attending an interview at the University of Nottingham. I had spent some time looking through prospectuses and that university was offering an in-service degree for practising teachers requiring just one year in full time study. I knew I would not be able to get more than one year's paid leave and equally I should not have been able to manage without any income. The decision felt a practical one and suddenly my dream was beginning to feel as if it could be realised. Somehow in interview, however, I felt I perhaps needed to convey that my decision was based upon idealogical rather than purely practical considerations!

Such a stance was to prove easier than I had expected. As I was welcomed into the study of the tutor who was to conduct the interview and we both assumed easy chairs I felt immediately at home. We spent the next half an hour chatting about our educational idealogies and I discovered somebody who cared about education as much as I did. Suddenly, beyond the practicalities, I found that I wanted to study here. I had found an institution which enshrined values that felt real to me and held fast to academic freedom. I knew now what was important to me.

Meanwhile the head had encouraged me to apply for a deputy headship in another county and I had duly sent off my letter of application. Thus I found myself attending another interview, having been short listed as one of four candidates. Interviews were conducted firstly at the education office and later at the school. It was during that final interview that I found myself saying that I had already applied for a place to read for a degree at the University of Nottingham which, if offered, I would feel bound to accept. At the time I reasoned that I was simply being honest. Upon reflection, I was clearly shooting myself in the foot, if not attempting professional suicide for a second time! Even though I did not immediately recognise it, that increasingly strong voice within was not going to be silenced. When I received an offer of a place at Nottingham just a few days' later, I knew what I had to do. The practicalities of finding the money to do it and securing that precious year's sabbatical leave would have to come later.

For the moment I had a slightly more pressing responsibility. The deputy head had clearly had the same feelings as I had during the previous testing year and had gained a place on the local in-service diploma course. It was generally regarded as the stepping stone for those seeking promotion. Hence, holding the post of deputy head more or less assured him the funding, provided that it had the head's backing, which was duly forthcoming. So accordingly that year saw us without a deputy head and hence the roles he had been filling we covered between us. I had quietly, with tongue in cheek, suggested he was leaving a sinking ship to which I recollect he replied in similar vein, "Don't let it sink till I get back!" Hence that rather more pressing responsibility.

I was appointed head of the 'wing'. We were a team of three and clearly the head had learnt some sort of lesson from the previous year as he made it clear that I had to organise it and make it work! The three of us had sat down together at the end of the previous term and had drawn up a timetable which we felt could work, that respected our different strengths and with which we felt reasonably happy. We agreed to meet again immediately before term started, but in the meantime, still suffering from shell shock after that previous year, probably agreed that we needed the six week break more than the children.

As I assumed my new role at the beginning of that new term, I began to understand some of the many roles the deputy head had been filling. He had been the unofficial head of audio-visual aids, swimming pool coordinator and coach to the school football team. When the head had suggested I lead the 'wing', he had somehow failed to mention the other roles. Perhaps, in fairness, he had not realised just how much extra curricular work his deputy head had been doing. I began to, as the head informed me that the area football tournament was in about a month's time. Teams from all over the southern part of the county met together for one complete Saturday morning and competed for the coveted area schools' cup. It was something we had never won and so I rather felt that when we lost that year no-one would be too surprised. The head clearly had different ideas as he said that all eyes would be on me that year to "bring home the bacon!". I quietly thought to myself how apt his phraseology was, as, given my own declared prowess in the game, we were most likely to be slaughtered or to put it another way, 'pigs might fly!'

Fortunately for me, I recollect that we had two particularly able and keen players who both happened to be in my class. I reasoned that we needed to build on that strength. I started by appointing them both as captains of two six aside teams and the three of us sat down together to select the two teams. I encouraged Gary and Jason, for their names still stay with me, to think carefully about the positions in which they would put the players in order to use their individual strengths. When it came to our first games lesson of that term I left those two teams to organise their own skills practice while I got all the other boys organised into some sort of a game. Going back to the two six aside teams, I did my level best to referee the match generally agreeing with my two captains when it came to any offside calls. I noted that even though they were playing against each other, they generally agreed on the calls. I could see how much the two boys respected each other and how much that spilled over into their respective players. When a couple of weeks' later I sat down with them, again to explain that the area cup was approaching and that we needed to get a team together, it was comparatively easy, as we now had enough players for a complete team, plus a reserve. It was again heartening to see these two working together as they drew up the team. I felt it important to encourage them and to give the team a sense of identity so I drew up the team on paper in as professional a manner as I could manage and posted it on the notice board. Their pride was palpable.

My only difficulty, I felt, would be the appointing of the captain. I need not have worried; the two boys between them agreed mutually that Gary should captain the team. I remember being quite humbled by their obvious maturity and respect for each other and felt that perhaps some adults might learn from them. It was a joy to see the team beginning to shape up and to pull together as they played against the other boys at the next games lesson. It was a rather unequal match and the result a foregone conclusion but somehow both teams came off the field exuberant; the school team because they had won and felt they had proved themselves, the rest of the boys because they had played against the school team. It is amazing what a little kidology can achieve. At this stage I harboured no illusions and did not seriously expect to win the cup, but, at least, I determined the team would enjoy themselves and gain a sense of pride as they represented their school.

Come that Saturday morning, it was an exuberant group of boys that greeted me as I drove into the school car park and got the minibus out of the garage. Most of the boys had been brought in by parents which ensured that they got a good send off. My mounting anxiety was not whether we would win, I was sure there was no chance of that, but whether they would be too deflated when they didn't. My advice to them as we drove along therefore was to enjoy themselves. The cup, I said, would be a bonus, but the object was to have the opportunity to play against other teams and to enjoy the football. My little 'pep' talk was really a mixture of, "Its taking part and not winning that counts", and, "Play on, play on and play the game"!

The first team they were drawn against was from a much smaller school and with less personnel to call upon, it meant that their team was basically made up of any older boys who showed the slightest inclination and possibly a few who didn't. I don't mean to detract from our team's efforts but I pointed this fact out to them such that they went onto the pitch obviously relaxed. As a result they played well and made their win look fairly convincing. The next match was a little more even but they managed to win that one too. This left them to play against the host school which happened to be the largest school with the largest playing field. The head was also quite keen on sport. I was aware of this as I had also taught his son. Unsurprisingly not only had we not won against them but, in truth, neither had any other school most of the time. My words to the team as they went onto the field for that last game were, "You've played really well. Just go on and enjoy it". They did, and the score at half time was one all. They were becoming quite exuberant and I felt that I needed to do my "coaching bit" at that moment. I gathered the boys round and we went into a huddle as I suggested that they needed to keep passing the ball between them, to be aware of where their back up was to pass to and where their counterpart was. In other words I was saying, "Mark your man and keep control of the ball". They looked at me earnestly and nodded. It was clear that the other team had resumed the field with considerable determination, but our team matched that with a growing mutual respect for, and trust of, each other. They were really beginning to work together as a team. If ever they needed to, it was now. It was a gruelling second half as teamsmanship and gamesmanship met sheer grit and determination. The opposing team knew they just had to get one goal and their whole game became centred around that, while our boys kept passing the ball between them and, although their game was slightly more defensive against a stronger theam, their ball control and teamsmanship held their game together. At full time, with no penalties, the score still stood at one all and the head of the host school approached me and asked me if we would be content with a draw and share the cup or did we want to play to whichever team scored the first goal. I accepted his gracious suggestion that we should take the cup for the first half and pass it to them for the second half of the year. I said to him in honesty that both teams had played well, had given it their all and were tired. They had done enough, I felt, but I put it to the team and they nodded their agreement. They knew they had agreed a draw, but they hadn't realised that, as a result, they were going to be presented with the cup.

If it was possible, it was an even more exuberant group of boys that I brought back in the minibus than the one I had taken out earlier that morning. As I arrived at school on the Monday morning it was clear that the news of the result had preceded me as the head greeted me with, "I hear we have won the cup. You realise you are now the official football coach". As I thought quietly to myself that accolades like that I could well do without, I explained to him that we had actually just drawn and should return the cup later in the year. I explained that I felt the boys had given it their all and that the agreed draw had felt the only honourable course. What I did not say to him was that given my "ability" in the game, I could hardly believe my luck and thought we should quit while we were ahead. I don't think the head would have heard any of that had I said it. He was too anxious to show the cup in assembly that morning.

I found stepping into the other roles that the deputy head filled rather easier. The swimming pool needed to be put into use for the first half of the autumn term, but as it had been used regularly before the holiday, apart from checking that the area, including changing rooms, was clean and tidy, I happily left the "hoovering" of the pool to the caretaker. Equally to ensure that the heating was put on sufficiently far in advance, I simply liaised with the caretaker and happily left him to it. The deputy and I had looked after the audio-visual equipment together so that did not present a problem. Thus I felt that perhaps I could turn my attention to the task of trying to maintain the smooth running of the wing. We had inherited the vertical grouping from the previous year and had been charged with making it work. In hindsight the head's response to the pressure placed on him by the County Inspector was not to change the system but to step back and make it our responsibility. His quiet word to me was, "You're the head of the wing. You need to make it work". My response was an acknowledging nod and, "Yes, O.K., Bill", remembering the head's preferred mode of address. I was tempted to reply rather more in the vein of "Gee, thanks!" but, not for the first time, restrained myself.

Somehow, we did need to make it work. We needed to overcome the problem of the children wandering about like displaced persons and we needed to help them feel that this was their area. They needed too to have a sense of structure and to understand that how they behaved mattered. While not being naturally into rewards on the grounds that it smacks too much of the use of treats in dog training and can put the wrong emphasis on the process of socialising, yet I understood that what had felt like the anarchy of the previous year needed to be addressed. Perhaps my description of the previous year and the head's attitude is grossly unfair and an exaggeration of the situation, but I perceived an expectation that we must somehow make this work. Hence I introduced star charts, so loved of yester year. At the end of each week the class with the most points got an extra break while the other two classes set to and tidied the wing ensuring that equipment was put away, cupboards tidied and even the sinks and paint trays cleaned. This was their space and they needed to be able to take a pride in it.

There is, of course, a wider philosophical issue here and a fundamental flaw in the system; some members of staff would tend to award stars more readily than others. Hence the class whose teacher was a little more reserved in the rewards would tend to lose out. My reasoning was that their being taught by another teacher from time to time would have a balancing effect. the other answer would have been to agree on a set of criteria for which a star may be awarded. The problem with criteria based awards is that no set of criteria can possibly hope to cover every aspect of meritorious behaviour while it encourages people to do only that which will gain an award while also engendering a legalistic mind-set which looks for the loopholes. There is little which is more undermining for the teacher than when a child says "Well you said..." or perhaps more infuriating than one who says, "Well I didn't actually (do or say whatever)". Beyond which such a degree of standardisation felt like a step too far and would have been impinging upon the professional freedom of one's colleagues. Perhaps there is a wider issue in this in our current criteria based curriculum and assessments. There was also a wider lesson for me which was brought home during that year.

I recall that when originally applying for a place for teachers' training college, I had approached the head of the infants' school at which I myself had been a pupil, and where I had started my own school career, for a reference. I had kept in touch and she was still the head. I remember our talking for some while about my own aspirations in teaching and recall her saying, "Children don't like being told off". That advice stayed with me and I remembered too in college being advised not to use the word, "no" if we could avoid it. "No" is a put down word. It is non-negotiable. It closes doors and cuts lines of communication. It does not encourage the child in further exploration. It is the final negtive. We were therefore advised to avoid, "You're wrong" and rather to find other ways of expressing that, such as, "That's nearly right", or, "That would be right if... but ..." or simply, "Not quite". The secret is to be alert to and to avoid those situations which will lead to one having to tell the child off; to so structure the question such that the child will be more able to answer it correctly.

Those experiences had led me to understand the need for structure. Just as teaching staff felt as if they had been run ragged the previous year and had felt exhausted, so children too needed structure in order to function. Structure, of course, if there are too many rules can be restricting and fail to facilitate growth. If we work in an atmosphere in which we are constantly looking over our shoulders, we are not free to discover and therefore not free to learn. In short, children need a space to learn. Similarly, however, if we are constantly bombarded by a multiplicity of random stimuli, then again we don't learn beyond how to switch off. Hence, not only does the learning experience need to be structured, but the learning environment needs to have sufficient controls in place to free the child to learn. I recollect that we three 'wing' teachers met together fairly frequently and informally in an effort to support each other and that we could express any concerns about what we were doing or was happening. Such concerns could range from whether we felt the timetable was working to availability of materials or equipment, and sometimes the behaviour of individual children. We needed to have a sense that we were keeping on top of issues instead of their being on top of us.

Such a need was to become apparent later in the year when I was again asked to host a student's teaching practice of six weeks. A student again needs to be free to attend to their own teaching. It is the class teacher's job to ensure that not only do they have the materials and equipment that they need but also a class of children that are free to learn. Such freedom ranges from lack of external distraction through to a sufficiently disciplined environment. I remember the joy I felt as I watched her grow in skill, as her lessons became structured, and in confidence as increasingly I saw her relating to the children and developing that all important rapport; a rapport which enables us to set self aside and to be truly present for the child.

Again the old adage which I had learned at college came to mind, "How can I hear what you are saying, when what you are is screaming in my ears?" Somehow I must have managed to provide that environment for not only do I recollect the joy with which I wrote my report on her work but also it was confirmed for me later in the school year.

Perhaps the findings of the County Inspector from the previous year had found their way upwards. I could not know, but the following term we received a visit from one of Her Majesty's Inspectors, not to be confused with OFSTED which replaced them. Again I had not been given notice of her comimg and therefore, rather like the previous year, she had to take us as she found us. She spent two days in the school, most of which were in the wing, just looking at our three classes of older junior children. She spent the time sitting in on lessons, looking at the children's work, talking to the children and talking to the staff. It became clear that whether or not I had fulfilled the task with which the head had charged me of "making it work" would be assessed as a result of that visit. In an extended chat that we had on the final afternoon of the visit, she commented that the children seemed happy and well behaved which was reflected in the good quality of their work. She also commented on my obvious confidence and that I had a good sense of what was happening. The head did not say much to me about it, but merely remarked that such a good report would not do my request for a year's sabbatical leave any harm. His relief, however, was evident.

The H.M.I. was not the only "fly on the wall" we were to have in the wing that year as the head, again unbeknown to the staff, had agreed to cooperate with some research which was being undertaken into different teaching styles and their efficacy. It involved an interview with individual teachers and a tape recording of a lesson. The object of the tape recording was to see how far the lesson was teacher led and how much pupils contributed to the learning process. The object of the interview was to understand not only the teacher's style but also how that tied in with the plan for that lesson, as well as the philosophy which underlay the approach. It, perhaps, was not surprising when the recording of my lesson clearly revealed quite an interactive style with pupils contributing to the lesson. At least that sounds better than chaos as normal.

I like to think that such an atmosphere sprang from mutual respect; the respect of the teachers for the children and for each other, and the respect of the children for the teachers, another prerequisite for learning. One incident remains in my memory as not only an example of that respect, but also of the privilege that teaching can afford.

With the boys' football team now welded into a cohesive group and given the respect of the team for its captain and vice captain, games lessons became a relaxed affair from my point of view; relaxed to the extent that I began to feel comfortably redundant. It was thus one particularly cold, grey afternoon when I was concerned to keep the children moving, which in the case of the boys' football was never a problem, that I noticed one of the girls, all of whom were playing netball under the supervision of one of my female colleagues, sitting out. I was immediately concerned not only because she was a member of my class, but also because, while I noticed that the teacher was muffled up against the cold, the child, like all her fellows, was wearing no more than a pair of shorts and a tee shirt. Beyond the obvious inequality, I was wondering why she should be sitting out and obviously getting cold. Feeling protective of the child and filled with a sense of righteous indignation, I immediately took the whistle from around my neck and handed it to Gary amid complaints from the rest of the team at the temporary loss of their star player. Confident he could referee the match perfectly well, I ran over to see what was amiss. In asking the child quietly what was wrong I learned that she had strained a muscle in her thigh. I spoke to the member of staff concerned asking if I might "borrow" Ruth, the said girl and, too, if she would just keep an eye on the boys. I took the child into the classroom and explained that I was concerned that she was getting cold and that the muscle would be stiffening up. She confirmed both and I realised that if I didn't do something fairly quickly that not only would she not be walking home that afternoon, but that she would be in considerable pain as the muscle gradually seized. I suggested that we needed to massage the muscle and to get it moving again. She sat up on one of the bench tops and I proceeded to massage the full length of her thigh, doing my best to relax the muscle which I could feel quite tense beneath my hands. She commented how much better it was feeling and was clearly most impressed by, as well as grateful for, my efforts. Having satisfied myself that she was safe to walk on it, I told her to rejoin her class suggesting that she ask Miss... if she could join in the game but to take it very gently in order to keep the muscle moving and to prevent it seizing.

I returned to the boys to learn that they had managed perfectly well without me which only went to confirm my redundancy although the team did complain that they were one goal down as a result of the loss of a player. Once their star player was returned to them, however, they quickly equalised and peace was restored. So apparently was Ruth's leg, as come home time I asked her if she felt able to walk home and she assured me that it felt much better.

It was only later in the quiet of my classroom that I reflected how easily my actions of earlier that afternoon could have been misinterpreted, but at the time my over-riding concern had been for the child with perhaps slight anger at what felt like my colleague's neglect, although I acknowledge that sometimes our care for the greater number comes first. That, of course, could have applied to the boys as well and it might be argued that I had neglected the welfare of a greater number for one individual. But what does it say of our society if the individual does not have value?

It was perhaps with a slight sense of relief, but certainly one of feeling affirmed, that the following morning I received a letter from the child's father thanking me for my prompt, timely and entirely approriate action, saying how grateful his daughter had been. Her father just happened to be a doctor. It was some weeks' later that I received an invitation to her baptism at the church she and her family attended. So I found myself sitting in the back of their 'camper' van with a group of her friends from class. Again I recall just how privileged I felt as outside the classroom my status as their teacher suddenly didn't seem relevant and I was able to spend a very relaxed, enjoyable and deeply moving afternoon.

This had indeed been a busy year for me in trying to prize order out of what had felt like chaos and to get the wing as a functioning unit, but the year was not over yet.

The start of the summer term meant that the swimming pool had to be got ready for use. When I opened the door to the enclosure I was greeted with an accumulation of rubbish and water lying in stagnant pools. I had been hoping that the caretaker would have inspected it and put the work in hand, but not so. I began to understand that if I wanted something to happen I was going to have to make it happen. I secured a broom from the boiler room along with a couple of large dustbin bags filling them with the accumulated rubbish which had clearly been thrown over the fence during the intervening vacations. I then set to and tried to sweep away the stagnant water that had accumulated during the winter, but while it got rid of most of the water, the rest just combined with the build up of dirt to form a mud which I found I was now spreading over the concrete area surrounding the pool. It became apparent that the children could not use the pool area in the state it was. At that point I found the caretaker, presented him with my two bags of rubbish and my broom and suggested that the concrete needed hosing down and the pool vacuuming. In fairness to him he did both and within the period of a week the pool was ready for use. The head's contribution was to say, "We shall have to get the pool ready for use". I wasn't sure if that was the royal "we". My response was merely to say, "Yes, O.K. Bill. I've got it in hand". Fortunately at least the caretaker had got it in hand and I was again reminded of how much had fallen to our deputy head. When was his sabbatical over? And when was it my turn?

The latter proved to be a little way off as yet. Before then there were the all important reading tests and standardised tests which could render all manner of quotients, including intelligence quotient and reading age. The former, on the whole, would tend to be fairly stable. The latter, hopefully, should have increased along with their chronological age. It was always a testing time for teachers as well as children. Indeed rather more so, I sense, as the scores were not for public consumption and the children knew that they would not be judged by them. Rather any judgement was of the teaching staff. How effective had their teaching been during the year? Had the children in their charge actually learned? Not surprisingly the scores of the older junior classes the previous year had been a little concerning, although not disastrous. One thing I was gradually coming to understand was that children would learn, whatever the teachers did, sometimes in spite of them!

How well the children had learned, how effective the teaching had been and whether the organisation of the wing had provided an atmosphere in which those two activities could happen was about to be assessed. I even introduced another reading test which gave a rather more accurate or broader picture of ability than the simple word recognition test. The scores, all round, were up; not earth shatteringly, but certainly up. We three teachers had pulled together, we had cooperated, we had respected each other, and we had made it work.

That became apparent at the end of the term as we prepared

to say goodbye to those children who would be leaving to go on to the village college. I felt we had afforded them a good foundation upon which they could now build, as in their maturing years they would have to take ever more responsibility for their learning. I so wanted to give them something they could hold onto and take with them and I had wanted to engender in them that same love of learning which signifcant teachers in the past had afforded me. Hence I gave all the leavers in the three classes a greetings card in which I had written a text from the Book of Proverbs, in the bible, which read,

"Happy he who has found wisdom, and the person who has acquired understanding; for wisdom is more profitable than silver, and the gain she brings is better than gold." Proverbs 3, 13-14

Unbeknown to me and quite independently the children had, between themselves, contributed to and commissioned a china tankard which was painted with my name and bore a picture of a knight in full armour, complete with lance. I was deeply touched and, it was clear, so were some of the children, as we said our goodbyes. I don't know if I had been their knight in shining armour but I like to think that I had at least afforded them a sense of chivalry.

Chapter Twelve

Precious Funding

"He that wants money, means and content."
William Shakespeare, "As you like it"

The beginning of a new term and the new academic year saw the return of our deputy head. I had the sense that it was a welcome return all round, certainly from my own selfish point of view. Was it my turn now? I had applied for sabbatical leave. Everything hinged on that year's paid leave. I asked the head if he had heard anything about the progress of my application. Was it my imagination or did I sense a slight cooling in support? Apart from confirming that he had not had any news, his only comment was to point out that as one member of staff had had a year out it was highly improbable that a similar award would be made to another within the same school. I understood that essentially our deputy head had been so favoured because of his seniority and that as I came lower down in the pecking order then my chances were considerably reduced. He confirmed my fears a little later in the year, saying that he had it from the grapevine that as far as my sabbatical was concerned, I should not hold my breath. Given his earlier encouraging noises I sensed the message was basically, "Don't rock the boat".

By this time I had started on what the university described as an induction year. As the course was intended for serving teachers and was therefore a B.Ed. the induction year was designed to get us back into the way of studying again and to help us acquire those all important study skills which are so easy to regard as unimportant but without which we can quickly find ourselves floundering. This involved my travelling to Nottingham on several occasions, particularly for half term holidays and the occasional weekend. Some friends from the village had married and had moved to Nottingham a little while previously and they were kind enough to put me up overnight on a few occasions. Later, however, when the husband's job took them farther north, I was left wondering where I could find accommodation as my salary did not run to hotels on a regular basis. As all the other students were local, I was, it seemed, the only course member to encounter this problem. As if sensing my predicament, without my having said anything, the secretary to the faculty asked me if I should like to stay with her and her husband. Apart from being touched by their kindness I was struck by how friendly the university felt, which reminded me of my initial interview and how relaxed I had been, which confirmed me in my resolve to obtain the funding I needed somehow.

Thus my perception of the head's lack of support for my application and my understanding that it was likely to be unsuccessful merely strengthened my resolve. This was at a time when our political masters were talking about an "all degree profession" and those who had entered it after three years' basic training were being encouraged to enhance their qualification by going to university to effectively "finish off their degree" by doing one year's further study. Thus I perceived a mismatch between what was coming from government and what was actually happening on the ground. This did not feel right and so, fired with a sense of righteous indignation, I wrote to my M.P. who immediately wrote to our Chief Education Officer. It was during the Easter term that I found myself invited to a dinner at the local university centre at which were present other senior education officers and county inspectors. I could not, at that time, make any connection and was at a loss to understand why I had received the invitation, but was glad enough to accept. I found myself sitting near the C.E.O. and we chatted about my aspirations and the work I was doing, including my present study. I was introduced to some of the other guests and I remember having a thoroughly pleasant evening. To me, however, at the time, that is all it was. Perhaps my readers may think me excessively naïve, but following that dinner I did not hear anything further and had no reason to expect otherwise. It was only later the following term that one evening after school the head came into my class and informed me that one of the county inspectors was coming out to see me the following day and that "it may be to my advantage" to have my classroom looking tidy. Bearing in mind that I was based in the art room which was being used by the other classes that was an ongoing struggle. I was fully aware that teachers tend to be judged by the quality and quantity of the displays of children's work. It was one of the ongoing tasks of any class teacher to keep the displays up to date so that they reflected the current and ongoing work of the children. Tired or faded pieces of sugar paper were a give away that the member of staff concerned was struggling and would be found wanting. Fortunately the children had just returned from a day's field studies trip, but it did mean that there was plenty of material for display. I had been working through this gradually each afternoon after the children had finished. Clearly 'gradually' would not suffice and I worked until about 7 o'clock that evening completing the display and washing any paint trays left out. Fortunately, after 12 years in teaching, my wife knew to expect me when she saw me.

The following day the said member of the county inspectorate came into my classroom. On seeing her, I realised that we had taught together briefly at my previous school in another county. As we greeted each other like old friends the head, looking slightly discomforted, hastily retreated. After we had caught up on each other's intervening years, we talked about my rather more immediate aspiration for the future. She seemed enthusiastic about my degree and wished me well. I am not even sure if she looked at the display that I had toiled over the previous evening! We parted on friendly terms my wishing her well for the future. My immediate future looked rather more secure when I received a letter a few weeks' later offering me one year's paid study leave, but it got better when I re-read the letter and understood they were paying my course fees as well! Admittedly I would still have to pay for accommodation and if my wife was to be able to get out of the village, given the state of the bus service, we were going to need to become a two car family, but suddenly everything felt a lot more manageable.

It was therefore with raised optimism that I continued my

induction year and my next weekend away, shortly after that, saw me knocking on the door of Prof's house for a tutorial. I had written a paper which he suggested we might discuss over coffee. I was warming to this more personal approach to learning. It suddenly got even more personal when he opened the door and two King Charles' spaniels both sprang out and bit me. As he called them off he apologised and explained that they were normally very tame and friendly. That made it even more personal; it was just me they didn't like!

Thus with a hole in my trousers he led me through into the kitchen, bathed the wounds on my knee with disinfectant, and made both of us a mug of coffee which we took through into the sitting room without the dogs, which I noted with relief.

He had already read my paper and was enthusiastic about it. He started talking animatedly about some of the points which I had raised suggesting I may want to take some of these further citing academics from other universities who were working upon particular aspects of my work. He was clearly not only familiar with their work, but also was personally acquainted with them as he explained that 'Fred' from Glasgow and 'Harry' from Cambridge had some interesting observations about various topics. He clearly seemed to assume that I would at least know of them as well as he didn't always mention their surname and certainly nothing as prosaic as giving me a reference that I might follow up in the library. With my knee still throbbing and my head still spinning from the affects of shock I was beginning to feel a little inadequate to the proceedings and it was all beginning to become a bit of a haze to me. Increasingly all I was aware of was his enthusiasm about my paper and my trying to nod sagely or to make the odd insightful remark which may at least convey the impression that I understood all that he was saying.

Even the title of 'professor' had been something which had been shrouded in mystery and hitherto regarded by me with awe. I had grown up with my father's assertions that "they" (academics) all lived in "ivory towers", but then that remark was usually made along with his assertion that teachers did not know what "real life" was about. Coupled with a neighbour's warning before embarking on this course that people in universities were "not like us" and lived in a different world, there was, for me, the initial expectation that I should not understand what he said. There was again something of the wide eyed little boy and even if I was a little bemused and still feeling a little the worse for wear, I knew deep down that this was an experience of which I wanted more.

That afternoon saw me sitting in the A & E department of the hospital which happened to be opposite the university, awaiting an anti-tetanus injection which, once administered, now left me with a sore behind as well as a sore knee. I really came to the conclusion that I was not safe to drive that afternoon as on a couple of occasions I found myself wandering over the white line that separated the hard shoulder to the A1. It was a few weeks' later that I related the incident to the departmental secretary and my accompanying feelings of inadequacy. I was comforted by her cheery response and her assurance that, "I shouldn't worry if I were you. None of us in the department understand him half of the time". She went on to regale me with a story of when he had walked into her office and simply asked, "Ah, Joyce, will you do it or shall I?" She reponded that she might be better able to answer the question if she knew what "it" was, to which he responded "Ah yes", and walked out of the office again. She simply explained to me, "He's got a brilliant mind, but he can be quite vague at times". When I next saw 'prof' he hadn't forgotten and enquired how my knee was. He was again full of apologies and went on to say that, in fact, the dog concerned had started to show symptoms of being ill shortly afternwards and had obviously been off colour at the time, his being at a loss to understand its behaviour otherwise. Clearly the story got round to the rest of our group of students who were in fits of laughter, suggesting that the dog had eaten something that hadn't agreed with it, that something being me!

In spite of the "fun" I was clearly having at weekends, school still had to occupy the greater part of my attention. The head had shared with me and encouraged me to undertake what he called three day projects. It meant suspending the normal curriculum for three days and undertaking a project on a particular subject. This could potentially be quite wide ranging but tended to be topics which immediately affected the children and was intended to be inter-disciplinary. In other words, it would take in all aspects of the curriculum including english, mathematics, history, geography, science etc. Hence 'milk', which I recollect was one such project undertaken some years' later, would cover some of the mathematics of dairy farming, including average percentage butter fat content for a given breed of cow and mean yields for a herd of a given size, as well as price paid to the farmer. It would include the history of dairy farming and current geographical distribution of dairy herds. It could also encourage creative writing such as the life of a cow from birth to maturity, through to calving and finally giving milk, thus helping the children understand the complete cycle. One can quickly see the opportunities it afforded for cross disciplinary working, while it helped to make their study of mathematics, social georgraphy etc. seem a lot more relevent. At least that was my rationalisation of three days of chaos which saw the teacher exhausted at the end of it, but with the walls of the classroom full of display. I began to see that perhaps the main motivation for the head was the end product of the classroom display. The exhaustion was incidental.

I recollect that the first topic which I undertook that year was "Me". No, not me, I was not that interesting, but the me which is individual to each of us. It is again perhaps easy to see how it could lend itself to inter-disciplinary working. Mathematics included some vital statistics, including the length of one's foot, as well as height, weight, and other statistics which could then be fed into calculating an average for the class. The opportunities for creative writing were obvious, while the biological sciences were again clearly an area of study. The latter was nearly covered in a rather unfortunate way.

I introduced the topic by inviting the children to sit in a circle and to contribute ideas of some of the things we might study in relation to ourselves. Some of the children felt that if we were to be taking vital statistics then these ought to include mine. It was pointed out by some that this was strictly for the purposes of comparison, of course, even if they did have a slightly mischievious grin on their faces at the time. I had suggested that they could draw round each other's feet so one enterprising child very kindly got a piece of paper and pencil and, standing in front of me, said, "Come on then, take your shoe off". My bluff had been called and I clearly had to comply. This was beginning to get personal.

It got slightly more personal, as while we were still sitting in a circle bouncing ideas around I noticed that the attention of a few children was being distracted. Following their gaze I understood the cause of the distraction. One of the boys who was wearing short trousers had his hand up his trouser leg and was clearly trying to masturbate. The boy concerned was quite highly strung and given to anxiety and I was aware that he came from a slightly chaotic family. At that moment he was in a little world of his own and this was his place of safety and comfort. I clearly had to do something if I was not to lose the class altogether. I equally wanted to avoid drawing further attention to the child which would simply have embarassed him, while my saying anything could easily have criminalised his behaviour. Instead I spoke quietly to the child sitting next to him and asked her to sit in my chair assuming the rather smaller chair myself. I put my arm around him and smiled, but said nothing. I simply carried on talking to the class, but could feel his tenseness beneath my touch on his arm. As I continued to conduct the brain storming I gradually felt the tense little body next to me begin to relax and his hand stilled. Peace was restored, my foot was drawn and we had got the project off to a start. I remember being deeply touched by the way in which the children cooperated together, not only in taking each others' vital statistics, but also in organising themselves into groups and sharing the work load between them. It was a very busy three days, and it had been a very productive time. Again I felt that it was not only the children who had learned, but my learning curve was to go through an altogether steeper turn in the second half of the summer term.

The head was not only in touch but also personally acquainted with the warden of the field studies centre based on the Fens and administered by the education authority. We, as a staff, had already taken our different classes out to the centre for a variety of activities, including pond dipping, plant identification and the like which had felt an important extension to the curriculum, introducing the children to a part of their local environment. I am not entirely sure how the next part of this saga came about, but it was suggested that, as a logical extension to the work which we had already started, the children should have a residential field studies week. When he pointed out that this would essentially just involve the upper juniors, particularly our fourth years, or 10 to 11 year olds, I began to realise this could involve me and began to listen a little more attentively.

While much of the Fens were, and still are, under intense agricultural use, one area had been set aside as natural fen. Hence it had not been drained and supported a wide diversity of vegetation and wild life. Beyond a visitor centre it also boasted a residential centre which groups could hire for the purpose of studying the surrounding environment. The head suggested that it would be a good idea if the upper junior class should spend a week in the residential facility doing a variety of field study based activities. This apparently was where I came in. In fairness I was not the only one to go as the deputy head also went and the following year the head was to lead one week himself. This particular year fell to me and as it transpired several years after that, but more of that later.

I recollect that week was the busiest and most exhausting week I had ever known; it was also the most rewarding. I was not on duty from 9-3.45, which had been the hours at school, but for 24 hours each day as I slept lightly in case any of the children needed me. To use a modern term, I was on duty 24/7 except this was only 24/5. I remember arriving back in school that Friday afternoon with a minibus bulging with luggage and a class of very excited, exuberant children. As the parents came up to meet us, I got my step ladders out of the back and started to untie the luggage from the roof rack, but I did not get beyond the first few knots before some of the boys had climbed up on the roof rack and were handing down the luggage to others below. They had again organised themselves. I was just beginning to feel redundant and thought to put my own luggage in my car, prior to readying my classroom for the following Monday morning, when all those children who were not unpacking the minibus clustered round me and ushered me into school in an impromptu, exuberant procession. I felt a little like Caesar in a triumphal march into Rome; returning from the wars perhaps!

In truth it had not felt like a war. Far from it, all the children had cooperated together and an enjoyable week had just flown by. More to the point, if I was like Caesar returning with his troops, then they all returned fit and well. Part of me wanted to report to the head, "all present and correct Sir" with an appropriate salute. In the quiet that followed as I drove home that sunny Friday afternoon, I felt perhaps a little more like Nelson whose last words had been, "Thank God I have done my duty." As I sat on the seat in our garden later that afternoon drinking tea I felt utterly exhausted but somehow complete. It had been a fulfilling week and again I had a sense of why I had joined the teaching profession.

My funding for a sabbatical secured, if I had been hoping for an easy time in which I could get some study done prior to my year off, I was clearly going to be disappointed. For having returned from the week's field studies, the work was just about to start. While the children had been able to see and draw a variety of insects and water creatures, this then left them with much research to do on their respective life cycles, chosen habitats and the like. Although they had seen the creatures in their natural habitat, that did not always answer the question of why they lived there and if they could be found elsewhere. This, of course, opened up the notion of interdependency of creatures, plants and habitat and began to afford the children a glimpse into the whole concept of ecological balance and an understanding of its fragility. The rewards were obvious as the walls of the classroom began to fill with the fruits of their labours, but all that work needed mounting and displaying. Even when everything ran smoothly and the children were well behaved and gainfully occupied which, I recollect, they were following our week away together, there is never a dull moment in teaching. It offers just one fresh challenge after another. When I had finished my A levels, my father had wanted me to join the civil service. As I reflected on that I began to see the whole idea as rather comical. I had learned quite early on in teaching to encourage the children to take it in turns to write the date on the blackboard at the beginning of each day. I reasoned, of course, that it encouraged them to take responsibility and to write clearly. That was my rationalisation of a simple truth that as often as not I could never remember the date! Given too my ability to even get my own name wrong if presented with a form, I think my father's career aspirations for me were perhaps a little optimistic in as much as he clearly wanted me to be something I could not. Teaching can make unique mental, physical and emotional demands upon us and as I continued in the profession I learned that it can be a fine line between whether those are sustainable or not, but it is never dull.

As that term, and therefore school year, drew to a close, I realised that the vacation ahead was not going to be a time to sit back and relax, where the summer break was one of those things which contributed to making teaching sustainable for me. I still had the minor technicality of finding somewhere to live in Nottingham for the next year, as well as providing myself with transport to get there and back. The latter was provided by the father of two of the girls in my class, their being twins, though fortunately not identical, which I had experienced once before in my career. I had realised that if my wife was to remain mobile and be able to get in and out of the village for even the basic needs of food, she would need a car, but so would I. The parent concerned happened to be selling an old "mini". It was stable in poor weather conditions, economical to run and served me well, provided I packed every square inch of space at the beginning and end of terms.

Thus provided with a car, there were only the usual end of term tasks and a final school assembly. It was my turn for the head to say goodbye to. As I was presented with a pen and pencil set, I recollect he said, almost sympathetically, that I would need them and that he hoped it would not be too hard a year. Similarly I recalled discussing my aspirations with a colleague the previous year and her asserting that she would rather it were me than her. The proverb runs, "One man's meat is another man's poison". Perhaps too one man's dream is another man's nightmare. When a few weeks' later I had managed to rent a room just across the road from the university and had secured one of the coveted parking places on campus, I began to feel as if my dream was ever closer to being realised.

Chapter Thirteen

The Eternal Student

"Beholding the bright countenance of truth
in the quiet and still air of delightful studies."
John Milton

The bonus of my study leave was that the university term did not begin until early October which therefore gave me time to make a start on the reading list we had been given. Without the teaching preparation for the following term I realised I needed to use that time effetively. Having purchased some of those titles which seemed more immediately relevant to my particular areas of interest and, blessed with a fine September, I recall sitting in the garden enjoying our "Indian Summer" and trying to look studious. I fear that maintaining the look was about as far as I could get.

I had always been interested in how children learned to read and as a primary teacher was aware of the importance of getting the teaching of reading right. It was the one fundamental skill which would govern how well children could gain all other skills. In our information age it is vital to every aspect of our life. I had often come across the term of "barking at print", but had never fully understood what it meant or how it could obtain. The term describes essentially the problem of reading without meaning or just reading words. I had been unable to see how that could be. "Surely", I thought, "If we can read a word then we must understand it". As I sat trying to read these new erudite works I began to see how hasty and wrong had been my earlier judgement. It reminded me of how arrogant teachers can sometimes be.

My apprehension, in some cases fuelled by well meaning friends and low self esteem acquired in childhood, left me feeling quite inadequate to this new demand. A rather self defeating voice kept saying, "Who do you think you are kidding? University is for intelligent people. You know that you will not cope". With that voice constantly screaming in my ears, it became quite difficult to concentrate. Given too that one of the books concerned had been written by the aforementioned professor with the dogs that had a liking for human flesh, well mine at least, then I was fast beginning to feel quite undermined. It is interesting how persuasive our inner voices and inherited prejudices can be. At all events I was fast beginning to feel a failure before I started. I, however, was not the only one who was starting at a new 'school' that term.

My son was also starting at the school in the village. He had always been a fairly quiet, conservative soul and arguably would find the school environment a little more difficult to adapt to than the more gregarious or outgoing child. He was also, however, blessed with an equally quiet determination. I had learned in my teaching to avoid confrontation with children where possible. "Because I say so" is a position of last resort and is not designed to engender cooperation. I had discovered too that confrontation was not a helpful stance to adopt with my son. Unfortunately his reception teacher had not learned such wisdom and his early days in school quickly deteriorated into a battle front as one immovable object met another. My wife and I went to speak to my son's teacher twice in those first few weeks before I went up to Nottingham and suggested that she might get a little further if she tried to come alongside him. Unfortunately her only repeated response was that "He must learn to do as he is told". That, equally unfortunately, seems to have been the general culture within the school as a whole, for in the summer term of that same academic year he encountered a similar approach to the teaching of swimming. Again, being a fairly conservative, if not slightly diffident child, when it came to water at least, it was clear that he was going to need a sympathetic approach. Sadly the teaching style seemed rather to resemble the one I had encountered in my grammar school at the hands of our frustrated ex-sergeant major. Again another visit as we tried to point out that it was becoming increasingly difficult to even persuade my son to attend school, to which the equally limited response was "He must learn to be a brave boy". As educational psychology was one of my areas of study, I could see the shortcomings of such an argument. Not surprisingly my son was never to become a strong swimmer. The damage done in our early years can so often prove immutable and again my son's own assertion, rather later in life, that school teaches us how to fail, was to prove true. A reminder of the huge responsibility that teachers bear; a reminder too of why I was undertaking that year of study. My only regret was that it had to be that particular year when I should have preferred to be rather more present to support my son.

As a student I found it rather difficult to know quite where I belonged. All those on the course were serving teachers and therefore mature. This clearly did not obtain over the rest of the university where nearly all other undergraduates were fresh from school and were therefore just 18+. For most that was not a problem as many were doing the course part-time over a number of years only coming into the university once a week for lectures. Only four of us were actually full time and of those, two lived locally and only came in during the day and therefore were confined mainly to the department. Only myself therefore and one other student (from Hong Kong) were having to live on site and were able to enter more fully into the life of the university. As a student I felt as if I was neither fish nor foul. As an undergraduate aged 35 the other undergraduates regarded me as "old", after all I was nearly twice their age. Equally I was not a postgraduate who tended to be separate from the undergraduates. There was a fairly well established group of students from Hong Kong on campus with whom my colleague tended to mix. That left me potentially rather isolated apart from those short periods when we were all together in the department. That was another problem, with just four of us studying together on a full time basis, where were we to work? Part-time students would work at home using the library when they were at the university for lectures. Full time students would tend to live on campus and work in their rooms. Again I found I did not really know where I belonged. We all need a sense of belonging. That is why class teaching and the class teacher are so important to those in the early years of school especially. In a university where rooms were at a premium we had to find somewhere to call our own. After scouring the department we found one room in an outbuilding which did not seem to be used; at least not regularly. We put a label on the door, "B.Ed. full time" feeling that possession was nine points of the law and, afterwards, asked if anybody knew if it was used. The general concensus seemed to be "yes, by you". Thus we had a room we could call home. This was to prove quite important, far beyond the question of identity and physically having somewhere to work; as we were having to fit all our studies into one year it meant we also had to accommodate extra teaching through seminars and the like. We were now able to cordially invite staff to come to us. After all, we pointed out, we even managed a kettle in our home from home.

Teaching, like so many courses today, was modular in nature and therefore rather like 'pick n' mix', except the range wasn't quite so wide as that offered by the old Woolworth's stores, and some were compulsory. Educational psychology, which had been there in my basic training and my diploma, was one such. If our teaching was to have a sound basis, it was unavoidable. As the four of us were working in the primary sector the teaching of reading was common to all our situations. The professor who held the chair at that time specialised in that area and he and another of our tutors had collaborated in writing a book which had been published that same year. It felt quite exciting in being part of ongoing research at that time. Beyond these two "basics" there was a third, truly optional, element. I had chosen sociology as I found peer groups, friendship groups and the social hierarchy of the playground naturally interesting since they governed so much of how the child perceived him or herself and therefore how well, or otherwise, they would function at school. I found that I was the only one of our group choosing this option. The practice was that we would prepare a paper in readiness for a weekly tutorial; the other three in the group had all chosen the same 'other' option which meant that they could share the load, taking it in turns to write a paper once every three weeks. Clearly I did not have such leisure. Furthermore my tutorial fell early every Monday morning. It was expected that we would offer a dissertation in the teaching of reading, submit a study of some 7,000 words as well as sit one paper in educational psychology while theoretically we had a choice between an examination paper and a dissertation for the third option. Given that I was having to write a paper each week, I rather felt that I did not want all that work to go to waste, so quite early on I opted to write a second dissertation, thus avoiding another examination paper. My fellow students clearly felt that I was a glutton for punishment and communicated their opinion accordingly. I even questioned myself as to whether I had made the right choice when I thought of all the extra work. As it turned out my choice was to prove to be vindicated, but more of that later.

I guess, like any academic, my tutor lived and breathed his particular subject area and in spite of the hard work, I recall how I valued those tutorials and experienced a real joy in engaging with somebody who knew their subject. I felt I was in the company of a true academic. Just how true that was I was to find out when one lunch time I encountered my tutor standing helplessly surveying a flat tyre on his car, wondering whether to telephone his wife or the emergency services first. I asked if he had a spare tyre to which he replied, "I suppose so, I don't know". A quick inspection of his boot, after he had fumbled through his car keys, declaring he didn't know which one fitted, confirmed that he had. It also confirmed the presnce of a jack and a wheel brace. As another member of the gang of four and I changed the wheel he declared that he had often wondered what those tools were for!

Having secured a room of our own, word must have got around for there tended to be not infrequent visits from undergaduates struggling with their essay for that term. With our workload of three essays per term, one assignment and at least one dissertation, in my case two, meaning a total output of approximatley 67,000 words, I remember how envious I felt. It also became clear that the university had not made too many concessions to those of us who were squeezing it into one year instead of three. Through these and other contacts, I very soon found myself fitting into the undergraduate population of the campus. I also found, however, that postgraduates and undergraduates were happily mixing in together and that my fears of where I belonged had been largely unfounded. I found myself welcome in their rooms and being invited out to meals in the homes of postgraduates who lived locally. I felt particularly honoured to be invited to a meal with a number of the Hong Kongese students who lived in a university flat. I was treated to a traditional meal and learned of some of their customs. I even learned how to say "thank you" in Cantonese. I have always experienced it as a real privilege to be able to learn about and share in the traditions of another culture, which can so enrich our understanding and our lives. It is sad when the politics of immigration and integration are mishandled, thus creating misunderstanding, resentment and prejudice.

It was during the second term that I found myself sitting in the back of a minibus with a number of mainly younger undergraduates crossing the North York moors on our way to a convent where we were to spend a long weekend; another new experience for me. An assistant chaplain was a member of the community at Whitby and had invited us "home" for the weekend. It was a very active community with a school abroad as well as outreach in this country. It was also a very welcoming and friendly community. Just how friendly I discovered on our first evening there when I managed to get locked in the library with one of their novices after their grand silence had started! Somehow silence seemed inappropriate in that setting as we struck up a conversation and learned of each other's situations. Silence also seemed equally inappropriate if we were to avoid spending the night together, and after some calling, we were finally rescued. It was after lunch the following day when I was helping to wipe up that I managed to drop and break a plate. I expected a shocked silence only to have my effuse apologies greeted with laughter. Having been accustomed to censure for such clumsiness when growing up, to find myself surrounded by such warmth, felt deeply enriching. In retrospect that was not only my experience of that weekend, but that year as a whole.

As much as that may have been true, however, I could not bathe in such warmth all the time. There was actually some work to do. Indeed as much as I enjoyed learning more about the sociology of the classroom peer groups and the like or, even more, as much as I found myself excited and stirred to eloquence by the philosophy of education by such proponents as Dewey and Carl Rogers, the beginning of the third term was a time of back to basics as I started to look again at the work of Piaget. Not only had Piaget featured prominently in my own basic training 15 years' earlier, but he was at the beginning of this saga and had underpinned so much of my teaching ever since. He had identified distinct early stages of learning, culminating in the notion of the conservation of number. Such conservation means that with a given quantity of a substance, sweets, counters etc. that no matter what container the substance is placed in and no matter how the sweets are arranged that quantity remains the same. It is quickly apparent that without that concept of conservation then the teaching of higher numerical or mathematical functions is in vain. Teachers have always experienced themselves under pressure, perhaps from parents, to raise the attainment levels of those children within their charge but never more so than now in our present target orientated culture and the expectation that places upon pupils and teachers alike. I needed to prove to myself that such stages, as proposed by Piaget, did indeed exist and were indeed within the experience of the children. Thus in the early days of the summer term and before the university term had started, I returned to school and put the theory to the test with a number of individual children ranging from 5 - 7 years old. I remember being fascinated to see that gradual development of understanding as the children got older. Thus with the yougest children if I placed a quantity of water in one container and then emptied that into a taller, thinner container and asked the child whether there was more or less or the same amount of water, they replied without hesitation that it was higher so there must be more. By the time they got to six there was clear questioning and reasoning was beginning to develop as the child typically said, "Well that's taller, but thinner and that one is shorter but broader. I think they're both the same, I'm not quite sure". With the seven year olds they would say without hesitation that it was the same and would often look at me in slight puzzlement, clearly wondering why I had asked such a silly question. Such research was clearly interesting and confirmed Paiget's original findings but, given such a small sample, could never render a statistically significant result.

Thus we were introduced to the administering of standardised tests which would render a statistically significant result. While we were afforded the opportunity of going into schools to apply such tests, be they for reading ability, IQ etc., we were first to try one such test on ourselves. Just for fun our lecturer suggested that we try out a liberal/conservative scale in which one had to make 100 choices, where a high score indicated a conservative personality, while a low score would suggest rather more liberal leanings. For example, if one favoured the teaching of latin in schools that might indicate conversative thinking, while being against competitive sport may indicate a liberal tendency. Reassuringly my three colleagues had scores of 70-75, indicating a fairly conservative personality, but not extremist. I, on the other hand, scored 36, to which my fellow course members commented that I was clearly a "confounded radical" From my colleagues' comments, not only did I make dogs ill, if they were silly enough to bite me, but now with such liberal ideas I wasn't really safe to be in charge of children either.

We were by now also beginning to undertake research for our own dissertations and I had designed a scale myself which I was able to apply to a group of first year undergraduates, and a class of 11 year old children, for comparison purposes. I then needed to apply a test of significance to the results. As I was now handling rather more scores some one from another department suggested I should feed the results into their computer. Back in early 1980, this was the first time I had ever seen a computer. It was at the time when the ubiquitous "BBC Model B" had just been brought out and was certainly way ahead of its peers. After the person concerned had loaded the necessary programme, he left me to it. I remember prompts such as, "Please enter your scores" appearing on the screen and thinking it must be almost human. When I had entered my final value and it said, "Thank you" on the screen I remember thinking how polite it was and by the time it displayed, "Please wait while I work out the results", I was really beginning to think it was magic. In my innocence, of course, I knew nothing of operating systems or programmes, and I did not realise that a programmer had written all this in advance. To me it seemed as if the machine was displaying all this of its own volition. Just a few years' later, and by the time that I was teaching the children how to use that same model of computer in school, I understood that it was merely a machine running a programme. Sometimes, however, if I telephone a company now and am told, "But the computer says", or, "The computer requires me to ask this question", I begin to wonder how many are still inclined to see them as capable of 'thought', or even as magic. Sadly the operators just don't seem quite so polite as that BBC Model B!

Having statistically validated my research I now had to begin the process of writing it up. It was one thing for me to undertake to submit two dissertations, but beyond the fact that I had to write them, it left my wife to type them up for me as I did not possess such advanced keyboard skills. My wife had been trained in shorthand and typing long before such skills were, apparently, rendered redundant, and therefore asserted that it just did not make sense for me to acquire the skill myself as it was unlikely that I would achieve the same speed as she and that it would not be an economic use of my time. As much as I readily agreed with her logic, it did mean that all the typing fell to her. She was thus fulfilling the roles of secretary, wife and mother, while for most of that time, apart from every other weekend during term, she had to fill those roles alone. Each week saw me sending another batch of writing through the post, only for me to pick it up the following weekend when I returned home. If ever I was to graduate there was a feeling for me that it should be my wife that collected the degree, not I.

As we had now got as far as writing up our assignments and dissertations, so it also meant that we had to sit the obligatory examination. I unlike my other three close colleagues, only had the one paper to sit. Every cloud had a silver lining! Just how true that was, and how wise had been my decision to opt for just one paper was to be brought home to me a week or so later when one of our tutors said that our papers had been marked. He made it clear, of course, that our marks had still to be moderated and equally would only form a part of our final degree award.

Standing in the foyer near the coffee area, I simply retorted, "Don't hold me in suspense. What were my marks?" To which he replied, "You are a fourth or borderline third". I was aware that a fourth class degree was the lowest award possible and that with it I would not even be awarded honours. At least with a third I would gain honours. I realised too, however, that if ever I wanted to go on to do a higher degree, I would have to gain at least a second class honours. Clearly I was going to have to pull the rabbit out of the hat with my two dissertations, but a fourth to drag my marks down was going to make that very difficult. However, my tutor had himself just said that I was a borderline third. "How borderline?" I questioned, and "Was there a possibility that I might cross that line?"

I think I may indeed have crossed a line when I responded immediately, "Let me buy you a cup of coffee. Perhaps we can talk about it. To that my tutor retorted, with a slight grin, "If we're into bribery you can make that a chocolate biscuit as well!" I nodded and said, "You're on!" I do not suggest, for one moment, that serious corruption took place that morning, but I was grateful for the opportunity to talk through the paper and as we discussed some of the questions, he was able to say, "I see where you're coming from now". I sensed that my responses had satisfied him that perhaps I really did know what I was talking about after all, as his parting remark was, "I'll see what I can do".

Just what, if anything, he did, I do not know, but a week or so later I submitted my plan for my dissertation in Education which sought to take a fresh look at the teaching of reading and to build and reflect on the work that had been undertaken by the professor and which had been published the previous year. My plan included devising a measure for assessing reading ability. I was tactfully reminded that as good as my plan was it would make a perfectly good Master's dissertation, but went beyond the limited scope of a first degree. Almost in the same breath, however, I was offered the chance of undertaking a Master's degree as I was invited to apply for a funded place on that programme. I was flattered and was greatly tempted to apply, but, not for the first time in my career, felt that my family and their security must come first as I realised I should have to resign my teaching post. Perhaps too there was a feeling for me that one step at a time was advisable. I still had to pull that proverbial rabbit out of the hat!

As the term drew to a close and our assignments were handed in, all we were left with was a submission date for our dissertations. The four of us had worked closely over the year and would miss each other; one of the group would be returning to Hong Kong shortly after the end of term and invited us to a celebratory traditional chinese meal. Were our celebrations a little premature, I wondered? Perhaps rather we were celebrating a very busy and fulfilling year together. The meal was held in a local chinese restaurant. At that stage I had only had a chinese meal once before in my life and that was during that same year. I really began to feel a little like "a boy up from the country". My horizons were broadened even more when our host declined the menu that we were offered and in cantonese said she wanted the proper menu. The waiter's demeanour changed immediately and became a lot more attentive. Again our host translated for us and advised on our choices. It was another very special meal and a very special occasion. I had again learned a lot and felt privileged.

I packed up my car for the last time with books, clothing and even an old television that a friend had loaned me and returned home with the summer holidays before me, and the submission date for my dissertations still a few weeks' away. Athough I tried not to waste my time and to apply myself to the job in hand, it became apparent that I was not going to meet my submission date. I telephoned the departmental secretary and asked for an extension, and to my great relief was told that shouldn't be a problem as I was only asking for two weeks. I reasoned I could not sensibly ask for any more as soon after that the new school term would be looming and I must change hats in time to resume my teaching post. I worked up to the wire, my wife typing as fast as I could write. I just had time to get them bound and to submit them. A very busy year had been completed. With just the four of us submitting where all the others had been part-time and thus continuing their studies, the marking of our major opuses did not take long and I learned my results over the phone before I returned to school. I gathered I had indeed pulled the said rabbit out of the hat as, in spite of my distinctly underwhelming performance in the examination, I had achieved the second class that I needed if ever I were to aspire to a higher degree. At this point I was just glad to have made it. Any future aspirations could wait. I had achieved my goal and got the pass I needed. I remember communicating the news to my mother who simply said, "Is that good dear?" to which I simply responded, "Yes that is exactly what it is". I felt too as if I would 'do'. When later, learning that I had managed rather better in both of my dissertations, I understood where my strengths lay and it wasn't with examinations! While it had been a fulfilling year for me I felt it had been a hard year for all of us; my son, my wife and myself. We all needed that summer break before my son and I, at least, started a new term.

Chapter Fourteen

Down to Earth with a Bump

"Once more unto the breach, dear friends, once more."
William Shakespeare, Henry V. Act lll, Scene 1

After a brief respite, the beginning of term signalled, for my son and I at least, a return to the battle front, except for him it was under a new commander, or class teacher. He was, unfortunately, to encounter the same authoritarian approach, except his reputation for insubordination in the ranks had clearly preceded him. This may, in part, have accounted for the fact that we learned fairly early on in that year that he was now a 'backward reader'. Thus I was to understand, first hand, how easily labels become applied. The labels stuck on by the hasty judgements of over stretched teachers, like any professional, are of the self adhesive variety; they are quick and easy to apply, but remarkably difficult to remove.

It was often said that teachers make the worst parents and, in my own case at least, I would not necessarily argue with that judgement, given the benefit of hindsight. Perhaps, however, my particular area of interest and the nature of my newly acquired post may just have been to my son's advantage.

I already held a scale post with responsibility for the library.

On my return to the school after my year's study leave I found myself with the title of head of language. Rather like my previous grand title of head of french, however, the post did not attract any extra remuneration nor did I lose my responsibility for the library. Rather, the head, anxious to justify my year's absence to the school governors, felt it would be politically expedient to create the post. Such a creation also enabled him to require me to write a paper, for the consumption of the governors, on the teaching of reading on which apparently I was now an expert. Hence I spent the Christmas holiday gathering a bibliography and writing my paper entitled, "The teaching of reading: some thoughts on current research". I was duly invited to attend the next governors' meeting in order to formally present my paper and answer any questions. My uncomfortable feeling that the whole exercise had been politically motivated predominantly for appearance sake was rather confirmed when, instead of the searching questions which I had been expecting and, perhaps, hoping for, I received a, "Well done, it all seems very interesting". A comment which, to my mind, translated to, "It looks convincing".

Additionally I suddenly found myself with the job of overhauling the school's stock of graded reading books, but with that, at least, came some money to acquire new stocks where any schemes were found to be incomplete or otherwise lacking. That was to continue into the following year, but more of that later. For the moment, and of more relevance for my son, it afforded me access to a now growing range of graded reading books. Meanwhile my year out had not only given me an interest in reading measures but had also given me access to a number of recently published tests which, as head of language, I could apply in individual cases to any children that my colleagues might refer to me, for my new post was also meant to be an advisory one. To me at that moment, even though he was at a different school in another county, that individual case was my son.

Given my slight puzzlement, if not incredulity, that my son was a backward reader which meant, in real terms, that his estimated reading age would be behind his chronological age, I gave him a reading test to confirm his teacher's judgement. To my further puzzlement I found that his reading age was, in fact, one year in advance of his chronological age. Given that he had only been at school for just over a year it meant that he had gained two years in one or had acquired a skill in reading at twice the expected rate. So much for the label, but how to unstick it? I had an uncomfortable feeling that if I were to confront his teacher I would only create resentment and make things even more difficult for my son, who, after all, had already been labelled in the minds of many as a difficult child.

If my son had been reticent to read at school I had some sympathy with him when I saw the seriously dated, uninspiring 'dog-eared' reading books that he was bringing home. That was the other problem. He was expected to bring the book home in order that his parents could hear him read and duly write on his record card the page he had reached, his not being allowed to read any pages on his own. Clearly trust had no more place in that school than it does in our society today. The limitation with such an approach to reading is that it does not encourage the child to read for meaning, but rather to replicate words. It also encourages a slow, word by word, reading habit and inhibits the use of context for acquiring meaning. Monitoring a child's reading is, of course, vital and, indeed, can take a substantial amount of a primary teacher's time, so very clearly if a child must be heard to read every page then his or her progress is going to be very slow. Thus it would be easy for a child's reading material to lag behind his actual ability if the teacher fails to hear the child read often enough when not trusted to read on their own.

One must assume that it was a combination of factors that had contributed to my son's acquiring "backward reader" status. This would inevitably have included the teacher's own disinclination to engage with what she perceived as a 'difficult' child and her consequent failure to hear him read often enough. Beyond that, if the teacher is naturally authoritarian or communicates her dislike of the child through subtle, and sometimes not so subtle, means and is constantly criticising the child for being "wrong", then he or she will be reticent to guess at a word, even if they are reasonably confident that they know it, just to avoid further censure. If the teacher further fails to obtain an accurate measure of the child's reading ability through the use of a properly standardised reading test, then he is inevitably doomed to fail in a situation where the blind is leading the frightened and therefore reticent. It is quickly apparent that the teacher must not only be punctilious in their own monitoring of the child's progress, but must also be sensitive to the various social factors which may discourage and therefore inhibit that.

In my son's case it would appear that the teacher failed in all the above and that her only response to his apparent failure was to label him as "backward", which in her mind was obviously linked to his being "difficult". When we perceive ourselves in a position of "authority", it is easy to use the resultant power imbalance to our advantage and also to assume that any fault must be with the person over whom we exercise that authority. Teachers, like any other professional working directly with people, need to be sensitive to this and to exercise self awareness in order to prevent hasty judgements and to maintain a good learning environment. It is clear that not only was the teacher concerned failing in all the above, but that the atmosphere or ethos of the school was not going to encourage the sensitivity towards the pupils' needs that would have been necessary to overcome those failings.

In short, it was clear that, had I complained, my son would have suffered, as in such a situation the only thing worse than being a difficult pupil was having a difficult parent. Hence, armed with the information I had, I felt I had to use the system to my son's advantage. When he duly brought his reading book home each evening, we read a page each, such that he quickly worked his way through the scheme. Having done so, he was put onto another scheme which was a little more up to date and which he was able to enjoy to a certain extent. It then became clear that the school's stock was patchy and that a number of books were missing from the scheme. As all the books were part of a continuous narrative, even one missing would have created difficulties. I thus covered the missing volumes from our own stock at school such that his reading was not interrupted. Having clearly highlighted the inadequacy of the stock, the teacher had little alternative but to cooperate a little more readily. We continued our practice of reading a few pages each, such that my son quickly worked his way through the entire scheme. It was clear, however, that my son's motivation had to be maintained, so we spent a few mornings in the local bookshop where he could browse through books to his heart's content, where I could read short pieces to him, and where he could then select any books that he wanted. I remember the child sized seats and remember thinking all bookshops should be like this. It certainly gave me ideas for the school library.

His reading at least picked up remarkably! However, one morning he announced that he did not want to go to school. I sat with him, ever mindful that I should be leaving for school myself, and tried to ascertain what was bothering him. Was he being bullied, I questioned, but I understood that he was not experiencing difficulty with any children. Unable to make headway I had to depart for school and with my wife's help my son agreed to go to school himself. It was only some time later we discovered that it was his teacher who was doing the bullying! In her own subconscious mind she was somehow holding him responsible for highlighting the inadequacy in the school's stock and in her own teaching. Clearly he was a difficult child.

Unbeknown to my son, he was not the only person who did not want to go to school. It was true for his father too. I remember an old joke among teachers which ran: "Mummy, I don't want to go to school". "Why not dear?", "Because all the children and teachers bully me". "But you've got to dear, you're the head!" I was not the head, but the rest felt true.

Having returned to school, I found that my classroom was based in the art room. That, in itself, need not have been a problem except while we were no longer teaching as a team we did still have vertically grouped classes who had to have access to the art room, such that I found myself relegated to the audio visual room on these occasions. This was clearly unsettling for the class when I was beginning to feel that my grasp on classroom control was tenuous enough. The circumstances which contributed to that sad situation were many.

Fresh from a year in which I had been able to immerse myself in, among other things, the philosophy of education and the works of Dewey, Rogers and the like, I had returned to the classroom, rather like my first year in teaching, full of high ideals. I had too, I am aware, removed my teacher's armour and was perhaps a little reticent to put it on again. My year out had had a profound effect upon me. I had learned much and I had changed. Rather, I had been changed, and I could not be the same. I had come to believe that if I showed care and respect for the children and could sufficiently motivate them, they would respond with enthusiasm and equal respect, where in an atmosphere of mutual respect, well motivated children would not need external discipline. In an ideal world, of course, that is absolutely true. Sadly, we do not live in an ideal world!

While I was not naive enough to really believe that I could abdicate all responsibility and expect that the children would not need any external constraints, my own increased awareness and sensitivity meant that I was just a little more reticent to apply such external discipline. Such a philosophy is not necessarily wrong. Indeed in a setting where all are mutually committed, it can be a joy to work in but teachers, as has been previously observed, rule by consent. The children bring their own expectations into the classroom which will have been shaped by parents and other teachers. To a large extent a teacher must work within those constraints. It is clear that the children and my colleagues perceived that reticence in me, and either did not understand it, or in the latter case did not want to understand it.

I was aware of a considerable amount of resentment on the part of a few of my colleagues. Again, with hindsight, it is easy to see the factors that would have contributed to that, but very difficult to see how I could have done anything about it. Perhaps, in my more forgiving or philosophical moments I can look back to that time and see that they and I alike were victims of our own perceptions. At the time I was becoming increasingly aware of how difficult that resentment was making it for me to function. There was, inevitably, the resentment felt by some that I had not only had a year off enjoying myself while they had been working, but that the county had even paid my year's holiday! Furthermore, on a staff in which nobody else had a degree, including the head and deputy, I had the temerity to return with one such. From some of the comments I received from one or two of my colleagues along the lines of "So you're going to tell us all how to do it now, are you?" their resentment became apparent and I felt that my protestations that I would not be so presumptuous seemed to do little to redress that. My appointment, by the head, to "head of language" did not help either, for not only was my paper on the teaching of reading for the consumption of the governors but the teaching staff were also given a copy. I can see, of course, that was only right and proper, but to some of my colleagues who had been teaching longer than I, and had specialised in the early years in which the acquisition of such skills was central to their work, it is easy to see that they may rather have felt I was seeking to teach my grandmother how to suck eggs!

If the staffroom became a place in which I no longer felt able to relax then the classroom was no better. As was explained earlier the class was one of three vertically grouped classes as I had worked with the year before I left. The only obvious difference was the children had changed. In my more paranoid moments I rather felt as if the class had been handpicked just for me. Indeed I was reminded of the words of Caesar immediately before his assassination as portrayed in one of the "Carry On" films of yester year, "Infamy, infamy! They've all got it in for me!" How else could I have a class in which there was one child who suffered from an hysterical personality, two with poor social skills and inadequate coping strategies and one child who was just sufficiently intelligent to exploit that. It is often said that every class has to have one difficult child and certainly at the beginning of a new year the teacher finds that it is their name which they learn first, but four went beyond coincidence. "No, Peter, you can't just run out of the classroom and go home" and, "No, Paul, you can't join him just because you've got a sum wrong". Meanwhile, "Gareth, you're encouraging him while trying to be the class entertainer is really not helpful", and, "While I recognise that this is very distressing for you, Zoe, your simply standing up and screaming really isn't the answer!" Not for the first time in my career I could rather see myself as Joyce Grenfell in one of her monologues. Unfortunately nobody was really laughing this time; least of all me. To add to this volatile mix, I had the pleasure of the company of the son of one of my colleagues, a reasonably intelligent child, who was bright enough to be able to exploit his perceived superiority. If I corrected him which, in spite of my inclination to the contrary, I found myself doing on an increasingly frequent basis, his response was to grin. I began to wonder what lay behind the grin, until I received a visit from his mother, my colleague, who told me that my poor class control was not helping her son's education. Tactfully pointing out that her own son was not entirely blameless, her response was to complain to the head. His response, in turn, was to come over to my classroom for a "quiet word". His "word" or rather "words" were few which he summed up in one phrase, "Shape up or ship out".

I began to realise, firstly, that I had no support, secondly that I had a spy in my classroom who was clearly gleefully relating all that was happening to his mother as I found that any slight altercation the child concerned had with another somehow became my fault, while any behaviour problems which I might have experienced were, in turn, being taken up with me by the head. I also realised that whatever I did was not going to be right. If I did do anything right, it would not be acknowledged and whatever displeased, be it right or wrong, was going to be counted against me. I quickly began to feel isolated and disempowered, such that I felt helpless to do anything about my situation.

It is a sad truth that we can very quickly be rendered helpless where the things which disempower us are manifold in our society. Many of our social institutions and large organisations disempower the individual through their very structures and practices, thus often creating the very problems that perhaps they were set up to deal with in the first place. It is, of course, every government's dream to have a docile, compliant population and we see how our health care, social care and social security are so structured to engender compliance and dependency but we do so at our peril for a sense of helplessness perpetuates the very problems they seek to address, where a population that feels powerless and disenfranchised can express its frustration in various antisocial ways.

I was not about to express my frustration by using the stock of paint that the art room afforded to daub grafitti about the place, although, looking back, I can see how my mounting frustration began to be expressed in various destructive ways. I became increasingly intolerant at home and given to angry outbursts, with my wife particularly. At the same time, aware how my performance was being "judged", I got caught up in a desperate, self destructive attempt to be the "perfect" teacher. I could be found working ever later at school, trying to ensure that my classroom displays were up to date and well presented. I attended more and more courses after school in a desperate attempt to be proactive in addressing those areas which may have contributed to my being the inadequate teacher and person that I began to believe myself to be. In that sense, perhaps, that year was not all bad, although I fear that neither I nor some of my colleagues, particularly the disaffected mother already spoken of, were able to see the good. I had been judged and found wanting and nothing was going to alter that perception, but it would not be for want of trying.

If I was going to be based in the art room with the adjoining kiln room which also housed a cooker then perhaps at least I could utilise all the facilities and enrich the curriculum a little. I hoped well motivated children would be the well behaved children I so desperately wanted some of them to be. Hence one of the courses I attended was a series of evenings on pottery. I had acquired basic skills in clay some years' previously when my wife and I had attended pottery evening classes, and we had progressed from slab work and coil pots to actually throwing pots on a wheel. We had discovered too how literally true the notion of throwing pots really was. No, not across the room in frustration, but onto the wheel. The first skill we had learned in pottery was "knocking up" in which the clay was worked into a convenient sized ball, not only for convenience of handling, but to exclude all the air which might otherwise expand when fired, thus causing the pot to break. Having so equipped oneself, the object was to throw the ball of clay onto the epicentre of the turning wheel. Thus with tongue clenched between one's teeth one took careful aim and hoped for the best.

Interestingly I find the skill similar to that of centering the mouse pointer in the middle of a tiny window on a computer screen on which is a suitably meaningless symbol (or icon as we delight in calling them) prior to clicking, hopefully, the right key, only to find that in doing so you have moved the mouse and clicked onto an adjacent icon which brings up a screen you didn't want, only to scan another row of meaningless icons as you try to work out how to get back to the previous screen before trying again.

With such skills, in clay that is, it made sense that I should be utilising the equipment and teaching pottery. What we had not learned in our evening classes were the technicalities of what clay body to fire at what temperature or how to make up our own glazes, which also had to be fired at their own appropriate temperatures. These were the technical skills I lacked, but acquired on the course. I well remember going into school during the half term holiday, taking my son with me, so that he could make a pot, which I later fired in the kiln, while I busied myself making up different coloured glazes using different oxides. Tin oxide produced a white glaze, while cobalt produced a deep blue. I even managed a wonderful honey coloured glaze, and left the recipe behind for future generations!

Following the half term break, having already gained the help of a 'mum's army', we organised a craft afternoon on a weekly basis in which each mother was in charge of a small group of children doing one particular activity. Activities ranged from making their own craft apron, cooking, fabric printing, exclusion fabric dyeing and other activities as the year wore on. The clay work, after my efforts, had to be included while other activities even extended to corn dolly making which a local thatcher had taught me one evening and a local farmer had provided me with a sheaf of wheat. I fear that many of the activities may not be allowed in our new safety culture as they necessitated the children using such things as a sewing machine and iron, not to mention the large saucepan of boiling fabric dye. It should be observed, however, that during those activities there were not, to the best of my recollection, any accidents. The head was particularly impressed by the corn dollies. Indeed I was beginning to learn that the head was impressed by anything that looked good or perhaps that he could impress parents and governors with. I was learning too that I was being judged on looks. It was not so much the feel good factor that counted, but the look good factor!

The head may have been impressed by my corn dollies, but I was aware that was as far as the accolades went. I was increasingly aware that like Belshazzar, I had been "weighed in the scales and found wanting". Indeed I might have seen that the writing was on the wall, but I was too intent on trying to maintain my grip on my work, the class and myself to look beyond that. I was aware of being judged and found wanting, given the freedom with which the same colleague felt able to walk into my classroom. That, in itself, felt disempowering, such that I began to feel increasingly isolated. Given the presence of three children in the class with clear emotional problems, if not borderline personality disorders, I had been inclined on a couple of occasions to send one of them to the head when their behaviour became difficult to contain and the general order of the class threatened. It was my hope that by sending them to the ultimate source of authority within the school they would be suitably chastened and my authority would remain intact.

Far from seeing, however, that I had the backing of the head, when one returned from such a visit he wore a broad grin and reported the head as saying that if in future he had any difficulties, he could go over to see the head whenever he liked. The child quickly realised that there would be no sanction to his anti-social behaviour and could basically walk out of my class whenever he wished and that he would always have a sympathetic ear. I felt completely undermined. My authority in tatters, I realised, not for the first time, that I could not look in that direction for support again. I saw rather that, far from being my support, the head was my judge. If the head was my judge, then I realised too that there was only one counsel and one witness, both for the prosecution. I knew increasingly that the counsel for the prosecution was my aforesaid colleague; the one witness the mole in my classroom. If all this begins to sound slightly like persecution mania, it must be borne in mind, as has been observed before, that teachers rule by consent. Furthermore children, like us all, feel secure when their teacher displays confidence and appears to be in control. I was displaying neither, I suspect.

Although by this time I had seen my doctor and was taking tablets for anxiety, the writing was clearly on the wall. I did not see it until I woke one morning ready to go to school as usual except that I couldn't. Deep within me I knew that the present situation was unsustainable; I could not go in. I went to see my doctor instead who gave me a certificate for three weeks, but made it very clear that it was only an interim one. We would review it, he said, at the end of that period but that I should expect it to be longer. Thus it was, I became a "school refuser" as we now term such children, in February and finally returned after the Easter holiday.

Meanwhile, armed with my certificate I felt several times lighter. I think I must have felt like one of the first astronauts on the moon in diminished gravity. I certainly felt as disorientated. This was totally new territory for me. I had never had time off school unless confined to bed. I felt a sudden rush of freedom. The certificate might just as well have read reprieve! I immediately telephoned the school. If I had been looking for sympathy I would have been disappointed.

When I did return after the Easter vacation essentially nothing had changed except that the children did seem genuinely pleased to see me. Perhaps it was a case of better the devil you know, but I sensed a palpable relief on the part of a number of the children. Such a feeling was not reciprocated by my colleagues, but they had kindly reserved the extra playground duties which they had had to cover before my replacement had arrived. Fortunately she had arrived fairly quickly, as otherwise I might have been on continuous playground duty till the end of term.

This time that phrase, "the end of term", had assumed a heightened significance for me. I only had to survive to the end of term. Somehow, in that knowledge, anything seemed sustainable and I did not want to think beyond it!

Chapter Fifteen

School in the Field

"Once you have a hierarchy you need rules to protect and administer it and you end up with some kind of chain of command which destroys relationship."
Paul Young, The Shack

The end of that term had been accompanied by the news that the following academic year I was to be in another classroom within the 'wing'. I wouldn't be in the art room again! Did the head hear my sigh of relief, I wondered? Furthermore I would be taking the 10 year olds or 3rd year juniors. Apparently the children were no longer going to be vertically grouped. We, as a staff, had not been consulted, but somehow I was not going to worry about that. Could it be that the head had learned a lesson from my own experience of the previous year to occasion the apparent U turn? Whatever the cause, I was glad enough to receive the news, quietly thanked divine providence, and said nothing!

That following year saw me starting with different children in a different classroom. If my experience of the previous year was still around for me, I did not let it show. The only visible difference perhaps was that I tended to spend rather more time with the children and rather less in the staff room. Was there still an atmosphere or was that simply my own paranoia? If those questions were in my mind nothing was said, either by myself or my colleagues, but I was aware of a slight change in me that felt rather more at home in the company of the children.

Thus it was that I was glad enough to lead my class on the week's field studies course on the Fens as I had the year before my sabbatical. That was to be the pattern for me thereafter as each year saw me leading a group on the annual field studies course. The previous year the head had, with help, led a group himself and returned to recount his experiences to the rest of us laughingly relating how an outbreak of diarrhoea and vomiting had spread through a substantial number of the children. He even related how one of the children had been sleeping in the top bunk above him in the staff bedroom and that he had been awakened in the middle of the night by a cascade of vomit from the bunk above. Apparently, too, one of the children had finished up in hospital because they had received a number of mosquito bites and had had a histamine reaction. Sufficient to say that, having had so much fun, thereafter he was happy enough to leave that responsibility up to me each year, and I was happy enough to fulfil it.

I can remember that each of those occasions were for me a time when I felt relaxed and happy; as relaxed as anyone can be when one has full and sole responsibility for not only the education, but also the mental, social and physical welfare of thirty children. I say sole responsibility because although I did have the help of a female member of staff for one week and of a student for another, there were as many occasions when I was indeed completely on my own with the children, but whether accompanied or not it was emphasised by the head that I had full responsibility. Whether or not that was so that he knew where to pin the blame if things went wrong, I could not know, but I acknowledged that somebody had to have ultimate responsibility which I happily accepted.

It is significant that while I remember much of those field trips, those memories have, in my mind, blended into an homogenous whole. I cannot pick out individual classes, although I can still remember the children concerned. Perhaps, therefore, if the reader will forgive the absence of a precise chronology, and feel it right that I should relate the field studies courses as a single narrative, this chapter will be devoted to it.

On the first of those occasions which had taken place just two years' previously, I was to have the help of a female member of teaching staff which perhaps was just as well as, having finally got all the children to the field studies centre that was to be our home for the next week, I began to realise just how much organisation really was needed. Acknowledging that organisation perhaps was not my strongest point, I realised too the things I had not done. In particular I had failed to bring any games equipment. I had also failed to draw up those precious rotas which I had been advised were essential. Thus leaving my colleague with 30 children and the suggestion that they make a cup of tea and take time to claim a bunk and settle in, I returned to school some 20 miles away, which had just about finished for the day, and borrowed some basic games equipment before returning to the field studies centre.

The term field studies centre sounds rather grand to apply to the facilities and perhaps needs a little explanation. On my first encounter my immediate reaction was to wonder if I had arrived at the right place or whether I had happened upon the local scout hut by mistake. There was no mistake! The timber building was indeed to be home for the next week. On further inspection I found it to boast a communal area with benches and tables. Venturing further, I found a kitchen area with a large gas cooker, a stainless steel sink and draining board, work tops and some open shelves underneath as well as some further open shelves at eye level. I noticed the shelves appeared to have a few black deposits on them. On closer inspection I discovered the deposits to be mouse droppings! Hopefully, I thought, from some time ago. I cleared them up and disinfected the shelves confident that would be the last of them. Next to the kitchen, also leading off the communal area, was the washing area which consisted of a slatted wooden shelf running around two walls with plastic bowls, served by a hot and cold tap. At least we had running water. Disposing of the used water was effected by emptying the bowl through a series of holes in the wall underneath the shelf. Next to this, at the far end of the hut, were the girls' and boys' toilets; the former offering two cubicles, the latter one cubicle and a leaking urinal with a bowl underneath it to catch the drips! I could see immediately that this area was going to have to be cleaned on a regular basis. Making onto the wash room via a door was the girls' dormitory with the boys next to it, both equipped with two tier bunks. Right at the end was a small room with just two bunks which served as a staff bedroom. the teacher accompanying me for that first year offered me the staff room, saying that she would sleep in with the girls. I accepted on the grounds that it would also serve as a first aid room. These were the sum total of the facilities offered. It was not exactly home from home and one could easily see how inadequate housekeeping skills would quickly lead to an outbreak of sickness as had been the head's experience.

Having returned from school with the games equipment, I sat and drank a cup of tea which a child put in front of me and suggested that we should think about preparing supper. Aware of my failure to produce rotas I simply asked for volunteers, My only difficulty was selecting who out of the sea of eager hands. I recollect that the menu was fairly simple that first night with sausage and mash and banana and custard. I will say in my own defence that they were fresh ingredients and that I demurred from packet mashed potato or instant custard. At least there wasn't any waste. Surprisingly there seemed to be just about as many volunteers for washing up afterwards!

Household chores completed and still putting off drawing up those rotas I called all the children together and I ran through the week with them. This was, I felt, a helpful time as it gave the children, still quite excited, a chance to settle before bedtime and afforded them the opportunity to raise any of their own concerns, questions etc. It also gave us an opportunity to agree ground rules between us. Somehow it felt important that the children should feel involved in setting their own parameters and agreeing their own rules. In practice we largely seemed to manage without the latter. I felt more at ease with a democracy and really was not keen on a dictatorship, even if I was to be the dictator.

The first thing we agreed between us was bedtime, following suggestions from the children ranging from 8.30 to 9. We thus agreed beginning to get ready for bed at 8.30, including making hot drinks for bed, and settled by 9. The next thing to think about, assuming a quiet night, was the following morning, and more particularly washing arrangements. There were 30 children in two dormitories who needed to complete their ablutions in one wash room offering about 8 places. Given the logistical nightmare, presumably this was where my rota came in. As I explained to the children, however, we could have a rota of girls or boys first, but that would necessitate one group of children all being ready at the same time and would put me in a policing role so that the first group didn't keep the second waiting. There was also the question of who would then be available to help prepare breakfast as they needed to be ready first. I really did not want to be chivvying children first thing in the morning, as I could quickly see tempers becoming frayed and children upset. We talked through how we would feel happiest and the children all agreed that those who were happy to wash in a mixed environment of boys and girls should go first so that some should be ready to help with breakfast, while those who preferred a little more privacy should wait until a little later. That somehow felt respectful of everybody's needs and respected modesty at the same time. In practice there were so many who were keen to help with breakfast that just about everybody washed together. It also meant that I could wash and shave along with the children so that the problem of supervision, should there be such a need, was also answered.

The meeting had solved the problem of rotas; there were none, and throughout that week and subsequent weeks during the coming years the children just cooperated together, freeing me increasingly to teach and look after their welfare rather than being a policeman, which had never been my forte. I ran through the itinerary for the rest of the week. Tuesday was spent on the fen, including collecting samples of vegetation and bugs which included pond dipping. Wednesday was a study of a fen edge village and involved the minibus. Thursday either involved transporting the children in one direction to the nearby cathedral or walking in the opposite direction to the local pumping station and river. The Friday morning was to be spent doing a brief study of the local village before lunch, then packing the minibus and returning to school in time for the normal end of the day. That seemed a long way hence. Would we all return intact?

Perhaps it was questions like this and whether I had left the note for the milkman in the right place that so exercised my mind that I did not actually sleep that night. Were all the children alright? I listened for any noise. The only noise I could hear was the mice scrabbling in the wall cavity between the outer boarding and inner hardboard cladding. By the noise they were making there were several families hopefully coexisting peacefully if any of us were to get sleep during the rest of the week. I gathered the following morning that the children had slept perfectly well. So, apparently, had my colleague. For as the morning sky got lighter so I heard a gentle buzz of conversation from the boys. I entered their dormitory as they were busy "shushing" each other so as not to disturb me. I smiled, but said that I thought the girls must still be asleep as all was quiet. One of the boys came into the kitchen with me to help me make the tea. The facilities might have been a little basic, but, come what may, I was not going to be deprived of my early morning cup of tea. Having started that process I realised that I still had not heard a sound from the girls' dormitory. What had happened? Had they all gone home during the night? Were they ill? I opened the door and entered quietly. All the girls were wide awake and several of them raised their fingers to their lips and then pointed in the direction of the still sleeping figure of my colleague. A couple of the girls got out of bed and joined me in the kitchen as we put out cups, milk etc. and finished making the tea. That being completed, some of the other boys began to drift out. I poured one cup of tea and re-entered the girls' dormitory. Some of the girls were getting out of bed quietly. How my colleague could still be asleep amazed me. Perhaps it was just envy on my part. I approached her bunk, coughed loudly and, proferring the tea, said, as she stirred, "Good morning. Room service!" I smiled. My smile was not returned. I simply said to the smirking girls around me that there was tea in the kitchen for those who wanted it. Very soon there was a group of children in the kitchen and sitting in the community room chatting about how they had slept the night before. Apparently they had slept like logs. A couple volunteered to wash up the cups and some wandered back to their dormitory.

I did the same, got my soap, towel and razor and went into the washroom where a number of the children were already washing. I took off my pyjama jacket and lathered my face. I was impressed by how organised the children were. I began to realise that I need not have worried about the washing arrangements or how the children would cope with the mixed facilities. They were too busy wanting to finish washing and to get dressed ready for the day ahead. As children drifted out and more drifted in, so a couple came in, fully dressed, and asked if they could help start breakfast and what they should get out. In answer I told them to lay the tables and put out the packets of cereal and then lay out the rashers of bacon under the grill ready, for breakfast that morning was to be cereal, bacon, eggs and toast. It quickly became apparent that we were not going to be short of help. I left the children to it and returned to my little room at the end in order to dress.

I had just got as far as taking my pyjamas off and was just reaching for my underpants when there was a knock at the door. I responded with "Er, Ye-es?" which my visitor clearly interpreted as, "Yes, come in". As the door opened I quickly began to pull my underpants up and, Jill, one of the girls walked in. Apparently unperturbed by my state of undress she asked whether the weather would permit us to get out onto the fen that day. She was clearly most concerned that we should, so I looked out of the window and suggested that we should see if we felt there was enough blue sky to make a sailor's suit. I shared with her that my mother had taught me that rule of thumb which had never failed me. As we looked out of the window and started patching together the bits of blue sky in our minds, I continued to get dressed as nonchalently as I could. Having satisfied herself that there was sufficient blue sky, my visitor departed happily, reassured that we should have our day on the fen. As I finished dressing I found myself anxious about how much of my nakedness she had seen and whether I had somehow traumatised her.

By the time I returned to the kitchen my colleague was helping the children get eveything ready such that I suggested the children start serving themselves cereal while I grilled the bacon. A couple of children insisted on frying the eggs which we cracked, about half a dozen at a time, into a bowl while I heated the frying pan ready. By the time we were ready, so were the children. It was a new experience for me serving breakfast to 30. I thought of our cooks at school preparing lunch for about 150. Whatever drawbacks teaching may have had, I knew which job I preferred. It was now our turn to sit down and start our own breakfast while a couple of other children started the toast. It was while we were gaily munching our way through that, with the conversation ranging from what sort of night they had had and who had heard the mice scrabbling in the wall cavity, to what we were going to be doing that day, that one of the boys, who perhaps had led a slightly more sheltered life than some of the others, announced, "I saw Sarah in her knickers". If it had been the intention to embarrass the girl concerned or in some way to gain some credibility with his fellows, he failed miserably as Jill retorted immediately, in strident tone, "So what? I saw Mr. Cutler in a lot less than that this morning and it didn't matter, did it Mr. Cutler?" I smiled quietly to myself and reflected on my previous anxiety before I said, with feeling, "No, you're quite right, Jill, it didn't". And for the rest of the children for the rest of that week it didn't.

That was generally the case in the years to come. Perhaps rather I should simply echo the well known saying, "You always get one", and interestingly in the years that I led fresh classes for their week on the fen I only recall one other such occasion. At the age of 11 children are becoming increasingly aware of themselves and nudity begins to become an issue which needs to be respected, especially by the "responsible adult" at the time, although in our presently sex obsessed age I am a little concerned that we may be robbing our children of childhood altogether. That growth in emotional maturity can occur at different stages, however, such that the difference begins to become noticeable by the age of 11, when boys can appear a little emotionally immature in comparison to their female counterparts. That was brought home to me one morning as we were all happily having a wash prior to getting ready for breakfast. As had become our custom by then, children were drifting in and out of the washroom where I continued to have my wash and shave and one of the girls had peeled off her night dress in order to be able to wash a little bit more than hands and face. That, in itself, was not exceptional. Clearly, however, one of the boys seemed to take exception to it as he pointed to the girl concerned and said to me, "Mandy's taken her nightdress off". He must have seen the look of puzzlement on my face as I managed to reply, "How very observant of you. And?" Clearly intent on justifying himself he replied indignantly, "But she's...". He couldn't say the word. "Yes, and?", I responded patiently. "But.." was his only retort. Clearly the conversation could have gone on indefinitely and not only was I concerned for the feelings of the girl who was the subject of the conversation, but also was beginning to grow a little impatient of the boy's immaturity and responded with, "Do you have a problem with that?" He very clearly did, but could only say, "But..." This conversation needed curtailing and I needed to do it as I said, "If you have a problem with that you know what to do. Come back later when you can have the washroom to yourself". The boy stood apparently transfixed. Either he had not really taken what we had agreed seriously, or had not thought through the implications. He looked surprised when I finally said, slightly impatiently, "Go along", and he departed looking somewhat crestfallen.

It had not been my desire to humiliate the boy, but that, whether by intention or not, is what he was doing to the girl concerned. There was also a wider principle that needed to be asserted and I needed to take responsibility for that and for the situation. As if to reassure and to draw a line under the episode, I turned to the girl and said, "Don't take any notice of our friend. You carry on". She did, and so did the rest of the children. The core conditions had been established and I had reasserted the ground rules we had agreed.

From my reading of educational philosophy as part of my degree I had studied some of the works of Carl Rogers who had asserted 3 core conditions of acceptance, empathy and congruence, which for practical purposes within this setting meant acceptance of each other, mutual respect of and feeling for the other's needs, and an ability to be truly oneself without the need to put on an act, which meant children and teachers alike. I wanted to assert those conditions if we were going to survive the week together and come out emotionally and physically whole at the end of it.

Remaining physically whole, apart from maintaining good housekeeping in spite of the limitations of our circumstances, also meant keeping on top of the problem of mosquito bites. As the hut was not suitable for winter time use, term dates really necessitated early to mid summer for field studies purposes which coincided with the height of the mosquito season. Given the head's experience of the previous year, I was anxious to avoid one of the children finishing the week in hospital. I therefore advised the children to see me if they were troubled by mosquito bites. I had not realised what I was starting as just about every child was either so troubled or at least decided to avail themselves of my offer, as it quickly turned into a bite parade every night. This generally meant that any exposed areas were likely to find themselves a target. As all the children wore long trousers or jeans of one sort or another, bites were normally kept to a minimum. Having said that, beyond exposed hands and face sometimes the more tender areas proved easier biting. On one occasion all the children were settled in bed and having just checked that all the boys were comfortable I went into the girls' dormitory to say my usual good night, whereupon one of the children announced, in her customary direct manner, "I've got a bite on my bum". One of the other girls, who clearly felt that such a complaint was socially unacceptable and was simply not the sort of thing that one should say in polite company, responded in shocked tones, "Samantha". Sam, however, as everybody normally knew her, was not going to be deterred by such a 'put down' remark and retorted defensively, "Well it keeps itching and I can't get to sleep". At this stage I could not help but see the comical side of the "contratemps" between the two girls and doing my best to stop myself laughing so as to avoid offending either of them simply said, "Come on, let's have a look". Sam duly obliged and I cleansed the area with surgical spirit and applied some anti-histamine cream. Her honour satisfied and her comfort restored Sam settled down in bed and simply said, "Good night". As I responded in like manner, I hoped it would be.

One of the joys for me of those weeks away which, as I observed previously, I led on my own as often as not, was the unaffected relationship that existed between all the children and myself. Indeed it would have been difficult to maintain anything other than absolute congruence. Any falsity or 'political correctness' would have been seen through immediately. Such an open, honest atmosphere engendered mutual respect and would not have been sustainable without it. I hope therefore that the reader will forgive my diversion into our domestic arrangements, but I never failed to feel humbled and warmed to see a group of children, all from different backgrounds, cooperating together and respecting each other with what felt like little, if any, input from me.

To return to my narrative, however, breakfast completed, we did have our day on the fen and the blue sky had not let me down. After lunch of rolls, fruit etc. which tended to be our pattern, the children settled to drawing the various samples which had been gathered in the morning and researching in the limited library of books I had brought with me or which had been borrowed from the local field studies education centre. When 5.30 p.m. arrived and I suggested that we should pack away and start thinking about preparing supper or that some might like a break, it was greeted by a disappointed "Oh, do we have to?" I reflected how, if they had been at school, they would have finished two hours' previously. I think the children worked a lot harder during those weeks away than they generally did at school, but then they weren't having to prepare their own meals as well. It was a tired group of children that went to bed that night.

The Wednesday morning was again greeted by sun and after I had swept the mouse droppings off the tops in the kitchen and wiped over them with disinfectant (so much for my misplaced confidence earlier in the week) we were ready to start breakfast. I was concerned to be ready fairly promptly as the head was to join us to help transport the children to the neighbouring fen edge for a village study. Some of the children were just finishing the washing up and some were helping to prepare our packed lunch when the head arrived and asked if he was too late for breakfast! Clearly I need not have worried. Without a word from me, some children disappeared into the kitchen and a little while later proudly set a cooked breakfast in front of him. He was clearly most impressed. He asked how I was getting on with my rotas. To my response that I had not got that far, but that it all just happened, he replied, through a mouthful of bacon, that it clearly seemed to be working.

I remember that we had another busy day and while the children weren't working some could be found patting a donkey that was in a neighbouring field. It became clear, however, that the donkey must have supported a population of fleas, for when it came to our now established bite parade, I noticed that some of the children had been bitten at regular intervals up their arms which rather indicated a hopping flea rather than a mosquito. I spent the next quarter of an hour or so going through the bed sheets of those affected engaged on a flea hunt. I became quite adept at finding and squashing the offending creatures.

Before then, however, we had to welcome the parents who were customarily invited to visit for an hour on a Wednesday evening and the children would proudly show them all that they had been doing. I was aware of how protective I was becoming of the children and our "home", as a part of me slightly resented what felt like an invasion from another country or world. I remember, however, on one such occasion one boy, who had found it difficult to settle, had complained to his parents that he had not slept well. His mother said they would take him home for the night and promised to return him first thing in the morning. I was saddened and felt that he needed to be given more time to settle but accepted her assurance that he would return in time for another busy day. He did indeed return bright and early the following morning; at about 7.30 a.m. I greeted him and his mother as I was on my way to the washroom still in my pyjamas. As I suggested he might like to go into the kitchen and start setting out a few things for breakfast, his mother looked slightly disapprovingly at my pyjama clad figure and at children wandering about and clearly felt it right that she should have spared her son at least one night of such obvious chaos.

That day, being Thursday, would either be spent visiting the neighbouring cathedral or walking to the local pumping station which afforded the children the opportunity of learning about how the fens were drained and how the whole of the fen agriculture depended upon this elaborate drainage scheme. That particular year we were blessed with good weather and it seemed a shame to be indoors. It was as a fine day for the walk across the neighbouring fens. Our way took us alongside one of the lodes before crossing a bridge and walking up to the river and the pumping station.

The lode had to be crossed at the start of our walk to put us on the right side and on the tow path. The crossing was effected by a bridge made up of railway sleepers across two stout iron girders. There were no handrails but it was quite wide enough for children walking in pairs. For that reason I made sure children were lined up in pairs and then stationed myself on one corner of the bridge which afforded me a view of the front of the line while still being able to observe those still waiting to cross. I felt I was thus taking all precautions that I sensibly could. One boy, however, who was waiting to cross, thought to spend his time investigating the edge of the lode which, being man made, had sheer sides. The inevitable happened and just as I saw the child begin to slip I ran to the edge and heaved him out of the water by a handful of clothing at the back of his neck. I set him upright on the bank and he appeared none the worse for his brief dunking in the water other than to observe, "Cor, you saved my life". To which I replied with a smile, "Don't bank on it next time, you daft ha'p'orth. Go and get changed and we'll wait for you". Fortunately the hut was visible and so we only needed to wait where we were, by this time all on the right side of the lode. Some of the children did observe, however, that I had literally leapt into action and said, "No wonder they call you speedy". Certainly the name stuck ever after that and became my permanent nickname at school for years after.

Apart from the inevitable worksheets, I did my bit by pointing out salient features including drawing the children's attention to the fact that the river was higher than the surrounding land, not lower as might be the norm. Thus this irrigation scheme, started by the Romans, did not pump water from the river into irrigation channels, but from them into the lodes and then finally into the river. They also therefore understood that the only major development was on high ground which in the early days of the Fens would have been an island. On future occasions indeed I did take the children to the nearby city and its cathedral, but more of that later.

On this occasion, having been rejoined by our recently soaked member of the class, we were able to enjoy a fairly substantial walk as well as drawing and again collecting different samples before returning for a late lunch. We actually had a couple of hours recreation that afternoon during which some children went outside to play rounders, others carried on with drawing and writing up from previous days, while some visited the local shop to buy mementos and the like. It was on just one such afternoon that I became aware of a child who was not joining in with the others and seemed unaccustomedly unhappy. I asked what was wrong and finally learned that some of the children had been bullying her and calling her names. In the years that I led classes on that residential week this was the only occasion that I had experienced such behaviour and I was hurt for this child. I remembered how, when I was very young, I had been followed home from school by two boys who kept taunting me and calling me names. On that occasion I was met at the gate by my grandmother who immediately strode out and gave the two young bullies a piece of her mind. She had been my champion. Perhaps it was that memory that so filled me with righteous indignation now. It was later that day when we had finished supper and sat down in the community room for our customary sharing/debriefing that I spoke in stern tones to the children, explaining how saddened and shocked I was to learn of the bullying incident. "Never", I explained "had I encountered such behaviour in all the years that I had been bringing classes to the Fens". I felt a little like Churchill as he gave his rousing speech to the House of Commons, "Never, in the field of human conflict..." Having observed previously that I had learned to be honest with the chidren, I am aware that there must be a part of any teacher which is the actor. It is that part which enabled me now to convey my real hurt to the children. It was a very crestfallen group of children that I left to "reflect on what I had said" as I went into the kitchen to prepare evening cups of cocoa, carefully shutting the door behind me before collapsing quietly into laughter. The student who had accompanied me on that occasion looked shocked until I explained that I had been what might be termed "method acting" and needed to release the tension which had accompanied the energy that I had to summon in order to deliver my reprimand. Such a stance did not come naturally to me. Most of the time we were a lot gentler with each other and I found that my trust of the children was never disappointed.

That was borne out for me one Thursday morning when, instead of walking across the Fen, on this occasion we had visited the local cathedral. A slightly smaller group of children had enabled me to squeeze all of them into the minibus although I have an uncomfortable feeling that we probably exceeded the insured number. The cathedral had recently started making an entrance charge for individuals and groups. The charge was considerable and certainly would have exceeded our budget. Hence I drove the minibus round to the south side entrance rather than our entering by the main west door. I suggested that the children slip in quietly in pairs rather than our drawing attention to ourselves. It had not been my intention to defraud the cathedral, but I was unaware of the charge which had obviously been introduced since my last visit. Having planned our day round this I was not about to turn the minibus around and take an entire class of children away again. I equally did not want to run the risk of pleading my case with the person sitting by the door only to be refused entrance, as I suspected the person concerned may very well not have the "authority" to resolve such irregularities.

Thus I deposited our art materials, paper, crayons, pencils in the cloistered area just outside the door and said we would make that our meeting point and that if anyone got lost or separated from their partner they were to return to that point. The children

259

quietly dispersed around the choir and chancel, drawing or doing rubbings, for which again there was a separate charge, with one of each pair on the look out! Looking back, perhaps I should not have been encouraging the children in such dishonesty, but I reasoned that this was God's house and Jesus himself had said "Let the little children come to me. Do not try to stop them". (Mark 10:14). I was merely taking Him at his word.

Again the children were all busy and clearly rapt in the grandeur and atmosphere of the building as I wandered from group to group. As the morning wore on, towards midday the children began to collect around me in the crossway between the nave, choir and side aisles and I was busily pointing out things of interest. I noticed a few other visitors standing around listening. Clearly they must have mistaken me for one of the guides. At midday the clock struck and chimed the hour and one of the clergy mounted the pulpit to lead a few minutes of public prayer. I quickly lost my unofficial audience as I suggested to the children that they simply sit quietly and that they might close their eyes and join in the prayers if they wanted to. Benches with kneelers were placed around the crossing in an octagon and the children, without another word from me, went and sat down on the kneelers, closed their eyes and quietly bowed their heads. I stood and looked on. I then closed my eyes and said my own quiet little prayer. "Thank you Lord".

After the few minutes the priest concerned closed with "amen" and the children joined in. Perhaps he was not accustomed to such an attentive audience as I noticed that many others just kept wandering about, but as he came down from the pulpit he came straight towards me. Had he found out we hadn't paid? He introduced himself as the Dean and enquired which school we were from. Perhaps he had found out about our illicit entry and was going to send us the bill! He continued and said how impressed he was with the children's behaviour and how quiet and disciplined they were. Which church school, he wondered, had we come from? When I told him that we were from an ordinary primary school he looked around at the children who, by now, had gathered round me and said he was sure that we must have been from a church school from the children's behaviour during the prayers. I too looked around at the children and reflected quietly to myself, not for the first time that teaching did have its rewards. I smiled and thanked him, but glowed quietly inside. The children had not let me down.

It was not very often that children became homesick while we were away for that precious week and even less often that they would be in tears. Indeed I can only remember two such occasions. One stands out in my memory. The child concerned was a quiet, sensitive girl, not greatly given to crying, such that when a group of children rushed into the community room to say that Yvonne was crying I was immediately concerned and found her in her dormitory. It must have been a sufficiently rare occurrence for her tears were becoming the centre of attention and the subject of much speculation. I asked her if perhaps we should go somewhere a little quieter, to which she nodded her agreement. I led her into the small end room, known as the staff room, although by this time I was not using it for sleeping in, and we sat on the bunk together. It appeared that her parents had not visited her the previous evening when so many others had. She expressed how sad she felt and how she missed her family. She looked a little surprised then when I said how lucky she was. I went on to explain that the fact that she missed them suggested she must have a very special relationship in order to so miss them and that perhaps some of those who appeared not to worry had less to miss in the first place. I pointed out that, very often, missing people was a sign of how much we loved them and they us. Her face lit up as if with a new understanding, but at that point we were invaded by some of the children who were still so concerned. Our quiet moment was shattered but I hoped I had given her something she could hold on to.

Again it was a very tired group of children that retired to bed that night, to say nothing of their teacher. I was sleeping in with the boys as was my practice and slept very soundly. However I was awakened by the general stirring aware that this was our last day there and that there was much to do before we finally packed the minibus to drive back to school. I realised I must get out of bed and start the day. In my haste, I tumbled out of the top bunk and landed rather unceremoniously in an embarrassing heap on the floor, much to the amusement of the boys around me. I reflected ruefully that perhaps I too should have had something to hold on to. The news went round the entire hut that I had fallen out of bed. While I was still rubbing my bruises, concerned if not amused, children rushed in from the other dormitory to see the spectacle. Along with my nickname of 'speedy', this was something else I would not be allowed to forget.

The last morning there, the Friday, was spent doing a brief study of the neighbouring village, looking particularly at the use of local building materials and how one could date the buildings from that. Lunch was followed by packing, tidying and cleaning the hut and packing the minibus roof rack. By this time my wife had arrived with our car to transport some of the children back to school. This was to become a fairly regular practice as the years went on, sometimes with the help of a parent and their car, depending on the size of the class.

It was with a slight pang that I rolled out of the parking area and over the narrow plank bridge as I reflected on the busy week we had spent together. It was also with a sense of relief and fulfilment that I delivered all the children happy and intact back to school and their awaiting parents. The bond that the children and I had built during that week, and in the succeeding years, has always stayed with me as precious; a moment to treasure and perhaps to hold on to when the practicalities of 'delivering' the curriculum and other professional pressures conspired to make it seem like a distant dream.

Chapter Sixteen

Dog Days

"A hard time we had of it ...
with the voices singing in our ears, saying
that it was all folly"
T.S. Eliot, *Journey of the Magi*

Those pressures became ever more present for me in the years that followed. The next three years were spent in the 'wing' as it became known, working with the older junior children. At least that and my classroom remained a constant and a refuge in what was otherwise a shifting and sometimes threatening landscape. My experience of that previous year, when I had been finally forced to take time off, had had a profound affect upon me. I had visited a place in which I had come face to face with my own limitations. Before then perhaps I had enjoyed an optimism which had enabled me to deal with each little challenge as it came along. Suddenly that was no longer the case. I had walked, or been driven, to the brink and had looked down into that abyss which, once visited, is never forgotten. Those of my readers who have visited that place will know what I mean. Some may visit that place and, with help, recover and eventually become stronger for their experience.

Others may not. But all, like the ancient mariner, will be "a sadder but wiser man". (Samuel Taylor Coleridge - "The Rime of the Ancient Mariner")

I could not be the person I had been and, more to the point, in that setting I could not be the teacher I had been. I could not immediately see that, although I sense that my colleagues and the children did. The latter responded to that in different ways; some more positively than others. My glimpse into the abyss had so shaken me that I no longer had the same confidence which, in turn, afforded me a greater sensitivity. That expressed itself in different ways. I found it slightly more difficult to tell children off; my judgements became less hasty. Discipline tended to be rather more by consent. As has been observed before, teachers rule by consent or not at all. I was just a little more aware of that truth. Perhaps outwardly there was not a great deal of difference, but one thing the head had picked up on the previous year was a source of serious criticism on his part as he said, "You are very polite to the children". This had been noticed once before by another colleague when I was training. I rather felt like Martin Luther as he stood before the then rulers of church and state at his first hearing in 1521 when he was reported to have said "Here I stand, I can do no other." Put simply, I could not stop being me.

Children can be remarkably perceptive and clearly saw that 'me' which perhaps I was the last to recognise. Looking back I realise that I began to enjoy a different relationship with many of the children. Again nothing markedly different, but I noticed that the children became rather more open and trusting and the relationship became slightly less formal than I had been in the habit of enjoying hitherto. It must be said I had always been a rather serious young man but my brief encounter with that place and a rather more extensive encounter with the philosophies of Dewey and Rogers, had softened my earlier approach a little. Beyond that I had experienced a different sort of relationship with the children during the field trips and they had responded. Most of the children responded positively to this changed 'me'. There was perhaps the occasional child who needed a little more containment. This slightly changed 'me' and my altered teaching approach relied on and encouraged a greater self discipline in the children. Such an approach also requires a level of maturity. It is, of course, true that maturity enables self discipline which encourages greater maturity, and so on. It is the teacher's job, like that of any parent, to recognise and provide the right level of support and containment commensurate with the child's level of emotional and social development. While it is true that children don't like being told off they can equally become quickly distressed and out of control if they do not experience the level of containment they need. That is equally true of society as a whole, and not just in the home. If well meaning politicians, bent on protecting our children, succeed only in undermining the parent or teacher such that they become frightened to apply those external constraints, then they ill serve the needs of our children. Equally, if through our failure to provide that external discipline the child becomes out of control and is then excluded from school, we do not serve their educational needs either.

I remember one such child in particular. Coming from an

unsettled family background, he was finding it very difficult to cope with his own conflicting emotions. He was a frightened, angry child who desperately needed, but hated, a proper level of control. He craved the holding or containment he did not experience at home but rebelled against it if ever a teacher tried to apply it. I remember his mother coming to me in a very distressed state telling me his difficult home circumstances. I could sympathise with her son's social difficulties, but in the classroom setting, I had the needs of thirty other children to balance against his. It was not an easy balancing act.

On one occasion it became clear that the external pressures upon him such as work and sitting still were getting too much for him to contain as he stood up on his chair and started to shout abuse at some of the other members of the class. I approached him, asking him simultaneously to sit down. This had little effect beyond causing him to raise his voice even more. There were two ways of approaching this; one was to back away and try patiently and quietly to defuse the situation, the other was to seek to exert my authority and try to contain him. Such decisions are never easy, the only clear understanding I had was that I had to do something. Given that the desks were of the collapsible kind and that the child was therefore in danger of falling, possibly hurting himself and others, I chose the latter option. As I continued to approach him, my voice now a little more stern, I intended to lift him down off his chair and then suggest that he sat on it. He must have guessed my intention as he stood, first on his own desk and then jumped onto his neighbour's, thus proceeding around the classroom at desk top level. I eventually headed him off and gaining a secure hold of him lifted him down onto the floor. As I did so he proceeded to kick me in the groin. I remember it hurt quite severely at the time and ached for some days afterwards. At that precise moment, however, I really could not afford to nurse my own wound. I had to keep him secure and move him to a space away from desks and children for the sake of his own safety and that of others. Having got to the front of the class I addressed the class over his screams and merely told them to continue with their work as Roger was a little upset at the moment! Meanwhile he continued to scream, "Let me go" and to kick my lower legs repeatedly while I continued to pin his arms to his side in a bear hug. I clearly needed to immobilise his legs and so sat down on the floor, in front of the class, pulling him down with me. I then wrapped my legs around him and placed them on top of his, thus securing his legs to the ground. I had at least managed to contain him and keep him from harming himself or others. From that position I continued to conduct the rest of the lesson answering questions above his screams as best I could. It is a testimony to the children's sense that they maintained their composure and did their best to continue with their work. Had just one other child decided to exploit the situation I should have been lost; another reminder of how fragile our hold on authority can be. Indeed very often authority can seem illusory and those who would see themselves as lion tamers, confident in their own perceived position, do well to reflect upon that.

Fortunately lunch time was imminent and I was able to dismiss the class, still from my position on the floor. I dared not let go of my charge. The class, again to their credit, left in a quiet orderly fashion as I reminded those who were staying to lunch to wash their hands! The need of the many, as well as the few, still had to be remembered. I managed, through my talking to calm the child, to relax my grip just a little before leading him into a smaller more containing room next door and sitting him on the step beside me. I continued to talk to him until I felt he was sufficiently calm to let go of him altogether as the storm passed and I felt safe to dismiss him and send him to have his lunch. I could start to think about my own wounds, although I did not spend too long doing so and did not realise that the blow I had received earlier had caused lasting damage which, some years' later, would lead to my having surgery.

Somewhat shaken, I followed him into the dining hall and related the incident to a colleague who admitted that she had had similar problems controlling the child's behaviour. On the basis of our shared experiences I spoke to the head who was also in the dining hall at the time, firstly on the grounds that he should, as a matter of course, be acquainted with any incidents, and secondly hoping that I might gain some support so that, should there be a recurrence of such problems, he might back me up in any future approach I might make to the parents, if not speaking to them himself. His response was to say that he didn't have any problem with the child himself and if I could not control him, then he would teach him himself and explain to his parents that I could not cope!

I tried to think of any occasions when the head had actually taught him but reflected that, had there been any such, they would have been in a one to one setting in his own office. On reflection I should simply have called his bluff and said, "Fine, you do just that". As it was, given my experience of the previous year, his bluff worked. Thus again I felt isolated and undermined. The signal from the head was clear; "Put up and shut up". I was still sufficiently shaken and undermined to feel that I had no other option. Not for the first time I was again left feeling professionally and personally isolated. My perception was to be reinforced later that term.

Shortly before Christmas I found myself on playground duty. It was a typically grey winter's day and the ground was wet. Over the years, experience had taught me how much the weather affected the behaviour of the children. When it was windy, they correspondingly would tend to be "as high as kites". On bright, sunny days they similarly were bright and cheerful. On dull, oppressive days, like this one, they would often become argumentative. They found it difficult to organise their own games but would then become disgruntled not knowing what to do with their energy. At that point it could so easily degenerate into arguing and pushing or shoving. I had learned therefore that active children were happy children which all went to contribute to a harmonious playground.

On this occasion they were trying to organise a game of tag or 'it', but could not decide who should be 'it' to start with. I might have suggested that they try one of the many rhymes for the purpose, but some of those that I could remember from my own childhood would not have been politically correct. Admittedly the disease of political correctnesss was not quite so endemic then and I was happy to wear such constraints lightly when need or children's welfare dictated, but on this occasion I felt we needed to get things moving. The quickest way of doing that was for me to be 'it' and then the first one I caught could take over the role. The sight of me haring round the playground making a fool of myself was always guaranteed to get the children joining in the fun. This time was no exception, except the fun did not last very long as my foot slipped on mud on the edge of the playground while I was in the middle of a tight turn. My foot went from under me and my face came into contact with the ground with some force, along with the rest of me.

Fortunately nothing was broken, not even my nose, which very quickly became quite swollen as well as the area around my right eye. My cheek was grazed and my head was spinning. I hurriedly picked myself up and asked one of the group of concerned children who had quickly gathered round me to be kind enough to go to the staff room to ask the deputy head to come to the playground. I was fast becoming aware that I was not in a position to adequately supervise the children, although it should be added that most of them had already gathered round me and did not need much supervising. As he arrived on the scene and saw the state of my face I did not need to offer much explanation. I excused myself and went to clean up. Somewhat shaken I returned to my class and continued teaching until the end of school. By this time my face was beginning to feel quite uncomfortable. I did the bare minimum to leave my class straight before driving home.

By the following morning it became clear that I would not be driving to school as one eye was partially closed due to the swelling and by now had changed colour. For the first time in my life I had the archetypal 'black eye'! Beyond that, my nose was also swollen and the graze was looking rather angry. When I telephoned school with my news it became clear that the head was not expecting me in school. Indeed, being quite near the end of term, I was surprised to learn that he did not expect me in school for the last few days. I was not sorry, but I was surprised to see the head the following day, visiting me at home. However I began to understand the reason for his visit when he asked how I managed to fall. As I explained that I had slipped on mud on the edge of the playground he immediately responded that he had spoken to my class and that, should I ask, they would say that there was no mud on the playground. The look on his face said everything and conveyed the truth of my position.

I began to understand the head's priorities and to recognise his vulnerabilities when he came over to my classroom, immediately before a parents evening after my colleagues had left, to ask me about the progress of a particular child. I replied honestly that his behaviour was hindering his work and that I would mention it to his parents when I saw them at the open evening. The parents concerned were articulate people who held fairly responsible jobs and enjoyed some respect in the village. The head told me not to mention the child's obvious difficulties. In my innocence I thought that is what parents' evenings were held for. Instead I was told that I should avoid the child's behaviour altogether and put as positive a slant on his work as I could, at which point I confronted his suggestion with, "You mean I should lie? I'm sorry I can't do that". Having failed on that tack he then turned to the attack and said that if the child's behaviour was poor it was my fault and proceeded to criticise my teaching. While I did not necessarily believe in my own perfection, I began to suspect that he was seeking to undermine me and encourage me to believe that it was all my fault in order to obtain my compliance. After my previous experience of his use of this strategy, I started to see through it. I reasoned too that he must have known there was a problem with the child to seek me out in the first place. "And," I questioned in my own mind, "Why wait until immediately before the parents' evening to express his concerns?" As he now proceeded to criticise my teaching, bearing in mind that he had not been in my class for some time, I felt my suspicions confirmed and finally met his remarks with, "I think you had better leave my classroom".

It was thus because I perceived my isolation and in an attempt to prove myself that I threw myself into my teaching even more. I spent long hours in my classroom preparing work and putting up displays. Very often my car was the last one to leave the car park in the evening. I organised classroom projects as I sought to ensure that my displays were up to date and reflected the work being undertaken. I involved more parents in my craft teaching which became ever more adventurous, which now included fabric printing as well as the exclusion dyeing. I particularly remember one project which focussed on the Elizabethan period. I managed to organise an educational visit to a local stately home which each year held experiential days for the general public and school parties, the idea being that the children and their teacher should go in costume. Again I remember how enthusiastically all the children entered into the project and how I enjoyed the support of the parents as they helped provide, and often made, costumes for the children. I had mine lined up too.

Unfortunately I never got to wear my costume as shortly before we were due to go, I fell ill and the children went with one of my colleagues and a number of parents. It was a source of great regret that, having worked up to the moment, I could not now share it with the children. This time, however, my illness was not stress, although I do not doubt it was stress related. Instead I contracted a virus which was associated with a particularly high temperature and severe muscular pain. My doctor was puzzled and offered a variety of diagnoses as the virus systematically worked through my body throwing up a range of debilitating and painful symptoms as it went, finishing up with my heart. I did not return to school for the rest of that term. I gradually recovered and we were able to enjoy a fairly relaxing boating holiday which we had already booked some months previously. My seven year old son was in his element.

I returned to school the following term to a new class confident that my illness had been "just one of those things" and an isolated incident. My optimism proved misplaced as I started to experience periods of illness with ever greater frequency. They always started with a virus, usually towards the end of term, as I began to become more tired. I noted too that those periods of illness seemed to become longer. I slowly began to realise that this trend could not be sustained indefinitely, but I was not really ready to admit that to myself. After all, what else could a teacher do but teach? Teaching had become a part of me. It is how I identified myself, beyond which, politics apart, I enjoyed the job I did inasmuch as I enjoyed working with the children. I believed, at that time, that what I was doing was important.

That position was gradually to change, but for the moment I soldiered on. The after-school swimming sessions had now become twice a week. Meanwhile it is clear that I had changed, or rather been changed by my experiences of the previous two years. The children became more relaxed with me and more trusting of me. Such a realisation, perhaps, comes with the gift of hindsight. At the time I just responded to whatever needs the children presented. I was too busy to look at myself; my position said I must look to the children.

The latter understanding was borne out for me during one swimming lesson. I had suggested an exercise that some of the children could try in the water if they felt comfortable doing so. Whether he was trying the exercise I had suggested or not, I am unsure, but one boy missed his footing, slipped under the water, and quickly found himself floundering. As I have previously noted, it was my practice to wear as little clothing as was sensible; it was less to dry afterwards. I immediately shook off my rubber flip-flops and vaulted over the side of the pool. On reaching the boy concerned I placed my hands under his arms and set him upright on his feet again. As I did so he smiled and seemed to be none the worse for wear. A couple of the children commented on how quickly I had cleared the side of the pool with apparently just one hand on the edge and a clear vault over. As I reflect, I am not sure to this day how I managed it. It was clear, however, the sight of me leaping over the side of the pool was sufficiently entertaining for the children to want an encore, as during the remains of that lesson and a couple of lessons that followed, the occasional child would jump up and down waving their arms and shouting "Help, I'm drowning!" To which, I have to confess, I retorted, "Then please drown quietly!" That experience taught me that a pair of shorts was probably the most appropriate wear which would allow me to enter the pool if I needed to, for some 'hands on' teaching.

As the children seemed, increasingly, to find my teaching, or perhaps just my antics, such fun, so I found that they became more relaxed around me. Shortly after the incident just described and immediately following a lesson, while the children were changing, I needed to impart some information. I went first to the boys' changing room and then to the girls'. In an effort to respect their modesty, I opened the door just a little and with my eyes looking down to the floor started to impart my message, to which a number of the girls called out in chorus, "Oh, for goodness sake, Mr. Cutler come in and shut the door. It's cold". I meekly obeyed.

Although I found a welcome with the children, the same did not seem to be true among some of the staff or in the staffroom. I could not know what was the cause of such hostiliy, but it showed itself in many subtle ways. I noticed a coolness towards me by some colleagues; particularly the female colleague already spoken of earlier in the book and, inevitably, those who must work with her. I found that I could not do anything right. If I were eating an apple with my packed lunch, I was criticised for peeling it. My explanation that I did so to avoid the spray residue on the skin was ridiculed. If I were washing up the tea mugs I was criticised for the amount of washing up liquid I was using. As the stress I experienced started to affect my digestion I was criticised for drinking peppermint tea. I started to avoid the staffroom, but the criticism continued in my absence. As I approached the staffroom door on one occasion I heard the shrill tones of one of my female colleagues. In response to the deputy head's statement, "He didn't", she asserted "He did, I tell you". Whereupon she repeated what I was supposed to have said. What was repeated bore little resemblance to the truth, but had been taken out of context and embroidered. I stood outside the door, my hand nearly on the handle, transfixed, as if traumatised. By this time I felt sufficiently isolated such that I was rendered powerless to confront or contradict my accuser. I felt a sinking in the pit of my stomach and turned and walked away.

In hindsight, I can see how the ongoing stress of my situation was contributing to the continued decline in my health such that after what, in my more paranoid moments, felt like an orchestrated campaign, I was becoming ill at the end of every term. My colleagues' response was to save up the extra playground duties for me that they had had to cover in my absence before a supply teacher could be found.

The only thing which made teaching sustainable for me was the continued support and trust that I experienced from the children and parents. I was, by now, recognising that my situation was unsustainable and I began to look at alternative areas. It was equally clear, however, that I did not really have the aptitude for office or administrative work. That was reinforced for me when, after one year of serving as treasurer for the Youth Club in my home village my wife commented, "Please don't take it on again. I haven't got the time!" I was to administration what snow is to the Sahara Desert. All other areas of work that might use whatever aptitude I may have would require further training. If I simply resigned I would be completely without income and, as my wife reminded me, "What were we to do without money?" All my doctor was able to offer was anti-depressants which left me feeling disorientated and even less in control. After the first week, I declined his offer. I soldiered on increasingly forcing myself to return to school before I felt fully recovered, both out of a sense of commitment and to avoid causing the atmosphere in the staffroom to become any cooler or more hostile than I already experienced it.

The head approached me at the end of the term and asked me to take the reception class the following academic year. His rationalisation was that, as head of language, whose main responsibility was to contribute to language development within the curriculum, it would be "good" for me to see where it all started. This was, I gathered, essentially about getting back to "grass roots". I could not help but reflect that my training had been for the junior/secondary age group, or 9-14 year olds, that all my experience had been with middle to upper juniors, 8-11 year olds, and that now I was to be taking 5 year olds. I had gradually gone lower and lower. Where could I go after this? Would I simply slip off the end? Such reflection is in no sense a judgement of my colleagues who presently teach the youngest age groups. Their job is vital as they help lay the foundations upon which others will hopefully build. A building stands or falls on its foundations. Aware of the responsibility that my infant colleagues had, I did question if I was adequate to the task. I had no experience or training in this age group. I think, at this point, the head muttered something about "challenge".

For the moment the summer vacation beckoned. The challenge could wait. All I could think about was unwinding. I did not have the mental energy to contemplate the distant scene. The future was tomorrow. All I wanted to do was to survive today. It is a basic truth of human behaviour that the more stress we experience, so the shorter our sight becomes; survival in the here and now takes precedent over planning for a future that we dare not even contemplate.

Chapter Seventeen

Back to Basics

"In my beginning is my end"
T.S.Eliot, East Coker

If I was to survive that following year I realised that I should need to be equipped for the challenge or rather I was aware that the classroom would need to be equipped. In spite of my personal inclination to simply play the ostrich, bury my head in the sand and hope that the situation might just go away, my sense told me that it would not, while my professional sense demanded that I should be properly prepared. Hence I went to see my colleague, whose classroom I was to be inheriting, only to find that she fully intended to take all work materials with her in spite of the fact that she would not need them for the age group she would be taking. I am aware that teachers can become very protective of materials and resources that they have collected over the years but in this case what she intended to take with her extended beyond personal materials she had made herself. Taking a reception class is a unique challenge as the children often arrive quite unable to read which immediately renders all published materials redundant, which a teacher of older children might naturally rely upon. With just a basic set of "Janet & John" reading books and nothing else besides, the task went beyond a challenge to an almost impossibility.

I expressed my concerns to the head pointing out I was going to be faced with a class with effectively no teaching resources. He, in fairness, immediately understood my concern and said that such a situation was quite unacceptable and that he would have a word with the member of staff concerned. She made a few concessions which were still going to leave me badly under resourced. I tried to gain whatever concessions I could but determined that there would be little point in going to the head any more on this particular issue. 'Telling tales', I reasoned, was not going to achieve the support I was desperately going to need. I was still going to have a busy vacation.

Fortunately the class was small in comparison to what I had been accustomed to, being approximately 20 in number. Each of those twenty children, however, were all at different stages of educational development such that all needed work tailored to their individual needs. In practice, that meant preparing their work assignments in the evening, normally immediately after the children had gone home, ready for the following day. As has been observed, however, there was not the pile of marking to which I had been accustomed. At least when I did get home my work would often be finished; a rare luxury. I still had work cards to produce, but I learnt to prepare those as the need dictated. My teaching had changed, perhaps simply in response to my changed situation. Where I had been used to planning the work in line with curricular requirements, I found that the children's needs dictated what I prepared. My teaching, if I could still use that term, was now very much child led. It somehow did not quite feel like teaching as I had known it. Rather I simply responded to the children's educational and developmental needs as they presented.

I was also aware, however, that their educational needs were not the only consideration; social development was also an intrinsic part of the child's overall growth and that if they were to develop intellectually, then the social aspect of that could not be ignored. It is only through play, and hence conversation, that we develop language. That could, of course, be seen as a rationalisation for the fact that afternoons could so often find me sitting in the wendy house drinking imaginary cups of tea. The afternoons tended to be spent in what were essentially play based activities which, apart from the wendy house, also included a dressing up box as well as slightly more cerebral activities such as jigsaws and the like. All such activities were again to encourage that all important social and psychological development. Dressing up allows us to explore different identities. The children could, through play, begin to gain a sense of how they saw themselves, while exploring their 'alter ego'. Jigsaws demand that we be able to hold a lot of visual information in our mind in order to be able to make a reasoned deduction of where a piece might fit. If all the above sounds immediately obvious, for me as the teacher I was beginning to understand practically what perhaps my early educational psychology lectures of 20 years previously had been trying to teach me. What I heard then as second hand I was now experiencing first hand, which, again, underlined the simple truth that I had learned as a student, "What I hear I remember; what I do, I know".

I began to see the vital role that education played in encouraging and enabling the children's early development on all fronts and as I saw how, even then, the children were at different stages within that particular spectrum, I began to gain an understanding of the vital role of parenting which had been going on for the five years before they even entered the door. Such learning for me was again like having a light turned on in my mind such that I could see things, that I had only dimly sensed before, in a new, and clearer, light. Here I was, not for the first time in my career, like the mole in "The Wind in the Willows" blinking in the brightness of the spring sunshine and saying, "Oh my, oh my, oh my". Mole, as he sat in the stern of a boat and looked about him, was seeing and learning so many fresh things. It was perhaps a little like that for me. I was learning a lot. I am not sure how much the children were learning, but they seemed happy doing it!

Again, with their social and language development in mind, sharing news was important. Thus each morning we would spend time together in the "quiet area" in the classroom simply sharing news. That might typically range from where they had been the previous weekend to where they hoped to be going, from what they had done to whom they hoped to visit. Again that was always a precious time to me when I could relate to the children as young people with their own identity rather than simply seeing their developmental age and as potential receptacles of education. How well they were able to relate to and trust each other with their news was underlined for me one morning when one little girl stood up, lifted her dress and announced, "I've got new knickers". The children received the news just as if she had been saying, "I've got a new bicycle". I recollect that girls' briefs printed with the different days of the week were in vogue, perhaps intended to encourage their being changed daily. I recollect she was wearing one such pair and, being ever the teacher, I saw an opportunity for learning as I responded with "Ah, but the question is can you read what day they're printed with?" I couldn't help but see the funny side of the situation as all the children turned and were craning their necks trying to read the girl's knickers as she proudly displayed them. Just to make life more difficult I have a vague recollection that it was Wednesday!

Those precious times together when we could simply enjoy relating to each other demonstrated another truth which was to lead me to reassess my outlook on teaching. I was reminded of another truth I had learned when training; "How can I hear what you are saying when what you are is screaming in my ears?" I began to see that how I related to the children as young people would have a very real impact on how they learned. If they perceived me as caring about them and interested in them as individuals, they would be more inclined to relate to me and hence to what I was saying. Suddenly I saw that it was not so much the curriculum that mattered or how carefully I had planned the work, but how I was able to relate to them and whether I could engender an atmosphere of trust in which the children could feel free to learn. When children feel valued and loved they grow in confidence. As they grow in confidence so they feel better able to handle the challenge of learning.

Very often, faced with situations, we may not consciously examine our motives or worry about the psychological implications, but with hindsight I recall an incident in which my response could have engendered or destroyed trust. It could have helped build the child's confidence or undermine it.

One of the girls who had been working quietly for some time came up to me and said, just a little apprehensively, "I've wet myself". My immediate response was to smile at her and laugh as I explained, "I'm not surprised. I saw you sitting there wriggling a little, but you were so absorbed in your work you just couldn't stop to think about it. If it is anybody's fault it's mine for not reminding you when I first noticed. Not to worry, you go into the toilet and get the wet ones off and I'll go and get you a dry pair". During the vacation, aware that I should be teaching younger children, I had taken a trip to M & S and had purchased 3 pairs each of boys and girls' pants for age 5, just to be on the safe side, and had kept them in my stock cupboard. With the older children I had always kept spare P.E. kit and plimsolls, just another part of a teacher's 'hump'. I was merely adopting those contingency measures. The wet pants being exchanged for the dry ones, I simply smiled at her and thanked her for telling me. The smile she returned said it all for me. When I met her mother at the door of the classroom later that afternoon I handed her a rinsed pair of pants in a polythene bag. As her mother looked just a little disapprovingly at her daughter and said, "Oh dear...", I was quick to say that "she should be praised for being so sensible and making no fuss, and that she could hardly be told off for being absorbed in her work". Significantly perhaps that was the only such incident and I noticed children were a lot readier to go to the toilet when they needed to, either coming up to me and saying, "I need to go to the loo" or simply looking in that direction and signing. Again that one incident had taught me something and had helped establish that all important atmosphere of trust.

Some children would inevitably arrive in class with a lot more social confidence than others. Such a precious commodity can be a product of many things and, as a result, some will need a little more encouragement in that direction with an acceptance of where they are. One such child had been with me since I had taken over the class in the September and being one of the oldest children was to move up to the next class at the beginning of the summer term. During the two terms that she had been with me I had watched this quiet, bright child begin to bloom. Metaphorically she was a lively, if slightly tender, plant that needed potting on, and with the right potting medium I had no doubt she would go on to blossom.

I could remember from my own early days in school just how large and daunting a playground could seem to a child from an otherwise sheltered background. On my first day in school I had spent the entire break hiding by the corner of a wall watching all the other children running around, just hoping that no one would see me, and that I could just slip in unnoticed at the end after my ordeal was over. I therefore had empathy with this rather quiet child. She had gradually grown in confidence during those first terms, but as she started in the next class, I noticed how very subdued she had become and would spend the entire break time, if I was on duty, clinging tightly to my hand. I was accustomed to having a string of children trailing from each hand as I walked around the playground, but this child, as far as she was able, tried to ensure that she was the first in line and therefore the one who was actually holding on to my hand.

I was happy to be her safe place, but I was concerned because I could not always be on duty, and I would not always be there, arguably not beyond the end of that summer term. It was with those concerns in my mind that I went to see my colleague to whose class she had moved in order to alert her to this particular pupil's needs that she might be sensitive to them. I explained that it was my hope that she should eventually be able to replace me with peer friendships while I was aware of her need for a safe place. I questioned if my colleague might find her and a friend a job for some break times in the interim to afford her time to settle in to her new and larger class, and perhaps space to form a friendship bond. That at least was my thinking. How much my awareness of the socio-political climate and of the possible judgement of my colleagues for being seen to encourage a "questionable dependency" influenced my thinking I cannot say. However when I saw the child in the playground the next time I was on duty I noticed that she was staying to the edge of the playground alone and looking very unhappy. I noticed too that she kept looking at me shyly but did not approach me. I, however, approached her and asked if she was all right. She explained that my colleague had spoken to her and told her that, "She was a very silly little girl and that I didn't want her hanging around and she must stop pestering me!"

I felt angry, guilty and hurt for the child. I was angry at my colleague's insensitivity, aware of the emotional damage that could have been caused. So much for all my concerns for the children's social and emotional development. I felt guilty as I realised that it was my approaching my colleague which had occasioned the reproach in the first place. I felt too the child's hurt as she was now isolated and felt unable even to approach me. She was alone and robbed of what seemed like her one place of safety and love. My response was to hold out my hand to her and say, "Of course I don't want you to keep away from me. You're not pestering me. I think what Miss really meant was that she was concerned for you and just wanted you to feel free to play with others if you wanted to. Short of saying, "Don't take any notice of my colleague, your class teacher", I did not know what else to say. She looked relieved and took my hand but I was aware that she had been hurt and her capacity to reach out and form those precious friendships had perhaps been set back. It was another reminder to me of the responsibility that we, as teachers, parents or "responsible adults" bear towards children and how easily one insensitive remark can hurt and cause a scar which only becomes visible many years' later. My awareness of that became ever more present for me.

Apart from the usual entourage of children at playtime I remember on one occasion a rather different following, as I found myself surrounded by a pack of hounds from the local hunt, closely followed by the "whipper in", mounted on a 16 hand hunter. The head, who had witnessed this incursion from the safety of the staffroom, summoned me and proceeded to assert that this "was not good enough", that he was trespassing and should not have brought his horse into the school. I tried to point out that he couldn't very well stay outside the school if he was to round up the hounds. My argument did not impress him and he insisted that I should remonstrate with the huntsman and basically give him a piece of the head's mind. By the time I reached the playground, I found that the hounds had got there before me. Interposing myself between the pack and the children I did my best to calm the situation by explaining quietly to the children that the dogs would not hurt them. I noted that the pack comprised of the dogs and therefore felt a little safer in my assertion. The last thing I wanted was a playground full of children running away screaming, closely followed by the hounds thinking that the chase was on. The "whipper in" came up to me full of apologies. I did not actually think that the head's words would help the situation where any remonstrating would merely have prolonged the incident. Apart from which, I reasoned, if the head felt so strongly, he could easily have come out himself. By this time some of the children had started to stroke the hounds and seemed quite disappointed to see them go!

So, spring gave way to summer. At least we would not be bothered by the hunt again as the season was over. The summer term was to prove busy, not only as I now had to fit swimming into the timetable, but also because I decided to start a project on "where we got our milk from". Perhaps as the year progressed I found my confidence growing; certainly my classroom displays did. In fairness all the children had been with me for at least two terms by now and were beginning to gain some skills in the

3Rs which made such work possible. It was also great fun, especially an outing to the local dairy farm that had a guernsey herd. My wife did some part-time work for the landowner concerned which made organising it very easy. Although we took children from all the surrounding villages, the reader will have gathered we were still very much a rural school.

Swimming again was a completely new experience for me with such young children and clearly the teaching style I had been accustomed to was not going to be appropriate in this setting. Fortunately, at the suggestion of my infant colleagues, I was able to enlist the help of a number of willing and very able mothers who happened to be competent swimmers as well. It should be added that all this was before teaching assistants had started to appear in schools, unless indicated by a particular child's physical needs. The mothers' willingness and ability really made the whole thing quite easy. Changing intially was effected in the classroom and what would otherwise have taken a long time without help was quite quickly accomplished. All I had to do, it seemed, was to help a few children with zips and to line them up.

To save the children having to trail through the school wet and cold, drying and changing afterwards took place in the changing rooms. At that point I found all the mothers willingly helped the girls change, while I was left with all the boys. After just one lesson the unequal division of labour became very apparent and I did have to tactfully ask for reinforcements. I could now understand why my infant colleagues tended to wear waterproof clothing as my previous slightly more hands on approach seemed a little redundant with so much help in the pool as well as out. Such redundancy, however, I could very easily cope with!

It might therefore seem that, perhaps, teaching was easy and that, given the project now under way, I was confidently in control. If I gave that impression, then the picture of the swimmer's head above the water smiling confidently while paddling frantically beneath the surface perhaps better describes the truth of how I felt about my situation. For, in truth, my confidence over the previous few years had been seriously eroded. I had, in a sense, come face to face with my own mortality. I understood my position which dictated that, for the sake of the children, I had to remain in control. I had taken from my initial training one guiding principle which had been stated and underlined by more than one lecture, that the needs of the child came first, second and third. My own may come a close fourth. How closely that accords with a modern understanding of 'professionalism' I am not qualified to judge nor to offer an opinion. It was my reality and, rightly or wrongly, I worked with it and lived by it. The cost of maintaining such a position was beginning to make itself apparent. Apart from my own perceptions it should perhaps be pointed out that I was now having to work closely with, and immediately next door to, the colleague with whom I had experienced so much difficulty, and by whom I felt so undermined. I felt a little like Daniel in the lions' den. The stress showed itself quite plainly one afternoon.

The children were in a colleague's class for story time during the last half hour of school, their coats and bags sitting ready at their tables. I sat momentarily and contemplated the scene and my own situation. As I got up to start my preparation for the following day I experienced a tightness and pain across my chest, accompanied by a pounding in my ears. At that point the deputy head came into my class and enquired if I was all right. I simply responded that I must be a little tired. He suggested that I should either go home or go and sit in the staff room. I was grateful for his concern but said that I would be all right in a few minutes and that he should not worry. Needless to say I was not all right and I was forced to keep my preparation for the following day to a minimum before driving home. I did not share my experience wih my wife. I did not wish to alarm her, beyond which I doubted her capacity to be able to hear or receive my deeper concerns. I was clear in my own mind that my colleagues would not and so determined to keep my experience to myself. I felt completely isolated and the problem was mine. Perhaps I should have heeded the warning signs, but I did not feel able to afford that luxury and soldiered on.

That was not to be my last experience of what, in hindsight, I assume to have been angina; such was the realisation that my situation was untenable. With that realisation gaining upon me, at the end of a particularly difficult day, I did the bare minimum to ensure my survival the following day and drove home. With what felt like the hopelessness and isolation of my position staring at me, as I drove home I found myself looking for a suitably stout tree that I might wrap my car around. However my cynicism told me that, knowing my luck, all I would succeeed in doing would be to write off my car and give myself a headache, with a broken arm being my best hope, resulting in my having to catch the bus to school which would have made a very long day.

I did not know to whom or where I could turn, so I turned instead to the tiny country church to which I was licensed as a lay minister by that time. I went in and broke down. I sobbed out to God that I could not go on any longer. In the absolute silence that followed my outburst, I heard a voice as clearly as if it had been audible, "I know. Now trust me". I could not know what it meant, but somehow I knew that I had really been heard by somebody else for the first time since my trial had begun some five years previously. That, in itself, afforded me a peace that I had not known throughout that period. I put the incident from my mind, or perhaps rather it was put out of my mind by all that remained to be done during those last few weeks of term. As for "now trust me", how could I know what that meant? I did, however, dimly observe that I did not have any more attacks and my health held up to allow me to keep going to the end of term. That goal was sufficient in itself, but I did learn from the head that I should be taking first year juniors (8 year olds) the following school year. That, at least, I reasoned, might be a little easier. For the rest I was content to stay with the words of the hymn, "I do not ask to see the distant scene; one step enough for me".

Chapter 18

The Horizon in Sight

"Then Aslan said 'Now make an end'."
C.S.Lewis, *The Last Battle*

After what had felt like a brief exile in some ways, I was back in the junior school. Perhaps the labelling of years 1 to 6 instead of infants and juniors has done away with the demarcation and the distinction that one experienced. I remember a fellow student who undertook his initial training with me, and how he was the only man to train for 'infants' teaching. Indeed I recall that he was just one of three men in the country training for that age group at the time. I am equally aware that the rise of a three tier system in some counties may also have helped to lower those barriers. For the moment, however, I felt rather as if I had been restored to the fold. Indeed I could not help but reflect that I was now back where I had started 19 years previously with first year juniors. I had come full circle. So had my confidence, for after the battering it had taken over the past five years I might just as well have been back in that 1C with the high window and its limited view of the world.

That, at least, had changed for this was a light, modern building with a carpeted floor, its own stock cupboard and its own indoor toilets. Some things had changed and in spite of the similarity of age group, so had I. All those experiences of the previous 22 years since I had started training had transformed me more than I recognised. Particularly my year's sabbatical study and the battering that followed it had made me more sensitive to the needs of the children. Like a good steak perhaps, the battering had tenderised me!

The beginning of that latter period in my teaching career had seen Margaret Thatcher come to power. I recall how quite early on in her period as Prime Minister she had said that there was no such thing as society merely the individual. Although I fundamentally disagreed with her views, and still do, that, in some ways, described how my own teaching had changed. I could no longer see just a class, but the individual children all with their own needs that made it up.

Thus as I watched the children coming into class on that first morning of term in September I saw two things in each of them. I saw an eagerness and I saw apprehension. I saw the eagerness of children who had left the infants' department behind and were now embarking on what felt to them like a new and hopefully exciting period in their education. They were growing up. I saw also an apprehension as these children had now been launched onto another playground where all the children were bigger and older than they. For all of them, too, this was their first encounter with a male teacher. I could understand their apprehension. However, the latter was not quite such a trauma as I might have imagined for I later understood from different sources that a number of the children had been happy, indeed relieved, to learn that they were going to be in my class. My reputation, whatever it may have been, had preceded me!

Although I had disagreed with Margaret Thatcher at a professional level, I could almost sympathise with the notion. I fundamentally disagreed because I could see how the emphasis on the individual may engender a selfish culture of "look after number one". It also denied a very clear truth of how individuals can adopt a corporate identity and are often very anxious to fit in with what they see as the prevailing social norm for it avoids criticism and individual responsibility. Somehow, what I wanted to encourage in the children was the complete antithesis of that. In the mini society of the classroom I wanted the children to take individual responsibility for their learning and for their actions. I wanted to encourage a culture where children were considerate of each other's needs and I wanted them at the same time to have a sense of a corporate identity in which they could feel safe and of which proud to be a member. Those conditions could only obtain if I started by respecting them as individuals and therefore taught by example. To that latter point I can only say that, along with my colleagues, I tried.

Apart from seeing the children's eagerness and apprehension there was a third thing which I saw in varying degrees in many of the children. That third element I can best describe as their 'back pack'. Beyond the satchel or duffle bag and the like, which so many of them carried, there was that other baggage which had only slowly become visible to me. It was the largely unseen luggage that we all carry around with us; our emotional hurts and needs which, as adults, we learn to keep increasingly to ourselves, but which make themselves felt nevertheless. That was very evident in the eyes and expression of one child as he walked into the classroom one particular morning. It did not require a lot of empathy to understand that he was very unhappy. I took him to one side as he entered the classroom and asked, "What's wrong?" In response to my question, his eyes filled with tears as he explained that his cat had died that morning. He had wanted to stay at home, but his parents had insisted that he attend school, thinking, no doubt, that the activity would help take his mind off his recent loss. The reverse, of course, was true; his recent loss took his mind away from any activity. He needed time to grieve, and anything I might have taught him that day was going to be in vain. How could he hear what I was saying when his emotional needs were screaming in his ears? That became clear when it came to the morning break. He seemed reticent to move. Indeed he was unable to move. I may not then have called it post traumatic paralysis, but it did not take a qualification in psychotherapy to recognise it. We spent that break talking about the nature of death and understanding that, given the nature of mortal life, we needed to be as thankful for it as we are the gift of life in the first place. He seemed happier as he walked home at lunch time. From a personal point of view, as a pragamatist and a teacher, as often the two must go hand in hand, I was just glad he could walk!

That experience merely reinforced my understanding that, as a teacher, I must be sensitive to the emotional as well as the educational needs of the pupil. Indeed I was reminded again of the hierarchy of human needs, and that physical and emotional needs must be satisfied before we are free to attend to the others. Educational needs, though important, tend to come lower in the pecking order. Indeed, our emotional status can directly affect our ability to learn.

That was never more evident than with one child whom I had encountered a couple of years previously. He had joined my class late in the October of that year, having just moved into the area. As I looked at the records which had been sent from his previous school it was clear that his reading was seriously retarded. It did not take me long to see that his mathematical attainment was similarly behind. It was clear, too, that his poor reading ability was the main cause of his difficulty with mathematics which, at that time, was increasingly 'problem' based and assumed a commensurate reading ability. As I talked to this child it became obvious to me that somehow he had acquired a label which simply said, "backward". His previous teachers clearly felt he was, and had been teaching him accordingly. He had most recently been reading a book which was well below his chronological age. As I tested his reading I learned that he was well in excess of two years retarded. In that sense, arguably, the book he had been reading was right for his level of ability. Unfortunately it meant that the nature of the material was of very little appeal to his age group, which resulted in his very poor motivation. I also learned that there were other emotional issues which I felt would be impinging on his educational development. As my area of responsibility was language development, it meant that I had a battery of measures that I could apply and approaches that I could use to seek to address his presenting difficulties.

My concern was, however, that no matter what I did it was merely going to reinforce his low self esteem. This child had learned that he was a failure and his experience of school to that date had merely gone to strengthen that opinion. If together we were to have any success, we had, somehow, to reverse that earlier learning. I had a sense that any remedial measures I might, or indeed under normal circumstances should, apply would negatively reinforce his acquired label.

Instead I talked to him. I talked to him about what he enjoyed doing. We talked about the sort of books he would like to read. I told him that I did not really think that his ability at reading was as bad as the books he had been reading would suggest. Rather I said, in truth, that I gained the impression he was really rather bright and that he was not reading very well because he had not been given anything worth reading. I had previously colour coded all the graded reading books within the school so that I was able to tell him to choose anything with a particular coloured sticker. I suggested that he should choose initially something just a little more advanced than he had been accustomed to. I heard him read it. I commended him on his ability and when he had finished his book suggested that he should go on to the next colour. He began to warm to this, so I spent time just sitting with him in the library discussing his reading interests and encouraging him, urging him on through the different coloured bands of ability. He began to improve. Above all he began to believe in his own ability. Instead of learning, "I can't", he learned, "I can". If I could believe in him, then he could believe in himself.

At the end of that year he had to move up to the secondary school in another village. Accordingly I tested his reading in order to send up to date records to his next school. On looking at the results, I found that he was now as far in advance of his chronological age as he had been retarded when he joined my class. I reflected on what I had done to warrant such a result and I concluded that, in short, I had not done anything beyond showing a little bit of interest. I was equally sure that, had I followed the measures that might normally have been expected of me, he would not have made such a remarkable gain where there was every chance that I would have reinforced his poor level of attainment.

Those two incidents, plus my experience of teaching the reception class the previous year, merely added weight, or perhaps volume, to that dissenting voice within that questioned the very nature and purpose of my role. It made me question what I was doing and why. Ultimately I asked myself if I could spend the next 20 years doing something which I could no longer really believe in. I do not wish to detract from the valuable work which teachers do day after day and the incalculable contribution they make to the educational development of many children. Rather I was uncertain if it should be me doing it. I was experiencing something akin to a crisis of conscience and began to question my raison d'être.

I kept my questions to myself and if that nagging voice was gaining in volume, it apparently did not show in my teaching. It was a little later in the spring of the following year that the head, unannounced, brought one of Her Majesty's Inspectors (HMI) into my classroom. Some of the children looked up as the visitor came into the room, the rest just continued working. I looked up from my position sitting at one of the children's tables helping someone who was having difficulty and had become distressed. On becoming aware of their tears, I had asked the person sitting next to them to exchange places with me. Hence, when the HMI came into the room she glanced at the teacher's desk only to see a child sitting there working and then continued to look round at head height, clearly expecting to see another adult in the class somewhere. The head quickly came to the rescue and said, "Oh you have to look much lower than that in this class if you want to find Mr. Cutler". Having received the assurance of the child I was helping that they were happy, I smiled, turned and got up to greet our visitor. I was struck by her sensitivity as she quickly said, in response to my greeting, "Please don't let me disturb you. You look busy". She went on to ask if she could look round and have a word with some of the children. Having introduced her to the children I turned to the child at my table and asked if he would like to resume his place. I gained the impression he had rather enjoyed his brief promotion. Our visitor spent some time in the class before thanking me and leaving.

She returned later that day during the last lesson of the afternoon. That last half hour was always precious as it was a time when one could sit and be still with the children. As was my custom, I was sitting in the quiet area with the class, reading a story to them. I asked one of the more able readers if they would carry on reading and again greeted her. We stood outide the quiet area where I could still see the children and, more importantly, where they could still see me and be reassured that I had not left them. Young children need the reassurance of the presence of their class teacher, for, regardless of the precise legal standing of their position, they are still in "loco parentis". The HMI seemed most impressed by the ability and confidence of the child reading as well as with the behaviour of the children as they continued to listen attentively. She spoke of her earlier visit to the class and said how very happy all the children seemed and was impressed by the fact that they all had a clear sense of what they were doing and what they wanted to achieve. In short, she experienced them as happy, confident and well motivated.

I reflected on the head's earlier remark about the apparent lowliness of my position in the class as he had clearly been saying something of my teaching style, to which perhaps I had not given a great deal of thought before. I had always, and had at that moment, simply responded to the child's need as it presented. Now this HMI's comments made me reflect more deeply on that. I recalled my own training all those years ago when we had been encouraged to work at the children's level and to relate to them, as individuals, within their own frame of reference, and I also recalled with fondness and some amusement the many hours spent sitting on the floor. As I looked back I understood how all our training and teaching had in those post Plowden years of the sixties and early seventies been child centred. I reflected too how much my own teaching had developed such that I had increasingly been adopting a similar stance. At the same time I saw how the curriculum, in response to political pressure, had been moving inexorably in the opposite direction. As I had become increasingly child centred, so schooling in the late eighties was becoming ever more process centred. Where the curriculum had been adapted to the children's needs, now the children were being increasingly governed by the requirements of the curriculum. That trend, of course, has continued such that different "key stages" dictate precisely what the child is required to have learned at any given age. The children now, when they enter school, embark upon a programme rather like the very computers which they must learn to use.

So I contemplated my position as I saw that just as I was moving in one direction, so teaching was moving in the opposite way. In spite of the Inspector's very positive comments about my teaching, my colleagues had detected that change and had judged me accordingly. It was clear that the stress of my situation was taking an ever greater toll on my health. Earlier, and just one month into the first term, I had become ill once more. The usual symptoms of a virus, which again seemed to affect my heart which was confirmed by the local hospital where I had been rushed. The incident had been sufficient to convince my wife and my G.P. that all was not well. Suddenly somebody was hearing me and I was now able to admit to myself that my situation was unsustainable. For the first time the true nature of what was happening became apparent and my way became clear. I contacted my Union and went to see the local secretary. He agreed that I should seek early retirement on health grounds. He contacted the then Department for Education and Science, particularly the teachers' pension department, and without any more effort on my part the machinery swung into action. I am aware that often such machinery can grind exceptionally slowly. Not so in this case. Within one month I was offered an appointment with a doctor. That, too, felt easy and civilised as he made a quick telephone call to my own doctor. The conversation was brief, which the appointed doctor summarised as, "The right man in the wrong job". He put the phone down, made a brief note before he turned to me and said, "You're out!" My fate apparently decided, I had just been invalided out of the service. Twenty years of service had been brought to a close in just a quarter of an hour. It was the 23rd November, which just happened to be my birthday. It was a wonderful birthday in more ways than one.

I reflected on how painless the process had been, but then I recalled too those words from the previous June, just five months' previously, "Now trust me". I did not feel that I really had much choice. The process was not entirely complete, for I had to await for a letter from my employing authority confirming what I had just been told. That arrived towards the end of term and just before Christmas. The head brought it through to me in my classroom. I was indeed 'out' and with that all important pension. As I read the letter again, however, I learned that my pension would be enhanced by 5 years, my reckonable service having been increased. As I had completed 20 years in teaching, my pension would be based on 25 years. Not only had I had an unexpected birthday present, now I was being given an early Christmas present as well. I had six months in which to accept the offer. I knew I would not receive such an offer again.

I cannot say that I rushed to accept it, for now the full

implications of what had happened began to dawn upon me. Education had always been so important to me. It was what had given my life purpose. With another 20 years of working life theoretically ahead of me, I suddenly felt rudderless. The practical me took over. I wrote accepting and offered my resignation to take effect from the May half term of the next year; the longest I could leave it if I was to accept retirement on health grounds. I should have liked to see my class through to the end of the school year in July, but the terms of the offer would not allow that. I would soldier on for as long as they would let me. The guiding principle that the child came first still obtained. That was my understanding of professionalism. I am aware of a shift in emphasis where "professionalism" in many areas of work seems more to equate with officiousness and not exceeding the "service level agreement". On reflection, however, given the then state of my health there may have been some wisdom in the latter position. Such reflection, however, is idle for I am aware that it is a position I was simply unable to adopt.

I had no option now but to tell the head that I had applied for and would accept retirement on health grounds. He expressed no surprise or regret. Indeed he asked how I had gone about it as he thought he may try himself!

Meanwhile nothing changed. Giving the right impression seemed to be the guiding principle. Perhaps such a comment betrays the naive idealist in me. I recall that year saw the appointment of a younger colleague to a post of responsibility for audio-visual aids. The deputy head and I had been fulfilling this role between us ever since the new wing, complete with its audio-visual room, had been built. I began to understand the rationale for what seemed such an inappropriate appointment. She had expressed the desire to start applying for deputy headships and the head wanted to be seen to be encouraging her in her career. It was clear that she had to be able to show that she already held a senior position or post of responsibility and any sinecure would do. I began to see how promotion worked. It became clear that the original arrangement would not change as our colleague did not even know how to operate the equipment and showed no desire to do so. Thus it was that we agreed that I would borrow the video recorder for the Christmas vacation.

That Christmas saw the televising of an animation of Kenneth Grahame's book, "The Wind in the Willows". I remember how my son and I sat entranced as we watched this magical tale of the river bank. I had read and been totally absorbed by it as a child. It brought back fond memories of holidays spent on the river Thames on board my uncle's boat which had been a family project to convert a wartime hulk to a cabin cruiser over a number of years. Could I share some of that magic with the children with this recording?

The following term, my retirement now confirmed, I felt suddenly freed from so many constraints. I no longer feared what other staff members thought about me, nor of the repression of curriculum requirements. Suddenly I felt free, for the first time in my career, to be truly and fully present for the children and to respond to their personal and educational needs as I saw them regardless of external or political constraints.

Recalling how much I had enjoyed the televising of, "The Wind in the Willows", I wanted to share some of my sense of wonder with the children. I was not quite sure how I might reconcile that with the needs of the curriculum, but rationalised it on the grounds that I was introducing them to a classic of English literature, beyond which I was not sure I cared too much. The children were as engrossed as I was and we were able to enjoy an hour together watching the video recording. It is so easy to fill the curriculum and our life with 'oughts'. I have since come to recognise the condition as a hardening of the 'oughteries' and I fear that is becoming ever more true of our schools. Yet was it not W.H. Davies who wrote, "What is this life if full of care, we have no time to stand and stare?" Beyond which, was I not still responsible for language development within the school? Literature was surely a part of that?

As I observed before, nothing changed, but I had. My care for the children or my teaching was not diminished but I cared less about the judgement of my colleagues. What a shame I could not have achieved that position earlier.

That, however, from my perspective, was the only change. The head was concerned that I should write a letter of resignation to the Chairman of the School Governors stressing that my leaving was not a reflection on the school. My letter, finally, was like any carefully written reference. The secret lay in what was left out! Again, looks were everything, but was it not said by Henry IV in Shakespeare's play of the same name, "Uneasy lies the head that wears a crown". I can only say that particular head must have been very uneasy. That was apparent one afternoon later that term when I was called to the office to attend to a rather severe cut to a child's head.

Some years previously I had attended a course in first aid, and duly earned a certificate, which meant from the school's point of view, at least, I was a qualified first aider. The head, of course, was not slow to capitalise on my newly acquired status as he now sought to assure the parents that the school boasted a qualified first aider. Over the intervening years I had had to attend a number of incidents when my first aid training had been put to good use. I had been able to diagnose a broken arm which I had immobilised and taken to hospital and I had also attended a child in the playground with a suspected back injury which I had again immobilised until medical help should arrive, earning a personal commendation from the doctor who attended. I had even attended a workman who had been laying some paving stones outside my classroom who, in dropping one of the slabs, had caught his hand between it and the adjoining one, severing a finger. I remember his colleague's consternation when I told him to go and retrieve the other half to the severed finger from underneath the slab. I was aware of cases where the severed digit had been sown on again. I washed the severed end and bandaged it in position. It was worth a try. I was quite disappointed when I later learned that the hospital had failed to restore his finger.

This particular afternoon, near the end of the day and immediately before the half term holiday, it was a gash to the front of the head above the hairline. Aware of the need to apply pressure to stem the bleeding and to keep a dressing in place I had to employ a triangular bandage such that it covered the boy's head. The head informed me that he had to leave early and that I would have to take the child home. On seeing the bandage, however, he told me that I was not to take him home looking as he did. After all, he protested, "What would his mother think?" I pointed out the need to secure the dressing, to which he questioned if I could not simply put a plaster on it, "or something". Again, I pointed out that it would not stick to his hair, to which he finally blustered, "Well just put a small bit of bandage round it. You're not to take him home looking like that!" I reasoned that there was little point in prolonging the argument but reflected quietly to myself how the head was clearly more concerned about what the parent might think, and feared how that may reflect upon him, than he was the child's welfare. Apparently, however, his concern did not extend to taking the child home. There was a quiet but determined voice in me that said I was not going to compromise the child's welfare just to help the head save face. After all, I reasoned, would not the child's mother be concerned to know that we had done all we properly could for her son? That same quiet voice also said, "Besides, whose the first aider?" The head left. The person taking my class for those last few minutes of the afternoon had dismissed the children so I duly took the boy home, complete with bandage, and suggested that his mother might take him down to the surgery, which she did, after thanking me warmly.

On returning after the half term holiday, the head's first words to me were to question whether I had taken the boy home and how his mother had received the casualty. Commenting that she was naturally concerned, he quickly replied, "You didn't take him home with that bandage on, did you?" His look, to my reply, suggested he didn't quite believe me.

Perhaps it is not entirely true to say that nothing changed, for that year saw the school's acquisition of its first computer. In the 1980's the computer appearing most widely in schools was the BBC Model B made by Acorn. Succeeding the Model A it boasted twice as much memory, namely 32 kilobytes. As we have become accustomed to mega- and even gigabytes, such memory limitations seem hardly credible, but there has been a marked shift in the way we use computers during the intervening years. I am aware that now much of that memory is taken up supporting what we delight in calling a "graphical user interface". The Model B then was simply command line driven. Therein lay the fundamental difference between computing then and as it was to develop. That difference also governed how computing was taught.

Essentially if one wanted a computer to do anything it had to be programmed. Then, as now, commercial programmes were available, but educational programmes were aimed at encouraging the children, in turn, to programme the computer to perform a number of tasks. Increasingly programming has become the preserve of large organisations such that software companies even dictate what commercial systems may do. Control has shifted from the hands of the individual computer user to the software company. When the micro computer first started appearing in the home, and certainly in schools, there was much talk about how it would empower the individual. It was thus the job of schools to equip children with the skills necessary to harness the potential of the new computers. Not then the delight of trying to manoeuvre a pointer into a tiny box on the screen and 'click' on a symbol, the significance of which was known only to the programmer. If one wanted to load a programme one simply typed "load" followed by the name of the programme. I remember how a number of books began to appear on programming aimed at the popular end of the market. It was indeed an exciting time.

One such programme which was designed by one education authority enabled the user to move a pointer round the screen or a small robot or 'turtle' around the floor. That, in turn, enabled one to draw a figure on the screen, or on a sheet of paper if the school could afford a turtle, with the child writing a simple programme such as:

Forward 80, Left 90, Forward 80, Left 90, Forward 80, Left 90, Forward 80. Which would draw a square with sides of 80 units, where left 90 indicated turning left through 90 degrees.

At that time we boasted just one computer between all the junior classes so that when we did not have access to the computer I could teach some of the basic principles of computing. I explained that computers counted and worked in binary rather than denary; hence base 2 rather than the base 10 that the children were accustomed to. This could be demonstrated by asking a number of children to stand at the front of the class such that a child standing represented 1 and a child sitting represented 0. Hence in binary 16 would be represented with 10000 where 17 would be 10001. So much for the basics, but it became much more fun when it came to moving a robot about the floor especially where I was the robot. On one occasion we cleared the desks out of the way and the children were moving me about the floor. It was made easier as the floor was covered in carpet tiles such that "forward 3" meant I moved forward 3 squares. Right 90 meant that I would turn right through 90 degrees. What could be more fun than having a life size robot at one's command? It also seemed a perfectly sound teaching strategy which was meant to bring the curriculum alive and make it real for the children. Thus the class, through a series of commands manoeuvred me around the room - and right into the stock cupboard. They then carefully locked the door behind me. I had walked straight into that, literally, so I could hardly complain!

The children's timing was perfect as by then it was break time and they thoughtfully dismissed themselves to go outside, my suggesting, perhaps rather lamely from inside the cupboard, that they should do so quietly. Ever resourceful, however, I did request that one of them might be kind enough to get me a cup of tea from the staff room! In fairness, not only did my cup of tea arrive and I was duly released, but a number of the children stayed behind to tidy the tables ready for the next lesson. It must be admitted that I was greeted with a few slightly apprehensive looks as I went out into the playground at the end of break to collect the class. The looks did not last long as I smiled and winked. Again I reflected that teaching did have its rewards and its 'fun' moments.

The first day of April could always be guaranteed to produce its own fun moments. On this occasion I had avoided the object balanced over the door designed to fall when I walked through it and I had recovered the missing register and text books. I was turning into a real "spoil sport". So the least I could do was to sit on the whoopee cushion which had thoughtfully been placed on my chair. After all it was April fool's day and I had already proved myself the fool.

The children's humour had a freshness and trusting naivety which I have always treasured. It was going to be difficult to say goodbye, but that time was approaching fast. It is said, after all, that time flies when we are having fun. That remaining month certainly did fly by and the last day of half term arrived.

That Friday morning saw the final assembly before the half term holiday. Parents were always welcome to join the children for the Friday morning assembly. That particular morning there was a considerably larger number than usual. A collection had been made for me and I had been quietly appraised of this by the head and asked to give some guidance on what I should like as a leaving gift. Given my love of English literature and language I had suggested a dictionary of quotations. It transpired that I had been a little conservative in my wish list, for that morning I remember I felt quite overwhelmed with gifts. Perhaps even more overwhelming were the letters and cards from parents and children with their many and various wishes and thanks, all of which I have kept and treasured. I believe I felt more loved than I had ever done before in my teaching career. That perhaps was my failing.

When the end of that school day arrived it was the hardest goodbye I had ever said. It was always difficult to say goodbye to a class at the end of the year as they prepared to go on to another class or another school. This had a finality I had not experienced before. I said my goodbyes, watched the children go and started to tidy my classroom. After all another teacher would have to take over my class for that last half term. Many of the resources I had built up over my 20 years in teaching I left in my stock cupboard. This felt like letting go of my last piece of security, my teacher's "hump", but I reasoned that the teacher following me would be grateful for it while I, arguably, would not need it. Beyond which if there were a question of ownership it belonged ultimately to the children for whom it had been built up.

While I was busily performing the last rites on my teaching career, for that is what it felt like, two of my colleagues came in to say goodbye. One of them even said I should write a book about my experiences! I was left alone in my classroom. For almost the first time in my career I had no books to take home, no marking or preparation to do. Apparently I was free. I gathered up what few personal possessions I still had and went out to the car park, which by now was deserted except for my own car. I was the last to leave as was so often the case.

As I drove out of the car park I was assailed by mixed feelings of relief, sadness and emptiness. As I went up through the gears and left school behind I reflected that, unlike the title of the book by R.F. Delderfield, I had not quite "served them all my days", but I had given my all.

Epilogue

As I write, all that seems a long time ago and much has changed both personally and in schools generally.

Following my retirement I registered as unemployed for the first time in my life and I discovered the truth of my earlier question, "What else can a teacher do but teach?" Fortunately the terms of my retirement had allowed me to retain my ministry number. I was still a qualified teacher and so I started doing home tutorial work for the local Education Authority where I lived, working mainly with school refusers or those, who through disability or other reasons, were unable to attend mainstream school. I remained fit for a year before my health broke down completely and I was diagnosed as suffering from myalgic encephalomyelitis (M.E.) I was completely unable to work, or indeed do little else, and spent the next three years doing a fairly good impression of a vegetable, staring into space or occasionally at the television, but the question still remained, "What else can a teacher do but teach?"

While I was still teaching I had undertaken a course in counselling in schools. That, and my introduction to the work of Carl Rogers while reading for my degree, had provided the seeds of an answer. As I continued to look at myself during that period those seeds began to germinate. I had too the words of the examining doctor who had finally retired me echoing in my head, "The right man in the wrong job".

Perhaps it had not been the wrong job initially. My training had introduced me to a new life and I had blossomed and grown, but the job had changed and so had I. In the 1960's, the years immediately following the Plowden Report, teaching had been focussed around the child's developmental needs; it was essentially child centred and over the intervening years I had become increasingly so. Indeed I found I still cared about the profession I had joined; about children and how we taught them. But teaching had changed. The advent of the Thatcher years saw an increasing direct political involvement in education. This started with contractual hours for teachers and the introduction of curriculum guidelines. The intervening years have seen the establishment of a National Curriculum. There have been subsequent Education Acts, such that when I was still teaching we had seen only the 1870 and 1944 Education Acts, while since my leaving teaching there have been almost twice that number. With the introduction of a literacy hour and the like, teachers are now told not only exactly what they are to teach, but for how long. A new method of assessment has been introduced in the form of key stage tests. This marks another significant change, for where teachers had been using standardised tests which offered an assessment of the child's true ability and educational development, the new tests are criterion based and show the extent to which the child has absorbed and can regurgitate the material pertaining to the relevent key stage. In short, education has become process centred instead of child centred such that when children start school they embark upon a programme which has become increasingly politically led and employment centred. Just as I had learned "Educare - to draw out", education, it seems, has become "Dictare - to dictate" or, perhaps, "to bang in".

I note too that the prevailing culture of fear has now crept into our schools such that parents are now locked out and children are locked in, while teachers may no longer have any physical contact with pupils. Indeed I remember visiting somebody recently when she received a telephone call from the local primary school where her daughter was a pupil, telling her that the child had fallen over in the playground and could she please come and attend to her. She found the child still lying on the ground where she had been left.

I began to see in those years immediately following teaching how I had cared more about the children than I had about the increasing political pressures. I saw too that regardless of how the curriculum might change, unless children are free to learn, then it will be irrelevent. I began to understand that unless we can attend to our personal luggage then we are not free to learn or indeed free to attend to the many other things which life may demand of us.

Those seeds had germinated into an idea which, after a couple of false starts, saw me enrolling for a Master's degree in Counselling at the same University where I had spent that precious year. I had found where I belonged and it felt like coming back home. My research told me too how stress can so contribute to our physical health, including M.E. Again I had learned a lot and grown a little. I went on to become a registered psychotherapist and hope that I can now help others grow. Indeed, just recently I received a letter from a client, saying simply, "You have given me my life back. Thank you". In a strange way, and after a tortuous route, I feel that perhaps the same may be said for me.